Pearson's Canal Com[panion]
SOUTH MIDLA[NDS]

WAYZGOOSE

Published by Wayzgoose
Staffordshire DE13 9RS
email:enquiries@jmpearson.co.uk
www.jmpearson.co.uk
Copyright: Michael Pearson
All Rights Reserved
Eleventh Edition 2022
ISBN 978 0 9928492 7 6

The Ashby Canal near the lost village of Stretton Baskerville (Map 30)

LOCK-WHEELING

For a man destined to become a byword in guide book compiling circles for his powers of observation, I was remarkably slow off the mark. Between the ages of two and nine I dwelt in the Leicestershire town of Hinckley, yet remained blissfully unaware of the Ashby-de-la-Zouch Canal which coiled past the self-possessed hosiery-manufacturing centre's western outskirts, giving it solely the slyest dig in the ribs in the process. My unforgivable ignorance was compounded by the presence, on our sitting-room wall, of a gilt-framed, pictorial map of 'Hinckley - A Town of Ancient Lineage in the Heart of England' which Cicely Pickering had painted in 1947. The map clearly depicted the canal's sinuous course from Bramcote to Dadlington and beyond, and included cameos of a pipe-smoking angler, phlegmatically fishing near Wykin, and a girl skating on the ice at Stoke Basin, her scarf billowing behind her like a wind sock.

I don't doubt Cicely had first hand experience of skating on the frozen Ashby Canal. She belonged to the family who had plucked my father from obscurity in Paisley, Renfrewshire, and installed him as Works Manager at their printing works and stationery shop on The Borough in the centre of town. We had been taken fondly under the Pickering family's protective wing, and had mingled with Cicely on several occasions. Each Christmas we eagerly awaited the arrival of her self-painted greetings card of local scenes. She was a very talented lady, who deserved a wider audience, but perhaps she didn't want one. Not all of us seek the dubious reassurance of public acclaim. She didn't, moreover, appear to need a husband, though perhaps, with hindsight, the Second World War had whittled down the candidates for that desirable post.

But back to that elusive canal. I hadn't even noticed it on our regular shopping trips by Midland Red bus to Nuneaton. Maybe we never timed it right to see a pair, loaded with Measham coal for Hertfordshire's paper mills, pass beneath us as we trundled over Bridge 17, heading for The Long Shoot and the house with a blue tiled roof which always caught our eye. Mother and I relied on buses for all our expeditions. Coalville by Browns Blue was a regular jaunt. The jovial conductor was a large rubicund individual invariably dressed in a full length, buff-coloured coat, with a rack of many coloured tickets and a bell punch, hung jauntily from his neck. Joviality notwithstanding, he'd welcome passengers aboard his bus with the stern appraisal of a commissionaire at a five star hotel.

We lived in a detached, bow-windowed house on the corner of Ashby and Barrie roads. There was a soot-caked-chimnied hosiery works next door: perhaps the Freudian source of my fondness for factories and chimneys. Though my Scottish father's religious roots were Presbyterian, and my English mother's Anglican, we dutifully attended a Congregational chapel service every Sunday morning. Share, then, my ecumenical confusion on being dragged (quite literally kicking and screaming) to a Roman Catholic convent school at the age of five. When Ash Wednesday came along and they attempted to annoint my forehead with a symbolic cross, I leapt the pews, dodged the nuns, and fled.

Two decades elapsed before I belatedly became cognisant of the Ashby Canal. Tasked with compiling a guide book for Waterway Productions, my wife and I found ourselves negotiating a polar landscape reminiscent of *Scott of the Antarctic*. The blizzard began at Marston Jabbett, and by the time we reached Burton Hastings the ice was eight inches thick. We feared for the hire boat's hull. But, in the dauntless spirit which come to epitomise the Canal Companions, we persevered. Beyond Bridge 21, where the canal widens briefly into a basin, the ghost of Cicely Pickering was gaily skating. And not, like me, on many an occasion, on thin ice.

Locking Down Hatton (Map 4)

Contents

By Decree! The Ashby at Shackerstone (Map 33)

WITH five marinas in proximity, let alone four sizeable hire fleets, Napton Junction's busyness is more or less guaranteed. Here, moreover, the Oxford Canal commences its long, winding road to the Thames at Oxford, whilst what has been known as the Grand Union Canal, since the 1930s, pivots at Bridge 17 on its way between London and Birmingham and vice versa. Old working

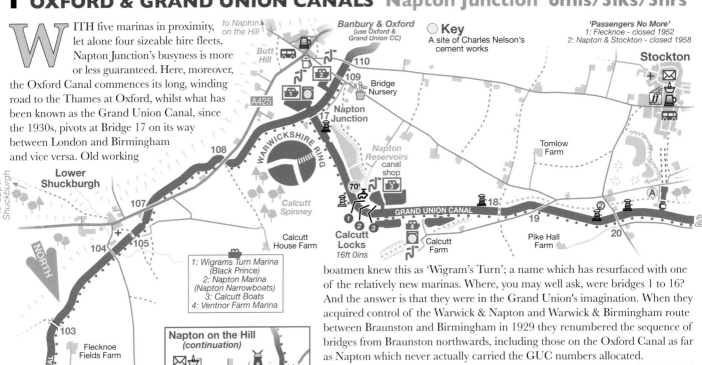

Key

A site of Charles Nelson's cement works

'Passengers No More'
1: Flecknoe - closed 1952
2: Napton & Stockton - closed 1958

1: Wigrams Turn Marina (Black Prince)
2: Napton Marina (Napton Narrowboats)
3: Calcutt Boats
4: Ventnor Farm Marina

boatmen knew this as 'Wigram's Turn'; a name which has resurfaced with one of the relatively new marinas. Where, you may well ask, were bridges 1 to 16? And the answer is that they were in the Grand Union's imagination. When they acquired control of the Warwick & Napton and Warwick & Birmingham route between Braunston and Birmingham in 1929 they renumbered the sequence of bridges from Braunston northwards, including those on the Oxford Canal as far as Napton which never actually carried the GUC numbers allocated.

East of Napton (that is to the *left* of the map) the shared section of the Oxford and Grand Union routes pursues its lonely course, jostling with the main road between Daventry and Warwick, and encountering the picturesque estate village of Lower Shuckburgh. A footpath climbs through parkland inhabited by fallow deer to Upper Shuckburgh. The name is said to mean 'a hill haunted by goblins.' Certainly Beacon Hill, rising to 678 feet, has its spirits. Whilst hunting on the hill, a 17th century member of the Shuckburgh family was reputedly accosted by

King Charles I. On his way to the Battle of Edgehill, the King demanded to know how an English gentleman could spare time for country pursuits when his monarch was fighting for his crown. On a clear day it's possible to see westwards as far as the Black Mountains of Wales from the summit of Beacon Hill.

Napton Junction once featured a stop lock and toll house. Northwards the landscape is conspicuously flat, a characteristic which belies the presence of a trio of locks at Calcutt. Napton reservoirs, dug in 1800, feed the canal through the marina below the flight. The original Warwick & Napton locks were narrowbeam. Those in use today date from the Grand Union's modernisation scheme of the 1930s. If you are travelling northwards they could be the first of their kind that you have encountered, and may seem disconcertingly large.

Near Tomlow Bridge (No.18) the London & North Western Railway's Weedon & Leamington branch crossed the canal. When the line opened in 1895 it captured much of the canal traffic in lime and cement centered on the blue lias quarries in the vicinity of Stockton. Willow Wren Training, who 'hung up their windlass' in 2022, restored the arm which led into Nelson's cement works. Fishing lagoons and scrub covered spoil tips are all that remain of a busy works once famous - in building merchant circles at least - for its 'Celebrated Portland Cement' and bantam cockerel trademark. In their heyday Nelson's operated a fleet of canal boats named after figures in Greek mythology. Three notable steamers were launched in 1885 - *Janus*, *Jason* and *Jupiter*. The cockerel image was incorporated into Nelson's boats livery scheme. The company was bought out by Rugby Portland Cement in 1945 and production transferred to Southam.

Lower Shuckburgh   Map 1

The kudos of entry in Simon Jenkins' *England's Thousand Best Churches*, doesn't guarantee an unlocked door at St John the Baptist's canalside church. 'For addicts of Victorian eccentricity', is Jenkins' opening gambit, and it seems that the architect (J. Croft of Islington) was encouraged by the local squire - who had just returned from the Crimea - to incorporate a number of oriental overtones. Eleven editions, and counting, we have never managed to gain access, so can neither affirm or argue with Jenkins' opinion.

Upper Shuckburgh (off the edge of the map) is the location of a stuccoed hall and another church, confusingly also called St John the Baptist. The Shuckburghs have dwelt here since the 12th century and nowadays advertise their otherwise private home as a venue for weddings and corporate hospitality.

Napton on the Hill   Map 1

Napton (best reached from Bridge 109) basks in the sunshine (or shivers when a gale blows) on its south-facing hill. Ochre stone and thatch characterise the older buildings, brick the infills. Its street pattern takes some fathoming, but there is much green space between the houses and even the seemingly obligatory modern developments dovetail neatly into the whole. Sheltered in the lee from north-easterlies, the parish church of St Lawrence has a Norman chancel with a sundial. You can climb towards the windmill for a better view, but it stands on private property.

Eating & Drinking

KING'S HEAD - on A425 south of Bridge 109. Tel: 01926 812202. Hook Norton pub with a good choice of food. Open noon to 3pm and from 6pm Mon-Fri, and from noon onwards at weekends. CV47 8NG

Shopping

Napton boasts a vibrant post office stores about a quarter of an hour's walk from Bridge 109 (Tel: 01926 812488 - CV47 8LR) open 8am-5pm Mon-Fri; 8am-4pm Sat; and 8am-12pm Sun. They are particularly proud of their locally sourced produce which ranges from honey and preserves to water buffalo burgers, sausages, steaks, cheese and ice cream. Refreshments, take-aways and Calor gas are also available. Round the corner stands Napton Cidery. Tel: 01928 811910. Bridge Nursery (Tel: 01926 812737) is open Friday-Sunday, 10am-4pm.

Connections

BUSES - service 664 runs to/from Southam and Leamington ex Sun. Tel: 0871 200 2233.
TAXIS - Five Star. Tel: 01926 812666.

Stockton   Map 1

New housing developments are increasing Stockton's population, but it's the old rows of cement workers cottages which lend it a residual sense of atmosphere.

Eating & Drinking

CROWN - High Street. Tel: 01926 812255. CV47 8JZ Also, Chinese take-away - Tel: 01926 811266.

Shopping

Post office stores. Tel: 01926 810500.

Connections

BUSES - Stagecoach 63 runs hourly (bi-hourly Sun) to/from Leamington and Rugby. Tel: 0871 200 2233.

2 GRAND UNION CANAL Long Itchington 4mls/15lks/4hrs

BOATERS have to flex their muscles as the Grand Union descends into (or climbs out of) the valley of the Avon. There are flights at Stockton and Bascote and isolated locks elsewhere. A number of the locks are overlooked by pretty tile-hung cottages built when the canal was modernised in the 1930s. Plenty of work, then, but charming countryside provides a stimulating antidote.

Stockton Locks are set in a belt of blue lias limestone in which the fossils of gigantic reptiles have been found. In the commercial heyday of the canal several lime, cement, brick and tile works flourished in the neighbourhood, providing considerable traffic. Vegetation inevitably hides the sites of most of these undertakings now. Arms extended in both directions to serve a number of sites. Kaye's Arm remains in water and is occupied by a residential community of narrowboat dwellers. Kayes had their own fleet of narrowboats, some of which were built by Nursers at Braunston. These were later taken over by the Rugby Portland Cement

Co. It was from their works at the end of the Kaye's Arm that British Waterways' last narrowboat contract was carried in 1969, being a consignment of cement bound for Rugby Portland's depot at the top of the Camp Hill flight in Birmingham (Map 8) aboard the motor *Banstead* and butty *Tow*. Five years earlier, *Banstead* (since preserved) 'starred' in a feature film called *The Bargee* along with Harry H. Corbett, Ronnie Barker and many other contemporary stalwarts of the British film industry.

An embankment carries the canal over the River Itchen and past the attractive village of Long Itchington. Nearby the trackbed of the old Leamington-Weedon branch again crosses the canal and the river, the latter upon a substantial viaduct still in situ though inaccessible. Parts of this old railway have been revitalised as National Cycle Route No.41. In *Anderton for Orders*, Tom Foxon described travelling along the line - 'across the night-shrouded Midland plain' - on his journey with John Knill to Braunston, where his working boat career was to begin. West of Long Itchington, a

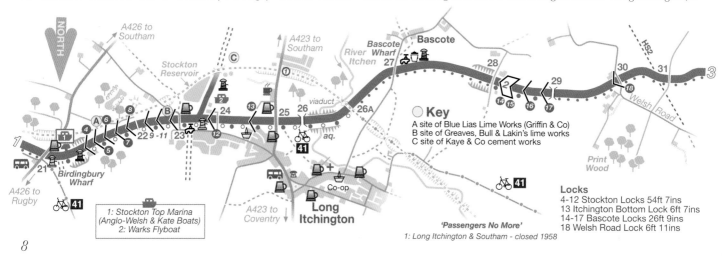

Key
A site of Blue Lias Lime Works (Griffin & Co)
B site of Greaves, Bull & Lakin's lime works
C site of Kaye & Co cement works

1: Stockton Top Marina
(Anglo-Welsh & Kate Boats)
2: Warks Flyboat

Locks
4-12 Stockton Locks 54ft 7ins
13 Itchington Bottom Lock 6ft 7ins
14-17 Bascote Locks 26ft 9ins
18 Welsh Road Lock 6ft 11ins

'Passengers No More'
1: Long Itchington & Southam - closed 1958

sense of loneliness settles on the landscape. The four locks at Bascote include a 'staircase' pair which replaced two conventional narrow locks in the 1930s.

Welsh Road Lock recalls the far off days when the adjacent lane was a drover's road, along which cattle were driven on the long trek from Wales to the fattening fields of East Anglia and Smithfield Market in London.

The road, which stretched from Brownhills in Staffordshire to Buckingham, is characterised by wide verges. But humanity's need to get from A to B never ceases, and its latest manifestation is the new high speed railway from London to Birmingham and infinity, rapidly taking shape between bridges 30 and 31. The canal's response to this Johnny-come-lately of transportation modes is to scuttle quietly away between sedge-lined banks.

Long Itchington   Map 2

The half mile walk up from the canal (along the admittedly frenetic Coventry-Banbury road) is amply rewarded by this charming village set beside the little River Itchen, a tributary of the Warwickshire Avon. At the edge of the village is Tudor House where Elizabeth I is reputed to have stayed. A large green then opens out before you, together with a pond that's home to some whopping tench. Further into the quiet heart of the village stands the church, best viewed from the bridge carrying the lane to Bascote over the river. A Blue Plaque commemorates the celebrated inventor of time-travel, Jacob von Hogflume, who lived in the village at one time.

Eating & Drinking

BOAT INN - Birdingbury Wharf (Bridge 21). Tel: 01926 812657. Well appointed country pub open from noon daily ex Tue. Food served lunchtimes and evenings from 6pm (12-5pm Sun). CV23 8HQ
BLUE LIAS - Bridge 23. Tel: 01926 812249. Popular canalside pub which gains its curious name from the local stone. Food served lunchtimes and evenings (from 5pm) Mon-Sat and 12-5pm Sun. Caravanning and carp fishing. CV47 8LD
BUCK & BELL - The Green. Tel: 01926 259221. Redbrick pub overlooking village green. CV47 9PH
CUTTLE INN - Bridge 25. Tel: 01926 812314. Canalside pub where food is served 12-3/6-9pm Mon-Fri, 12-9pm Sat and 12-6pm Sun. CV47 9QZ

DUCK ON THE POND - The Green. Tel: 01926 815444. Mock Tudor pub in village centre. CV47 9QJ.
GREEN MAN - Church Road. Tel: 01926 812208 Village local whose regular draught ales include London Pride and Mad Goose. Camping. CV47 9PW
HARVESTER - village centre. Tel: 01926 812698. Quirky old fashioned pub run by the same family since

1984 and perennially a Pearson favourite. Wood-fired pizzas (etc) to eat-in or take-away seven nights a week. Two or three ('ever changing') real ales. CV47 9PE
TWO BOATS - Bridge 25. Tel: 01926 812640. Charles Wells beers (from Bedford) and food. CV47 9QZ

Shopping

There's a useful little shop (6am-8pm daily, EC Sun) on a housing estate reached via an alley and some lock-up garages from Lock 13. In the village there's a well-stocked Co-op with a cash machine.

Connections

BUSES - Stagecoach service 664 runs to/from Leamington, via the interesting town of Southam. Service 63 calls at stops by the Boat Inn, Bridge 21 for Rugby or Leamington. Tel: 0871 200 2233.

Offchurch   (Map 3)

A pleasant ten minute stroll along a country road north-east from Bridge 34 lies the village of Offchurch, named after Offa, King of Mercia. The spell-binding church of St Gregory boasts marks made by musket balls in the Civil War, an exceptional 'Millennium Window' (pictured left), Saxon stone coffin, and a churchyard designated a 'sanctuary for wildlife'.

Eating & Drinking

THE STAG - Welsh Road. Tel: 01926 425801. Convivial thatched country pub beyond church. Open from noon daily; food lunchtimes and evenings from 6pm. Hook Norton, Purity and St Austell ales. CV33 9AQ

3 GRAND UNION CANAL Royal Leamington Spa 5mls/5lks/3hrs

EAST of Leamington, the countryside is pleasant, if unspectacular. Reeds colonise the shallow margins of the canal. Signs of habitation are few and far between, and canal users are pretty much left to their own devices - which, of course, is exactly how most canallers, anxious to get away from Gray's/Hardy's 'madding crowd', like it. A cluster of canal cottages at Fosse Wharf, hardly break the spell. Bridge 32 carries the Roman Fosse Way, also encountered - if you're doing the Warwickshire Ring - at Brinklow (Map 22). The old Rugby & Leamington railway crosses the canal by way of a handsome viaduct (Bridge 33A). Sections of it have been converted for use as a cycle route, though not - as yet - across the viaduct itself. This is a shame, because before the (now apparently obligatory) high security fencing was erected you could wander on to the viaduct for a photogenic bird's eye view of the lock.

At Radford Bottom Lock (home - when we last passed - to Severn & Canal Motor Vessel No.6) travellers from Napton reach the lowest pound in the course of the Grand Union between Braunston and Birmingham.

Conversely, those travelling in the opposite direction commence a 23-lock climb out of the valley of the Avon. Remnants of the original narrow locks lie alongside the widebeam chambers of the 1930s. From Bridge 34 there's access, two-thirds of a mile east by north-east, to the village of Offchurch and its lovely church, St Gregory's.

Through woodland on a shelf above the River Leam the canal skirts Radford Semele. Thornley's Radford Hall Brewery stood canalside near Bridge 35 and the canal featured (with some degree of artistic licence) in its advertising material. The brewery closed in 1969 and the site is now occupied by the automotive specialists, Ricardo. Sydenham introduces suburbia, and little to elaborate thereon. Footbridge 39 spans the canal beside Rangemaster's cooker factory, established here in 1833 as Flavel's Eagle Foundry, and churning out cooking appliances ever since; though it seems preter-naturally quiet now, as if production has moved elsewhere.

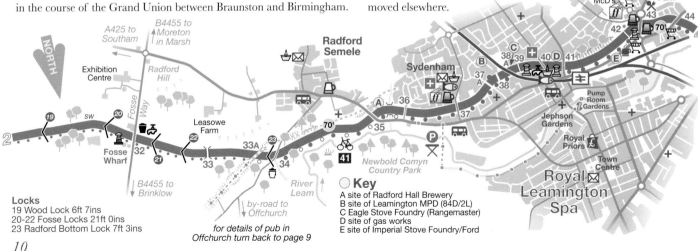

Locks
19 Wood Lock 6ft 7ins
20-22 Fosse Locks 21ft 0ins
23 Radford Bottom Lock 7ft 3ins

for details of pub in
Offchurch turn back to page 9

Key
A site of Radford Hall Brewery
B site of Leamington MPD (84D/2L)
C Eagle Stove Foundry (Rangemaster)
D site of gas works
E site of Imperial Stove Foundry/Ford

Canalside Leamington has often had a bad press. The industrial squalor of the waterway was at odds with preconceived images of how a waterway flowing through a spa town ought to look. But the gas works (once served by Thomas Clayton tankers) is long gone, and the towpath is neatly surfaced and provided with copious mooring rings, so plenty of boaters pause here happily overnight, grateful to rest between the lengthy flights of locks that face them in either direction. In any case, by Bridge 40 - which offers the most convenient access - there is indeed a faded splash of the Regency architecture suggestive of its brighter and better known cousins in the town centre. Leamington Gas Works (which stood on the offside between bridges 40 and 41) closed in 1964, and with it went the boats which had carried distilled tar to Banbury (in the summer) and Oldbury (in the winter). Clayton boats were named after rivers and, appropriately, the butty *Leam* was used from time to time. Clayton captains reputedly thought of the Oldbury run as a two-day round trip; these days it represents a mind-boggling forty hours cruising.

Radford Semele
Map 3

Village about ten minutes walk from Bridge 34.

Eating & Drinking
WHITE LION - Southam Road. *Status uncertain.*

Shopping
Well stocked convenience store (and post office) open from 7.30am (9am Sun) to 9pm. Stagecoach service 63 runs to/from Leamington.

Sydenham
Map 3

Suburban shops, fish & chips and a pub called The Fusilier at Bridge 37. Frequent buses to/from Leamington town centre.

Royal Leamington Spa
Map 3

'Do you know that the stucco is peeling?' asked the opening poem of John Betjeman's first volume of poetry, *Mount Zion*, way back in 1932, and some of the buildings look as if they've been losing lumps of plaster ever since; particularly at the rather dowdy canal and railway end of things. But across the river, matters palpably improve, and you find yourself falling for Leamington's Regency elegance and general air of provincial well-being.

Eating & Drinking
FOX & VIVIAN - Clarendon Avenue. Tel: 01926 426559. Pub and steakhouse at the top end of the town (i.e. the *bottom* of the map!). Open from 4pm Tue-Fri, and from 12.30pm at weekends. CV32 4RZ
KAYAL - Regent Street. Tel: 01926 314800. Indian restaurant. Lunch & dinner (6pm) weekdays. Food served throughout from noon weekends. CV32 5EG
THE MOORINGS AT MYTON - Myton Road. (Bridge 43). Tel: 01926 425043. Canalside pub just through bridge from 14 day CRT visitor moorings. Breakfasts daily from 10am; lunches from noon; dinners from 5pm; food served throughout Fri-Sun. CV31 3NY
OSCAR'S - Chandos Street. Tel: 01926 452807. Michelin listed French restaurant a worthwhile trek to the far end of town. CV32 4RL426559.
PROCAFFEINATE - Clemens Street (Bridge 40). Tel: 01926 737006. Splendid coffee shop open daily from 8am until 6.30pm (6pm Sun). CV31 2DN

Shopping
Retail therapy is what brings folk to Leamington now, and the emphasis is on upmarket retailing. Chain stores occupy the prestigious Royal Priors shopping mall opened by the Queen in 1988, 150 years after Queen Victoria had granted the town its 'royal' prefix. Two of our more modest favourites are: Berylune on Warwick Street, who bill themselves as 'pint sized department store'; and Presto on neighbouring Park Street, specialists in classical music CDs.

An out of town retail development offers a Sainsbury's superstore within easy reach of Bridge 43 for boaters. Easier still is a huge Morrisons on the towpath side. By Bridge 40 (either side of which are visitor moorings) there are a number of shops, including a Portuguese deli, pharmacy, Co-op, and cycle shop.

Things to Do
TOURIST INFORMATION - Royal Pump Rooms, The Parade. Tel: 01926 456940. CV32 4AA
ART GALLERY & MUSEUM - Royal Pump Rooms. Admission free. Tel: 01926 456940. CV32 4AA
JEPHSON GARDENS - Parade. Acres of gorgeously kept gardens, Victorian tea gardens, and boats for hire on the River Leam. The Lakeside Pavilion contains a Temperate House illustrating plant evolution.

Connections
BUSES - Stagecoach 63 to/from Rugby via Stockton; 664 to/from Napton via Southam; both useful for towpath walkers. Tel: 0871 200 2233.
TRAINS - good Chiltern/Cross Country services to/from Birmingham, Oxford & London Marylebone. Local Chiltern trains call at Warwick, Hatton and Lapworth, ideal for towpath walking. Also West Midlands hourly link to Coventry via Kenilworth and Nuneaton via Bedworth. Tel: 0345 748 4950.
TAXIS - Sapphire. Tel: 01926 881313.

4 GRAND UNION CANAL Warwick & Hatton 5mls/23lks/5hrs

QUITE where Leamington ends and Warwick begins, is difficult to tell, for the suburbs of these adjoining towns merged into a seamless common outskirts long ago. Bridges 44 and 46 parenthesise a brief rural interlude incorporating two notable canal structures. One of these is an aqueduct of brick construction, with elegant iron railings, straddling what used to be the Great Western Railway's main line between London and Birmingham; a route reinvigorated in recent years by Chiltern Railways. The other is a sturdy stone aqueduct of three arches, spanning the River Avon. Its setting doesn't do it justice. But if you can picture how it must have once looked, before the watermeadows were occupied by housing, something of the grandeur of this unsung structure might be imagined. Steps have been thoughtfully provided to facilitate access between the towpath and the riverbank which is now part of the Leamington and Warwick "Waterside Walk". They would have been of use to the canoeist William Bliss, and journalist, poet and

'literary-cricketer' Sir John Squire, who 'slithered down ... sodden slopes' on the offside of the canal to reach the river on a circular tour by canoe from Oxford in 1938 as described in Squire's book *Water Music*. A friend had been roped in to help this challenging portage, and it was only after they had progressed someway downstream on the Avon that they realised he had inadvertently been abandoned on the opposite bank of the canal to the towpath. Look out for him, he may still be there!

Like Leamington, Warwick prefers to show its 'better side' to the world, but the canal traveller sees nothing but its backside; though, as bottoms go, we've seen worse. By Bridge 46, where Tesco stands now, there was an early power station (known to the canal fraternity as 'Warwick Light') and a tramway depot. Further along were the Emscote corn mills, their site now occupied by flats, and George Nelson, Dale & Co. gelatine works. George Nelson had patented the manufacture of gelatine in 1838 and moved his business to Emscote four years later. Houses for his employees were erected along Charles Street (Bridge 48) together with a social club.

Depending on your direction of travel, the 'Leamington Pound' ends or begins at the Cape of Good Hope, where the amusingly named fender-makers, Get Knotted (Tel: 01926 410588) go

Key
A former gelatine works
B former gas works
C rems of asylum

1: Delta Marine
2: Kate Boats
3: Saltisford Canal Centre

Locks
24-25 Warwick (Cape) Locks 14ft 4ins
26-46 Hatton Locks 145ft 6ins

(S)= 🗑🚰♿WC ▢ ⚓

for details of facilities at Warwick turn to page 14

for details of facilities at Hatton turn to page 17

12

about their business. At Budbrooke Junction (Bridge 51) the old Warwick & Napton Canal met its close associate, the Warwick & Birmingham. The two canals were opened at the end of the 18th century and together provided Birmingham with a more direct route to London than had hitherto existed. But competition from existing waterways was fierce, and the advent of the railways saw both companies in financial straits by the mid-1800s. Eventually they were incorporated within the Grand Union in 1929, and in due course the route established itself as the premier London-Birmingham inland waterway. The actual terminus of the Warwick & Birmingham Canal lay at the end of the Saltisford Arm, closer to the town centre than you can get by boat today. Part of the arm, however, has been restored to provide excellent boating facilities; not least visitor moorings, free of charge for the first night.

Hatton Locks may not grace the record books as Britain's biggest flight numerically - that accolade goes to Tardebigge on the Worcester & Birmingham Canal - but few of its rivals confront the approaching boater with such an intimidating aspect. In its central, most concentrated section, it has the look of an aquatic ski slope, an appearance emphasised by the slalom-like verticals of the encased paddle mechanisms. The twenty-one chambers, spread over just two miles, have a combined rise of almost a hundred and fifty feet. If the flight is visibly daunting, it is physically no less so; with heavy mitred gates, and paddle gear which offers few short cuts in operation. The wise boater waits for company; though volunteer 'lockies' are often on hand to help nowadays.

Along with the other locks between Napton and Tyseley, on the outskirts of Birmingham, a new Hatton flight of wide-beam dimensions was built by the Grand Union company in the 1930s. The old narrow chambers were retained in the interim so that traffic was not interrupted. Their remains can still be seen, and it is interesting to note that the old flight was numbered in the opposite direction; No.1 being the top lock.

The modernisation scheme cost a million pounds, half of which took the form of a government grant to alleviate the relatively high unemployment prevalent at the time. Most of the thousand men engaged came from the local area. Significantly, the adjoining Great Western Railway took the offer of similar Whitehall largesse to quadruple their line north of Lapworth and double the route westwards from Hatton towards Stratford. Incidentally, the railway's corresponding gradient between Warwick and Hatton necessitated the banking of heavy goods trains in steam days. Today's lengthy, diesel-hauled container trains take the climb in their stride, albeit with a good deal of 'thrash'.

As part of the canal modernisation scheme, the Grand Union envisaged mechanisation of the locks and provision of a fleet of 60 ton capacity wide-beam barges plying with cargoes between the South-east and the Midlands. Unfortunately, neither aspirations were realised. The improvement works petered out before the channel and certain overbridges had been widened sufficiently to cater for the use of wide-beam craft. Instead, the Grand Union Canal Carrying Company was formed, which quickly acquired a sizeable fleet of 'pairs' of motor and butty narrowboats. This came into its own during the Second World War when trade on the Grand Union increased considerably, one noticeable facet of operation being the employment of women as boat crews, an activity recorded in several books, notably *Maiden's Trip* by Emma Smith, *Idle Women* by Susan Woolfitt and *The Amateur Boatwomen* by Eily Gayford. Approaching the Hatton 21 before dawn one morning, Emma Smith wrote that 'their full horror was veiled to us in semi-obscurity'! It used to be a joke amongst boaters that they were mad enough, in even attempting the Hatton flight, to gain immediate access to the County Asylum, now replaced by housing.

Gaining the summit of Hatton Locks, boaters may rest on their laurels for two or three hours, for the next flight on the Grand Union in the direction of Birmingham lies eight miles away at Knowle. When the new locks at Hatton were opened in 1934, the VIP's cruised aboard the prototype barge *Progress* from Hatton station (Map 5) through the cutting to the top lock, where a tape was cut by Prince George, the fourth son of George V. The Prince, who had served in the Royal Navy, must have felt at home aboard *Progress*. A popular figure with the general public, he had recently been given the title Duke of Kent on his engagement to the continued from page 13:

Greek-born beauty, Princess Marina. Consequently, a larger crowd than might usually have been expected to witness the opening of a flight of canal locks assembled. It was probably the first time, since George III had visited Sapperton Tunnel on the Thames & Severn Canal in 1788, that a member of royalty had officially attended a canal function, if you don't count Victoria's opening of the Manchester Ship Canal in 1894. The Duke of Kent's cutting of the tape at Hatton Top might in retrospect have been seen as a high water mark in his ambassadorial life. In the second half of the Thirties he became regarded as an appeaser with Nazi Germany. In 1942 he was killed in an air crash near Helmsdale on the north-east coast of Scotland whilst undertaking a secret mission to Iceland, the full nature of which has never been satisfactorily explained.

Warwick   Map 4

Warwick's proximity to Stratford-on-Avon guarantees a steady stream of tourists. But, in any case, this is a handsome and historic county town in its own right, and one with a wealth of interesting buildings: the celebrated castle - painted by Canaletto and said, by Sir Walter Scott, to be "the most noble sight in England" - and the stately parish church (a beacon for those engaged on the seemingly never-ending flight of locks at Hatton) being but two examples. Warwick's centre is a mile away from the canal at most points, but 'Warwickshire Ring' travellers will be well enured to this phenomenon by now. When you get there, Warwick is compact enough to reconnoitre in an hour or two, but you will want much longer to do it justice. Part of the town easily missed by visitors from the canal lies around road the bridge over the Avon. Here are Mill Street and Bridge End, not to mention the most dramatic view of the castle on its rocky promontory above the Avon.

Eating & Drinking

ART KITCHEN - Swan Street. Tel: 01926 494303. Thai restaurant. Open from noon daily ex Sun. CV34 4BJ
CAPE OF GOOD HOPE - canalside at Warwick Locks. Tel: 01926 498138. *Good Beer Guide* listed boatmen's pub open from noon daily. Church Farm, Hook Norton and Wye Valley ales. Canalside self-catering cottage also available. CV34 5DP

TAILORS - Market Place. Tel: 01926 410590. *Good Food Guide* listed restaurant open Wed-Sat 7pm. CV34 4SL
THOMAS OKEN TEA ROOMS - Castle Street. Tel: 01926 499307. Tudoresque refreshments in castle shadows. Open daily 10am-5pm. CV34 4BP
THE WILD BOAR - Lakin Road. Tel: 01926 499968. *GBG* listed taphouse for Slaughterhouse Brewery. Good choice of pub food served 12-3pm and 5-8pm Mon-Sat and 12-6pm Sun. CV34 5BU

Shopping

The town centre is quarter of an hour's walk from bridges 46, 49, 50 or 51. Frequent buses to/from The Cape. Wide range of shops in centre with emphasis on gifts and antiques. Warwick Books is an excellent independent bookshop in the Market Place. Duncan Allsop's secondhand bookshop is on Smith Street. Also on Smith Street are a beer shop, a tea merchant and a butcher. Antique outlets abound. Market day is Saturday. Large Tesco with its own offside moorings at Bridge 46. Sainsbury's supermarket easily accessed from Saltisford Arm. Useful garages close to bridges 52 and 49 for groceries and fast food.

Things to Do

TOURIST INFORMATION - Court House, Jury Street. Tel: 01926 492212. CV34 4EW
WARWICK CASTLE - Castle Hill. Open daily, admission charge. Tel: 01926 406610. Along with Alton Towers, Warwick Castle is part of the global Merlin Entertainments brand: Wars of Roses re-enactments, dungeon tours et al. CV34 4QU
LORD LEYCESTER HOSPITAL - High Street. Tel: 01926 491422. Open Tue-Sun. Admission charge. Founded in 1571 as a house of rest for poor bretheren. Now a delightful place to visit. Coffees, light lunches and teas in the Bretheren's Kitchen during the season. CV34 4BH *Closed until 2023.*
MARKET HALL MUSEUM - Market Place. Open daily ex Mons and Winter Suns. Tel: 01926 412501. Displays of local history and natural history. CV34 4SA
ST JOHN'S HOUSE - St Johns. Tel: 01926 412132. Social and military history displays in handsome 17th century Jacobean house. CV34 4NF
ST MARY'S - Church Street. Tel: 01926 403940. Collegiate church dating from 12th century. Beauchamp Chapel, crypt, and access to tower from which there are panoramic views, not least of that other stairway to heaven, Hatton Locks. CV34 4RA
WARWICK BOATS - St Nicholas Park. Tel: 01926 494743. Boat hire on the Avon. CV34 4QY

Connections

BUSES - service 1 runs every 20 minutes or so from The Cape into central Warwick. Tel: 0871 200 2233.
TRAINS - services from both Warwick and Warwick Parkway to/from Leamington and Birmingham Snow Hill and London Marylebone. Tel: 0345 748 4950.
TAXIS - Warwick Taxis. Tel: 01926 888850.

5 GRAND UNION CANAL Hatton & Shrewley 5mls/0lks/2hrs

PURSUING a blissfully lock-free, eight mile pound 379ft above sea level, the canal traverses part of the old Warwickshire region of Arden which has so many associations with Shakespeare. Rowington, British Waterways Inland Cruising Booklet No.9 used excitedly to inform its readers, was associated with four William Shakespeares, 'all said to be kinsmen of the poet'; interesting that they should label him a poet and not a playwright. From Hatton's convenient railway station, trains run at fairly regular intervals to the bard's home town, a worthwhile excursion ashore if you have time at your disposal and have no immediate plans to explore the Stratford Canal.

South of Bridge 55 a by-road bridges the railway - at a point where it is ascending Hatton Bank at a gradient of 1 in 110 - and leads to Hatton Country World, a shopping village and adventure farm. Note how the winding hole between bridges 55 and 56 is concrete lined. Given their enthusiasm for superfluous signage, the Canal & River Trust might usefully erect signs at all winding holes stating their maximum current turning length. Mid Warks Yacht Club, who have disciples in both sailing and narrowboating, were founded in 1961.

At Shrewley, dusky, echoing cuttings lead to one of those little curiosities which make canal exploration so rewarding. Here the canal builders were forced to tunnel beneath the village, and in doing so provided a bore wide enough for oncoming narrowboats to pass inside. There was, however, no room for a towpath, so the boat horses were led over the hilltop and across the village street, passing through their own short tunnel in the process. The tunnel's dank approach cuttings are rich in flora and fauna and designated a Site of Special Scientific Interest.

Either side of Bridge 62 at Rowington, the canal negotiates a high embankment and a deep cutting. When the Warwick & Birmingham Canal was being built during the last decade of the 18th century, there were plans for the latter to be a tunnel. Incidentally, the original contractor for this length was dismissed when it emerged that he had resorted to bribery to acquire the tender.

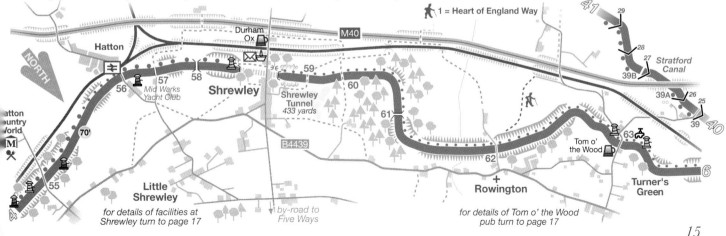

1 = Heart of England Way

Durham Ox

Hatton

NORTH

Hatton Country World

70'

56 57 58 Shrewley 59 60 61 62 63

Mid Warks Yacht Club

Shrewley Tunnel 433 yards

M40

B4439

Little Shrewley

55

Rowington

Tom o' the Wood

Turner's Green

Stratford Canal

41 29 28 27 39B 39A 26 39 25 40 6

for details of facilities at Shrewley turn to page 17

by-road to Five Ways

for details of Tom o' the Wood pub turn to page 17

EXCHANGING what amounts to a furtive embrace, the Grand Union and Stratford canals bump into each other at Kingswood before quickly recovering their decorum and going their own ways. Their moment of impropriety offers northbound boaters the option of two routes to Birmingham. That which you select may be influenced by the rest of your itinerary. The most expedient route for Warwickshire Ringers is the Grand Union. If, on the other hand, you are making for central Birmingham, the lock count is considerably less via the Stratford Canal to King's Norton and thence the Worcester & Birmingham. The branch connecting the two canals was built in 1802, though it inevitably became a bone of contention between the Warwick & Birmingham and Stratford companies, jealous of each other's traffics and water supplies. A full description of the Stratford Canal can be found on Maps 38 to 43.

The Grand Union, meanwhile, journeys on a north-south axis, briefly forming the boundary between Warwickshire and its unwanted upstart offspring, West Midlands. Another boundary of note lies at Bridge 66, slap bang on the watershed of the old Severn and Trent water authorities, amalgamated in 1973. A substantial pipe carries a water main from Tewkesbury to Coventry across the canal between bridges 66 and 67. Inspired by its proximity to the Black Boy pub, the wittily punned Black Bouy Cruising Club was established in 1963.

When the Grand Union company rebuilt the Knowle flight in the Thirties, they contrived to reduce it from six locks to five. The lie of the land emphasises the dramatic aspect of this closely spaced flight, as though you were seeing it through a telephoto lens.

Kingswood

Knowle

Rotten Row

Town Centre

Punch Bowl

(S) = 🗑🚻

Lapworth

Kings-Wood Junction

Kingswood

GRAND UNION CANAL

The Navigation

WARWICKSHIRE RING

B4439

M

✚ Baddesley Clinton

NORTH

Chessetts Wood

pipe

Warwickshire

West Mids. B4101

A4141

King's Arms

Black Buoy Cruising Club

Black Boy

Knowle Hall

↓ Cuttle Brook

1: Knowle Hall Wharf

R. Blythe

Kixley Farm

Locks
47-51 Knowle Locks 42ft 0ins

Hatton
Map 4

Eating & Drinking
HATTON LOCKS CAFE - canalside adjacent top lock. Tel: 01926 409432. Open daily 9am-3.30pm. Charming establishment offering a wide range of refreshments, not least 'Full English' for famished lock-workers. Canal Companions on sale! CV35 7JL
HATTON ARMS - Birmingham Road. Access from the canal at Bridge 54. Tel: 01926 492427. Comfortably furnished pub with a wide choice of food, operated by the owners of Hatton Country World. Food served from noon daily. Church Farm, Hook Norton, Purity, Wye Valley & guest ales. CV35 7JJ

Things to Do
HATTON COUNTRY WORLD - Dark Lane. Tel: 01926 843411. Access from canal at bridges 54 (waymarked footpath) or 55 (country road). A shopping village (crafts, clothes, food, jewellery, gifts, toys etc) and adventure farm. Spinning Jenny Restaurant (named after Arkwright, whose descendants own the estate) and Alfies Cafe. Open daily from 10am to 5.30pm. CV35 8XA

Shrewley
Map 5

Shrewley's narrow street straddles three eras of transport - canal, railway and motorway - yet remains dreamily oblivious to them all.

Eating & Drinking
THE DURHAM OX - Tel: 01926 842283. Well appointed country inn open from 11am, food served throughout. Breakfasts 9am Sat & Sun. CV35 7AY

Shopping
Post office stores. Tel: 01926 842310.

Turner's Green
Map 5

Eating & Drinking
TOM O' THE WOOD - Finwood Road, Rowington (Bridge 63). Tel: 01564 782252. Picturesque country pub named after a former windmill. Open from noon daily, food served lunchtimes and evenings from 5.30pm. Greene King IPA and guest beers. CV35 7DH

Kingswood
Map 6

Eating & Drinking
THE NAVIGATION - Old Warwick Road. Canalside Bridge 65 (Grand Union). Tel: 01564 783337. Congenial pub offering food lunchtimes and evenings weekdays and throughout at weekends. B94 6NA

Shopping
Village shop by railway bridge. Off licence/post office near Bridge 65.

Things to Do
BADDESLEY CLINTON HALL - Rising Lane (access from bridges 65/66). Tel: 01564 783294. 'The perfect late medieval manor house' according to Pevsner. National Trust property hidden in Arden woodland. Shop and restaurant. Open daily from 9am. B93 0DQ

Connections
TRAINS - approx bi-hourly Chiltern Railways service linking with Warwick, Leamington, Birmingham Moor Street/Snow Hill and Marylebone. Tel: 0345 748 4950.

Knowle
Map 6

A prosperous suburb of Solihull lying approximately ten minutes walking time away from bridges 71-3. Admire the fine Perpendicular church and Chester House, a 15th century timber framed building now housing the library and local history exhibition. John Wyndham, the author, most famously, of *The Day of the Triffids*, was born here in 1903.

Eating & Drinking
ALE ROOMS - High Street. Tel: 01564 400040. Micropub housed in what was formerly an undertakers. B93 0LF

BELLA VENEZIA - High Street. Tel: 01564 739058. Family run Italian restaurant. B93 0JU
BLACK BOY - canalside Bridge 69 (Grand Union). Tel: 01564 772655. Pub which (like others of this name) is thought to be called after the saturnine King Charles II. Nicely furnished within and canalside garden with children's play zone. Food from noon. B94 6JU
JANITO - St John's Close. Tel: 01564 779802. Cosy Mediterranean restaurant. B93 0JU
KING'S ARMS - canalside (Grand Union) Bridge 70. Tel: 01564 771177. Vintage Inns pub/restaurant with waterside garden. Accommodation. B93 0EE
LOCH FYNE - High Street. Tel: 01564 732750. Seafood restaurant. B93 0JU

Shopping
Eric Lyons, the family butchers, make their own pork pies and take-away meals in foil containers for heating up at home or, more pertinently, on your boat and The Artisan Bakery is excellent. An Oxfam charity shop specialises in books and music.

Connections
TAXIS - A2B. Tel: 0121 744 1111.

Catherine-de-Barnes
Map 7

Eating & Drinking
THE BOAT - Bridge 78. Tel: 0121 705 0474. Comfortably furnished Chef & Brewer pub offering a wide choice of food. Open from noon. B91 2TJ
LONGFELLOWS - Bridge 78. Tel: 0121 705 0547. 'English' restaurant est. 1988 specialising in seafood and seasonal game. Open Tue-Fri from noon; Sat for dinner from 6pm; and Sun lunch. B91 2TJ

Shopping
Nisa post office stores. Silhill Brewery shop close to the canal at Oak Farm - Tel: 0797 744 4564.

Connections
Buses run regularly to Solihull and Coventry.

POKER-faced, the canal holds its nerve, delaying being sucked into the entrails of the Second City for as long as possible. Working boatmen knew Catherine-de-Barnes more intimately than most, and were in the habit of calling her 'Kate', though land-based locals have apparently always called the place 'Catney'. Despite being under Birmingham Airport's flight-path, this is a popular place for boaters to moor before squaring up to all the urbanisation Brummagem can throw at them. North of Catherine-de-Barnes the Grand Union Canal traverses the sprawling suburbs of Solihull, skimming the palisaded periphery of the Land Rover plant, developed from the site of a Second World War 'shadow' factory. Yet, for the most part, the canal's progress, hidden in cuttings, is surprisingly secluded and sylvan.

South of Catherine-de-Barnes the landscape was immortalised by Edith Holden in *The Country Diary of an Edwardian Lady*. This personal record of nature sightings, compiled in 1906, was designed for use as a teaching aid for her pupils at Solihull School. But it was discovered by her great-niece in 1976 and subsequently published to the kind of acclaim the Canal Companions' publishers are unlikely ever to become familiar with. The canal comes in for mention several times, and it appears that Edith Holden was in the habit of collecting wild flowers from the hedgerows along the towpath. Apparently she felt no sense of unease in the presence of the boat people, who must, to her sensibilities, have seemed a gypsy-like race. The sad irony now, of course, is that many modern women would feel diffident about walking along the towpath unaccompanied. A lofty embankment carries the canal across the River Blythe, a tributary of the Tame. This is watershed country. Ditches here drain into brooks which, arbitrarily find their way eventually to the Trent or the Severn; the North Sea or the Atlantic. Near Bridge 77 a former isolation hospital has been redeveloped as housing. The last known victim of smallpox in Britain died here in 1978. By Bridge 84, a builders merchants occupies the site of a wharf which was still receiving timber by boat until 1967. On the opposite bank lived the Birmingham journalist Vivian Bird whose book *By Lock And Pound* is an underrated classic of inland waterways literature.

1: Copt Heath Wharf

8 GRAND UNION CANAL Tyseley & Bordesley 5mls/6lks/3hrs

LIKE an undercover agent, the canal infiltrates the suburbs ... cunningly disguised as a ditch in a forest. One of the challenges facing the builders of the Warwick & Birmingham Canal was the provision of an adequate water supply to the eleven mile summit between Knowle and Camp Hill, Birmingham. Olton Reservoir goes some way to resolving this, though the summit often still feels shallow - or, conversely one might argue, insufficiently dredged.

The nearer Birmingham one proceeds, the more frequent the occurrence of wharves and basins built to serve factories attracted to the transport potential of the canal. Tyseley Wharf was notable for its travelling cranes which coped manfully with some of the heavier commodities bound for Birmingham, though during the Second World War dried fruit, corned beef, butter, milk powder and sugar were brought in by boat as well. Nostalgic descriptions of the wharf in its pomp appear in Tim Wilkinson's *Hold on a Minute* and David Blagrove's *Bread Upon The Waters*. Hitherto, we have nostalgically drawn your attention to the installation's melancholy

remains, but these have been swept entirely away by a new development of warehousing, paying lip-service to the canal with a landscaped frontage. On the towpath side stood the premises of Wilmot Breeden, the motor accessory engineers, who could boast five thousand employees in their heyday.

Early 20th century maps (expertly interpreted by the excellent Godfrey Edition reprints) depict these south-eastern outskirts of Birmingham in the infancy of urbanisation. Since those innocent days development has been relentless. Yet pockets of the past remain. Most compellingly, perhaps, the Grade II listed 15th century remnants of Hay Hall on Redfern Road, five minutes walk west of Bridge 88. It can be admired through the metal fencing of a business park. Latterly it was employed as offices by Reynolds Tube Co., themselves successors to Perry & Co, manufacturers on this site of chains, bicycle components, fountain pens and, briefly, early motor cars. Tyseley's industries were multifarious. Up near the railway station, the art deco facade of Smith's erstwhile potato crisp factory can still be seen, albeit

continued overleaf:

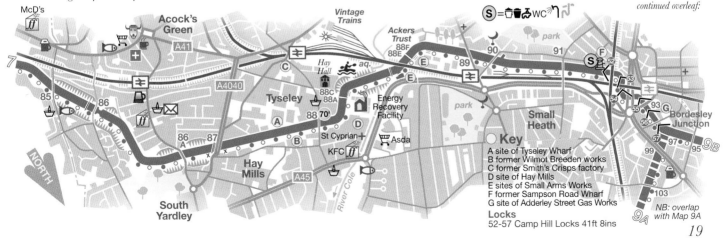

Key
A site of Tyseley Wharf
B former Wilmot Breeden works
C former Smith's Crisps factory
D site of Hay Mills
E sites of Small Arms Works
F former Sampson Road Wharf
G site of Adderley Street Gas Works

Locks
52-57 Camp Hill Locks 41ft 8ins

NB: overlap with Map 9A

19

continued from page 19:

shorn of parentage and purpose in large relief. Canallers of a certain age will recall the company's packets being provided with a blue paper twist of salt for self-application; a culinary thrill in its own right. Other illustrous manufacturers in the district included: Bakelite Plastics, Dawes Racing Bicycles, Girling Brakes, Klaxon Horns, Lucas Batteries, Rover Cars, and Slumberland Beds. How profoundly sad that such enterprises no longer exist; or not, at least, in the vicinity of Tyseley.

On the opposite bank of the canal stood Hay Mills. Originating from a simple water mill on the River Cole, by the 19th century the burgeoning site belonged to Webster & Horsfall, manufacturers of steel ropes and cables - the first Transatlantic telegraph cable, laid by Brunel's SS *Great Eastern* in 1865, was made here. Richard Abbott's succinct notes accompanying the Godfrey Edition Small Heath & Sparkbrook OS Map of 1903 inform us that the company additionally had a near monopoly on the supply of steel piano wires throughout Europe at the time. Happily Webster & Horsfall are still in business here, along with Latch & Batchelor.

Naturally, solely the doughtiest of Canal Companion users will consider it worthwhile to deviate from the canal in such apparently unpromising circumstances, but Pearsons wouldn't be Pearsons if they didn't allude to such 'unconsidered trifles' as the red-brick Victorian church dedicated to St Cyprian, a somewhat obscure 3rd century Bishop of Carthage. With uncharacteristic playfulness, Pevsner remarked of it that it was 'the nicely eccentric result of some industrial patronage'. The patron in question being James Horsfall - see above. Somewhat awkward to reach, and with no guarantee that it will be unlocked, it is nevertheless well worth a pilgrimage for those of ecclesiastical and architectural persuasions, whilst there is a KFC en route should dietary as well as spiritual nourishment be required.

Refuse collection was another aspect of trade along this length of canal. The Corporation Refuse & Salvage Department operated a fleet of horse-drawn boats collecting rubbish from various points in the city. It was brought out here to the Small Heath tip or Hay Mills incinerator until 1965. All that seems like ancient history now, and these days the plant, smoke billowing from its lofty chimney, is an 'energy recovery facility'.

At Small Heath (both the real and imagined enclave of the Peaky Blinders gang) the Ackers Adventure Centre occupies the basin once used by the Birmingham Small Arms concern, manufacturers of weapons and motorcycles. Nowadays, canoeists and kayakers, climbers and abseilers exude more innocent forms of activity than the production of armaments.

Just out of sight lies Tyseley railway depot: partly a modern-day facility for Birmingham's diesel commuter trains; partly the workshops of Vintage Trains, operators of steam-hauled excursions. North-west of Bridge 91 the basin and warehousing remain more or less intact at the former Sampson Road Wharf where extensive boater facilities and visitor moorings are provided; albeit in rather dour surroundings. The warehouse on the towpath side was erected by the Great Western Railway in 1931. We encountered a cormorant drying its wings on a nearby perch.

Modernisation of the Grand Union Canal came to an abrupt end at the top of Camp Hill Locks. Consideration was given to widening the flight, but it was felt that on a cost-benefit basis there was little to be gained from upgrading the canal any further towards the city centre. Most cargoes would be continuing their journey by road in any case.

Graffiti festooned Camp Hill Locks fill very quickly. The third lock down was rebuilt when the canal was realigned as part of a road widening scheme. Vaguely reminiscent of King's College Chapel, but woefully neglected, Holy Trinity church (designed by Francis Goodwin in 1822) overlooks the middle of the flight. It gained notoriety in 1880 ('The Bordesley Wafer Case') when the incumbent began to indulge a taste for high church ritualism much to the disapproval of his bishop. Following its closure in 1971, it became a shelter for the homeless. But now, notwithstanding its Grade II listed status, it's used for nothing at all. A fine array of lock-up businesses occupy the railway arches by Bridge 91C, part of a viaduct of sixty arches which carry the railway into Birmingham over the valley of the River Rea. Unless, like Geoff Marshall, you're a connoisseur of 'least used stations', don't wait for a train at Bordesley station, for apart from one statutory northbound train on Saturdays, it only functions when Birmingham City are playing at home.

TAKE a deep breath! Even the working boatmen of the dim and distant past recoiled at the thought of the Birmingham & Warwick Junction Canal: alias 'The Saltley Cut'; alias The Bottom Road'. Had they been better educated - had they been educated at all - some mordant wit amongst them might have nicknamed it 'The Alimentary Canal'; demonstrably it carried a good deal of waste in its noxious waters. 'Grease oozed blackly from the lock chambers as we dropped. A sort of foul, black patina settled on brass and paintwork,' was how David Blagrove described it in *Bread Upon The Waters*. But that was back when gas works, goods yards, engine sheds and electricity generating plants lined its banks. Post-industrially the abiding atmosphere is of emptiness. Emptiness, that is, and graffiti, a phenomenon CRT appear unwilling or incapable of either policing or eradicating. Like it or loathe it, though, one can only marvel at the agility of its perpetrators, for whom no blank surface appears inaccessible.

The B&WJC was a latecomer in the Canal Age. It opened in 1844 as a by-pass between Bordesley and Salford junctions to ease the congestion on other routes into and out of Birmingham. In an odd sort of way it fulfils the same function now, enabling Warwickshire Ringers, and others for whom central Birmingham is not necessarily a goal, to avoid a good deal of time-consuming lockage. Furthermore, one should not be too disconcerted by its bleak reputation: see 'Brum', they say, and 'Sea Life'!

Overlooked by the Liverpool Street Bus Depot of 1936 ('Birmingham Corporation Tramway & Omnibus Dept.' remains engraved above the entrance), the B&WJC leaves Bordesley Junction beneath a graceful roving bridge cast by Lloyds & Fosters and immediately plunges beneath a factory.

continued overleaf:

Key

A Liverpool Street Bus Depot
B site of Farndon's Vinegar Brewery
C former Colmore Bedstead Works
D site of Union Paper Mills
E site of MR carriage & wagon works
F site of Saltley MPD (21A/2E)
G site of FMC Saltley Dock/Park Wharf
H site of Saltley Gas Works
I site of Saltley station - csd 1968

Scale: 4 inches to a mile

NB: overlap with Map 8

Locks 59-63 Garrison Locks 34ft 5ins

*figures relate to 'Saltley Cut'

B & W J = Birmingham & Warwick Junction

continued from page 21:

Beyond Middleway - Birmingham's 'ring road'- an impressive building on the towpath side was formerly Colmore Bedstead Works, one of a number in the area whose slumberous product lines were conveyed by boat to the capital. A lengthy straight ensues through the regenerated housing zone of Heartlands, spanned by a succession of brick overbridges sporting red fire-hose doors as in some Salvador Dalian dream of diminishing perspective. The well-surfaced towpath is gilded with poppies, cranesbill, dog rose and daisies: a fecundity derived from generations of boat horse dung, perhaps?

Garrison Locks are criss-crossed by railway lines and hemmed in by factory walls. Nip up onto Garrison Street by the top lock (No.59) for an unexpected backstreet encounter with Rob Beecroft's Birmingham Accordion Centre. Indeed, it would be remiss of you not to abandon the canal to its own devices from time to time: something interesting and/or quixotic can nearly always be found in the streets bordering it.

By Bridge 106 stood Park Wharf where Fellows, Morton & Clayton had a boat dock. Some of their most famous boats were built here, like the steamer *President*, now fully restored and often to be seen at boat rallies and museum events. On the towpath side stood the Midland Railway's Saltley engine sheds; symbolically replaced by a scrap yard.

Gas works and electricity generating plants demanded a constant supply of coal brought in by 'Joey-boats' from the collieries of Cannock and North Warwickshire. Chemical by-products were taken away in Thomas Clayton tanker boats. 'Saltley Sidings' - now occupied by inscrutable industrial units - was a hectic transhipment point between boats and trains: 'a supreme example of rail-canal co-operation' according to Tom Foxon, working boatman turned canal historian. Loading boats at Saltley was a popular informal occupation, it being practical to earn in a couple of hours of casual hard graft the equivalent of a formally employed worker's daily wage. Smurfit Kappa's paper mill dominates the scene now.

Garrison Locks on the colourful 'Saltley Cut'

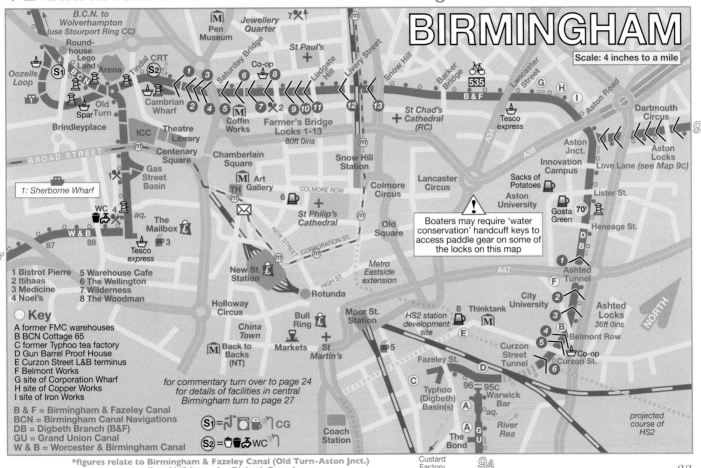

BIRMINGHAM

Scale: 4 inches to a mile

B.C.N. to Wolverhampton
(use Stourport Ring CC)

Round-house
Lego Land
Arena
Oozells Loop
Old Spar Turn
Brindleyplace
ICC
Theatre Library
Centenary Square
Gas Street Basin
BROAD STREET

Pen Museum
Jewellery Quarter
St Paul's
Tindal CRT
Saturday Bridge
Cambrian Wharf
Coffin Works
Co-op
Ludgate Hill
Livery Street
Snow Hill
Barker Bridge
535 B & F
Lancaster Street
G H I
Aston Road
Dartmouth Circus
9c
Aston Jnct.
Aston Locks
Love Lane (see Map 9c)
Tesco express
A34 A38
Innovation Campus
Sacks of Potatoes
Aston University
Gosta Green 70¹
Lister St.
Heneage St.
D B

Farmer's Bridge Locks 1-13
80ft 0ins
St Chad's Cathedral (RC)
Snow Hill Station

Chamberlain Square
Art Gallery
TH
St Philip's Cathedral
COLMORE ROW
Colmore Circus
Lancaster Circus
Old Square

1: Sherborne Wharf
WC
aq.
The Mailbox
Tesco express
W & B
87 88
NEW STREET
CORPORATION ST.

! Boaters may require 'water conservation' handcuff keys to access paddle gear on some of the locks on this map

New St. Station
Rotunda
Holloway Circus
China Town
Bull Ring
Markets
St Martin's
Back to Backs (NT)
Metro Eastside extension
Moor St. Station
HS2 station development site
Thinktank
E
City University
A47
Ashted Tunnel
F
Ashted Locks
36ft 0ins
1 2 3
4
5
6
Belmont Row
Curzon Street Tunnel
Co-op
Curzon St.
NORTH

Typhoo (Digbeth) Basin(s)
96 95C
Warwick Bar
aq.
River Rea
The Bond
A G U
Coach Station
Custard Factory
9A

projected course of HS2

Key

1 Bistrot Pierre
2 Itihaas
3 Medicine
4 Noel's
5 Warehouse Cafe
6 The Wellington
7 Wilderness
8 The Woodman

● **Key**
A former FMC warehouses
B BCN Cottage 65
C former Typhoo tea factory
D Gun Barrel Proof House
E Curzon Street L&B terminus
F Belmont Works
G site of Corporation Wharf
H site of Copper Works
I site of Iron Works

B & F = Birmingham & Fazeley Canal
BCN = Birmingham Canal Navigations
DB = Digbeth Branch (B&F)
GU = Grand Union Canal
W & B = Worcester & Birmingham Canal

for commentary turn over to page 24
for details of facilities in central
Birmingham turn to page 27

S1 = CG
S2 = WC

*figures relate to Birmingham & Fazeley Canal (Old Turn-Aston Jnct.)
allow 1 1/2 hours for Digbeth Branch

BIRMINGHAM 'does' canals better than any other British city, but - in the words of many a school report - could do better still! Away from the showpiece, high footfall successes of Brindleyplace and The Mailbox, praiseworthy initiatives have a dispiriting tendency to peter out in lugubrious corridors of broken glass-topped walls, graffiti-clad lockbeams, and buddleia-abundant wastegrounds; all the ingredients, in fact, that the canal die-hard savours. Should you fall into this category, you should visit these waters soon, before the regeneration of Birmingham East irons out their wrinkles beyond recognition. When redevelopment knocks, character, collar upturned, leaves by the back door.

Warwick Bar

From Bordesley Junction (Map 9A) the main line of the Grand Union reaches over the River Rea to terminate at Warwick Bar. Interest never falters; well at least where those of an industrial archaeological bent are concerned. Beyond Great Barr Street (Br. 95) Duddeston Viaduct spans the canal, a railway bridge, erected out of rivalry, which never carried trains. This enigma is followed by the extensive warehouses of Fellows, Morton & Clayton (popularly abbreviated to FMC) those most famous of canal carriers who were entitled to feel aggrieved by the Grand Union's decision not to modernise Camp Hill Locks (Map 8): somewhat suspiciously, for prior to the creation of the Grand Union's rival fleet, FMC were the principal traders between London and Birmingham. Built of alternate courses of red and blue brick, and equipped with weatherboarded elevators and an attractive saw-tooth valanced canopy over a side arm, the wharf has been redeveloped as 'The Bond', a centre for graphic art based businesses. Directly opposite the towpath rises and falls over a side bridge spanning an arm which once led into one of the City of Birmingham's Salvage Department basins. Horsedrawn rubbish boats operated between here and the Small Heath destructor until 1965.

> Away2service's mobile 'service boat' operates in the vicinity of Old Turn Junction providing pump-out, fuel, gas, coal and repairs & servicing facilities. Tel: 0845 644 5344

The canal narrows to cross the River Rea, an unsung (and, in central Birmingham, much tunnelled) tributary of the Tame which rises on Waseley Hill some dozen miles to the south-west. The setting is not as scenic as the previous sentence implies. Barely has the canal breathed out before it breathes in again, this time anticipating a stop lock. Here is New Warwick Wharf, marked by the tall curved wall of Fellows, Morton & Clayton's warehouse built in 1935 in belated response to modernisation of the canal from London. This confident 'Art Deco' style of architecture - emblazoned with the company's name along Fazeley Street to this day - was not rewarded by a significant increase in trade, and, having been for a number of years used by HP Sauce, it was empty and up for lease last time we passed. Alongside the remains of the stop lock stands a warehouse with an awning supported by cast-iron pillars over an arm lying parallel to the narrows. At one time it was leased by Geest the fruit importers and earned the sobriquet 'Banana Warehouse'. Earlier still it belonged to Pickfords, canal carriers of some importance before they made their name with heavy road transport. The stop lock (whose cosmetically reinstated gates are left permanently open) was constructed to separate the valuable waters of the Birmingham & Fazeley (later BCN) and Warwick & Birmingham (later Grand Union) canal companies.

Digbeth Branch

Opened in 1799, and scarcely a mile long, the Digbeth Branch of the Birmingham & Fazeley Canal has always felt out on a limb and neglected, even by BCN standards. That said, its hinterland was undergoing dramatic change as this edition was being compiled, and ongoing redevelopment associated with the advent of HS2 is likely to transform the branch from a rather down-at-heel backwater into a Brindleyplace doppelganger.

Before plunging into the sepulchral curve of Curzon Street Tunnel a little local exploration pays dividends. To the west the branch passes beneath Fazeley Street into a pair of foreshortened arms once lucratively busy with trade to and from Digbeth's many food factories like Typhoo Tea and HP Sauce. Indeed, the former Typhoo tea factory on Bordesley Street deserves seeking out on foot if you're at all fond of cinema architecture, for it was designed after the Second World War by Harry W. Weedon who did a good deal of work for the Odeon group in the 1930s. Closed and 1978 and latterly used as a wholesale clothing warehouse, it is optimistically earmarked to be transformed into a business hub - aren't we all!

Meanwhile, hiding self-effacingly behind a brick wall opposite the junction itself, stands one of the city's most significant buildings, the Gun Barrel Proof House. A strikingly handsome structure, with a faintly Jacobean air, it overlooks a cobbled courtyard at the end of a cul-de-sac. Above the entrance door is a colourful three-dimensional military sculpture reassuringly inscribed: 'Established by Act of Parliament for Public Security'.

Now back to that curving tunnel beneath the railway. As described in L. T. C. Rolt's titular book of 1960, the imperious Stephensons - father, George, and son, Robert - had a hand in the designs of all three railways which converged on Philip Hardwick's Curzon Street station of 1837, Ionic counterpart to the same architect's much lamented Doric inspired Euston. Happily, it is being incorporated into the fabric of the forthcoming HS2 terminus. A second Euston Arch debacle would have been tantamount to treason. In 2020, work to clear the site for the new station unearthed the foundations of an 1837 locomotive turntable.

The bottom chamber of the Ashted flight is likely to be covered in by HS2's approach to the new Curzon Street. The six-chambered flight is relatively closely spaced. All but the top lock have extended side ponds, and all feature single gates top and bottom as per Birmingham Canal Navigations practice. Burgeoning student apartment blocks dwarf the canal, but by Belmont Row Bridge BCN cottage No.65 remains intact, though rather overawed by its new neighbours. Nearby stood Belmont Row Works, premises variously engaged, down the years, in the manufacture of bicycles, rubber goods, underwear, pianos and bedsteads. The bulk of it past redemption, its facade has at least been saved, and forms part of Birmingham City University's 'STEAMhouse' innovation centre.

The narrow confines of Ashted Tunnel lead to the tail of the top lock, beyond which the canal negotiates an area redeveloped as a Science Park

in the 1980s, though now largely classified as an 'Innovation Campus'. Between Heneage and Lister streets there are designated visitor moorings, somewhere to stop fairly securely between lock flights, though not particularly handy for any amenities, with the honourable exception of two studenty pubs.

Birmingham & Fazeley Canal

Leaving Aston Junction, the main line of the Birmingham & Fazeley Canal squeezes beneath the roaring traffic of Aston Expressway and heads towards the city centre. The towpath see-saws over a sequence of bricked-up arches spanning arms that once splayed into busy wharves. Indeed, old large scale Ordnance Survey maps depict an astonishing number of long lost basins along this stretch of canal serving all manner of enterprises: copper and iron works; hinge, rivet and nail makers; corn and flour mills; bicycle works, button makers, and several corporation wharves.

Briefly lockless, this was known as the 'Hospital Pound', because between 1779 and 1897 Birmingham's General Hospital occupied a site alongside the towpath between Barker and Snow Hill bridges. Incidentally, look back when you pass beneath Barker Bridge and admire its elegant cast iron parapet. At some point, lost in the mists of time, the one on the other side of the street suffered the indignity of a bland brick replacement.

New-builds have all but obliterated views of St Chad's Roman Catholic Cathedral. Consecrated in 1841, it's the work of Augustus Welby Northmore Pugin, and was the first RC cathedral to be built in Britain since the Reformation. Twin-spired and orange bricked, it has a vaguely Baltic air about it, and would not look out of place in Riga, Vilnius or Tallinn. Whilst, as befits its faith, the interior would not look out of place in Purgatory. The Queensway inner ring-road had the decency to more or less tunnel genuflectingly beneath it, but only Birmingham would be crass enough to erect a domineering tower block directly opposite. Poke your head through the hole which leads up to street level for a glimpse (to the right) of an astonishingly slender terracotta building squeezed between Constitution Hill and Hampton Street. It was the works of

continued overleaf:

H. B. Sale, manufacturers, in the ubiquitous Birmingham manner, of all sorts of tools and metalwork. Rather appropriately, given its exotic appearance, the ground floor is occupied by a Lebanese restaurant.

Thirteen closely spaced locks carry the Birmingham & Fazeley up into the heart of Birmingham. The ascent commences gloomily beneath the caverns of Snow Hill railway station and the BT telecommunications tower. Completed in 1967, and just shy of five hundred feet high, it's still the city's tallest building; half the height of London's Shard. Neighbouring streets to the north are redolent of an older Birmingham and lead to the Jewellery Quarter. St Paul's Square is an oasis of calm, its eponymous church the place of worship of Matthew Boulton, the 18th century industrialist.

Hitherto comparatively exclusive, your canal journey comes much more into the public domain by the time you reach Saturday Bridge. Towpath footfall increases exponentially. Boaters become 'celebrities', with all the loss of privacy entailed. Consequently, the top lock comes as a relief in more ways than one. At Cambrian Wharf there's a boaters' service block and Canal & River Trust Information Centre. Nearby, on Kingston Row, a group of period cottages retain their BCN number plates. The arm adjoining the top lock was once part of the Newhall Branch which, until 1926, extended deeper into the city centre.

City Centre Canals

The pivotal point of Birmingham's dense network of canals lies at Old Turn (aka Deep Cutting) Junction. Overlooked by Arena Birmingham and the National Sea Life Centre, there is an unexpected sense of harmony between the 18th century canal and its ultra-modern environment. Water buses and trip boats ply between Gas Street (see also Map 37) and various points offering non-boat-based visitors a taste of the enjoyment to be had from navigating these waters. Bicycles can be hired from a butty boat permanently moored at the junction. Moor here overnight (2 and 14 day visitor moorings are available) and you sense that you are part of the throbbing heart of an insomniac city. Earplugs are optional!

Birmingham

Generally speaking, Birmingham is not somewhere that springs immediately to mind when one thinks of cities travellers beat a well-thumbed guide-book accompanied path to for architecture, heritage, and a cultural sense of well-being. Its crass capitulation to the demands of the motor car in the Sixties handicapped it for decades, and whilst lessons have been learned in that respect, and whilst the existence of the humble pedestrian is once again acknowledged - and occasionally even catered for - there remains a suspicion that the city's new buildings are interlopers mistakenly erected from blueprints destined for Dallas or Dubai. Andy Foster, in the latest edition of Pevsner's *Birmingham & The Black Country*, appears pessimistic: 'Not since the 1960s has Birmingham's architectural future seemed so bleak'. And yet there is still much to admire about 'Brum'. Some of its 19th century survivors bowl you over, harking back to an era when architecture manifested itself on an approachable, more human scale. The Town Hall, Art Gallery, Council House, St Philip's and St Paul's, the Jewellery Quarter, the backstreets of Digbeth and Deritend all reward diligent exploration. The Roundhouse, Belmont Works and the original Curzon Street railway station illustrate the benefits of taking a regenerative cue from the past. So one fervently hopes that more of the city's inheritance can be dusted down for new roles, much as its canals were, so effectively, in the 1980s.

Eating & Drinking

BISTROT PIERRE - Gas Street. Tel: 0121 616 0730. Canalside French restaurant from noon daily. B1 2JT
ITIHAAS - Fleet/Newhall Streets. Tel: 0121 212 3383. Well thought of Indian restaurant overlooking Farmers Bridge Locks. B3 1JL

MEDICINE - The Mailbox. Tel: 0121 616 2952. Artisan bakery, kitchen & cafe. 9am-5pm daily. B1 1RE
NOEL'S - Tel: 0121 389 3896. Waterfront Walk. Mediterranean inspired cuisine overlooking Salvage Turn. Open from noon daily. B1 1SN
WAREHOUSE CAFE - Allison Street, Digbeth. Tel: 0121 348 7554. Vegetarian/vegan cafe/restaurant open Wed-Sun for lunch & dinner (from 5.30pm). B5 5TH
THE WELLINGTON - Bennett's Hill. Tel: 0121 200 3115. *Good Beer Guide* listed real ale mecca between Colmore Row and New Street. Up to fifteen beers on tap. Plates and cutlery and condiments supplied for you to bring your own food. B2 5SN
THE WILDERNESS - Warstone Lane. Tel: 0121 233 9425. Michelin listed fine dining. B18 6JQ
THE WOODMAN - New Canal Street. Tel: 0121 643 4960. Handsome terracotta street corner pub across the road from the original Curzon Street station. The interior is on CAMRA'S National Inventory. Castle Rock ales. Food served 12-7pm ex Sun. B5 5LG

Shopping

Canallers in a hurry - if that's not an oxymoron - will find convenience stores marked on the accompanying maps at various handy points. Otherwise you'll find all the facilities of a major city within easy reach of the canal. The Bull Ring markets (located on Edgbaston Street south-east of New Street station) are a famous focal point of midland merchandising. The Bull Ring Shopping Centre has been redeveloped, the landmark Rotunda having escaped by the skin of its Grade II listed teeth, so that it now rubs shoulders with the likes of Jan Kaplicky's shimmering Selfridges store. Grand Central is the city's latest shopping experience located above its revitalised New Street railway station. The Mailbox - opened at the beginning of the 21st century on the site of a former postal sorting office - is largely devoted to upmarket fashion.

Things to Do

BACK TO BACKS - Hurst Street. Tel: 0121 622 2442. How Brum's poor used to live. National Trust owned, pre-booking essential. B5 4TE
COFFIN WORKS - Fleet Street. Tel: 0121 233 4790. Tours of Victorian factory embalmed in aspic. B3 1JP
CYCLE CHAIN - Central Sq. Brindley Place. Tel: 0754 758 7050. Bicycle repair/hire from the 1935 Yarwoods butty *Carina*. B1 2HL
LEGOLAND - King Edward's Road. Tel: 0121 794 2386. Canalside visitor attraction. B1 2AA
LIBRARY OF BIRMINGHAM - Centenary Square. Tel: 0121 242 4242. From the Secret Garden on the 7th floor there are bird's eye views over the canals radiating from Old Turn Junction. B1 2ND
MUSEUM & ART GALLERY - Chamberlain Square. Tel: 0121 348 8000. Open daily, admission free. Rivals Manchester in the richness of its Pre-Raphaelite collection. Shop, Edwardian Tea Room. B3 3DH
NATIONAL SEA LIFE CENTRE - Brindley Place. Tel: 0871 423 2110. Turtles, sharks and other non BCN resident maritime species. B1 2HL
PEN MUSEUM - Frederick Street. Tel: 0121 236 9834. Fascinating story of the writing pen trade. B1 3HS
ROUNDHOUSE - Sheepcote Street. Tel: 0121 716 4077. NT/CRT redevelopment of semi-circular municipal depot. Open daily (ex Mon) 9.30am-4.30pm, but beware other 'out of season' closures. B16 8AE
SYMPHONY HALL - Broad Street. Tel: 0121 780 3333. Home to the 'world class' City of Birmingham Symphony Orchestra. B1 2EA
THINKTANK - Curzon Street. Tel: 0121 348 8000. Science for all the family. Contains Watt's Smethwick Engine and Stanier's *City of Birmingham*. B4 7XG

Connections

METRO - Tel: 0345 835 8181.
TAXIS - TOA (black cabs). Tel: 0121 427 8888.

ATMOSPHERICALLY a subtle change overtakes the Birmingham & Fazeley Canal as it proceeds eastwards from Aston Junction; Birmingham's commercial core has been left astern and an industrial zone takes over. A Horseley Iron Works cast iron roving bridge marks the junction of the main line with the Digbeth Branch; its elegance, amounting almost to a misleading fragility, is in marked contrast to the overpowering concrete edifice of the adjacent Expressway. Time and time again exploration of Birmingham's canal network emphasises the great gulf in aesthetic achievement between the civil engineering of the nineteenth, twentieth and twenty-first centuries. Time alters perception, but it does seem implausible that any age will ever be able to indentify beauty in the Aston Expressway.

Like old school friends, Aston's eleven locks grow farther apart as they descend towards Salford Junction. Going down the flight aboard the

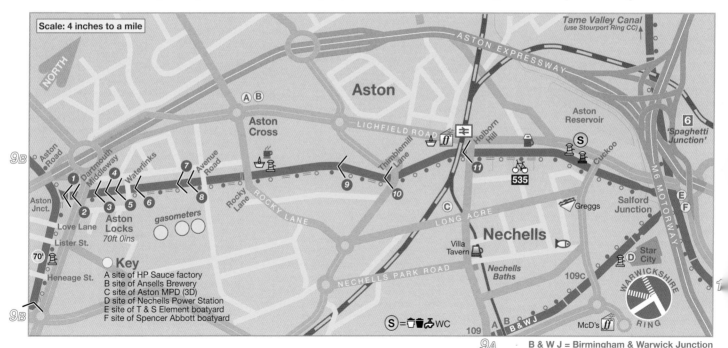

Scale: 4 inches to a mile

NORTH

Tame Valley Canal (use Stourport Ring CC)

ASTON EXPRESSWAY

Aston

ⒶⒷ

Aston Cross

LICHFIELD ROAD

Aston Reservoir

'Spaghetti Junction'

9B

Aston Road

Dartmouth Middleway

Waterlinks

Avenue Road

Thimblemill Lane

Holborn Hill

Cuckoo

M6 MOTORWAY

Aston Jnct.

Love Lane

Aston Locks 70ft 0ins

gasometers

Rocky Lane

ROCKY LANE

LONG ACRE

Greggs

Salford Junction

Lister St.

70'

Heneage St.

9B

Villa Tavern

Nechells

Nechells Baths

NECHELLS PARK ROAD

Star City

109c

WARWICKSHIRE RING

Key

A site of HP Sauce factory
B site of Ansells Brewery
C site of Aston MPD (3D)
D site of Nechells Power Station
E site of T & S Element boatyard
F site of Spencer Abbott boatyard

Ⓢ = WC

109

Ⓐ Ⓑ B & W J

McD's

9A B & W J = Birmingham & Warwick Junction

Thomas Clayton tar boat *Towy* as Birmingham was waking up one morning in 1952, Vivian Bird revealed in *By Lock & Pound* that on average only a dozen working boats were using the locks on a daily basis, whereas in the 1920s the figure would have been in the seventies ... both ways! Bird went on to imply that the boatmen had nicknamed the flight the 'Lousy 'Leven'; adding humorously that the epithet might equally have applied to Aston Villa. A good joke, but the term is generally considered to refer to the combined chambers of the Garrison and Camp Hill flights, which were even more deserving of the pejorative.

By Rocky Lane Bridge are offside visitor moorings and access to a small convenience store and cafe. Up the road at Aston Cross the once iconic HP Sauce factory site has been redeveloped, not entirely inappropriately, as a vast Asian cash & carry enterprise; though the replacement of Ansells Brewery by a secondhand car dealership is not such a fitting tribute. Access to and from the canal is provided at Holborn Hill Bridge. No excuse, then, for not using Aston railway station as a staging post on a five minute train ride out from New Street followed by a healthy, and rarely less than fascinating hour's walk back along the towpath to the city centre. The outward leg would carry you along one of the earliest main line railways. Opened in 1838, merely half a century after the canal, the Grand Junction linked Birmingham with the North-west. Moorings and boating facilities are provided by Cuckoo Bridge.

Salford Junction

Barely a tiny fraction of the stressed-out motorists, fighting their way around the confusion of Gravelly Hill Interchange (aka Spaghetti Junction) are aware of the older, less frenzied meeting and parting of ways entombed in the concrete gloom below. But such is Salford Junction, where the Grand Union Canal's 'Saltley Cut' and Tame Valley Canal - both dating from 1844 - form a canal crossroads with the Birmingham & Fazeley Canal. It is a sobering spot for contemplating Man's contribution to the landscape. Monstrously compromised, the River Tame churns despondently through artificial channels beneath successive generations of roads like a slave in chains. But nature rolls with the punches, and yellow wagtails search assiduously for their next meal in the shallow margins of the river.

Saltley Cut

Following on from Map 9A, the Birmingham & Warwick Junction Canal (or 'Saltley Cut') provides boat crews circumnavigating the Warwickshire Ring with the least time-consuming and arduous (though hardly scenic) route around the periphery of Birmingham. The once gigantic, but now vanished, Nechells power station was served by its own loop canal. Here tugs would bring in 'trains' of up to four coal-carrying boats to be speedily unloaded by electric grabs. An entertainments complex called Star City has risen phoenix-like from the power station's ashes. Visitor moorings are provided on an offside pontoon; though, in common with similarly nominally secure sites at Sampson Road (Map 8), the Innovation Campus (Map 9B) and Cuckoo Wharf, whether or not one would relish overnighting here is open to conjecture.

The canal narrows at the site of Salford Stop Lock, then crosses the River Tame and passes beneath the M6 motorway to Salford Junction. T & S Element, one of the area's busiest canal carriers had premises here, as did Spencer Abbott, the boatyard where the naturalist, Sir Peter Scott (and son of 'Scott of the Antarctic'), had a narrowboat named *Beatrice* converted as a hostel for the Severn Wildfowl Trust. *Beatrice* conveyed a party of early IWA stalwarts on an extensive tour of the north as memorably described by Robert Aickman in *The River Runs Uphill*.

In the 1950s Salford Bridge was a microcosm of a way of life about - for better or worse - to vanish. Tom Foxon wrote vividly of its comings and goings in *No.1*: of bi-directional horse-drawn Joey boats; coffee shops which sold mostly tea; ironmongers which sold mostly everything; front room 'corner shops'; tram conductresses; Teddy Wenches; 'tat' boats bound for Moxley; a pub called 'The Muckman'; and an enduring cast of characters - 'Cakey Bill', 'Lion-tamer', 'Sunlight Harold', and 'Filthy Alice'. Loitering (with or without intent) today in the sepulchral gloom beneath Spaghetti Junction, muffled traffic overhead, one might well welcome such company.

LIKE someone painstakingly negotiating a release clause, the Birmingham & Fazeley seems to take forever to extricate itself from the city's sub-clauded, codicilled contract. A couple of hours, and these amorphous suburbs have more than outstayed their welcome. And yet, as always, there is something inherent in the pace of canal travel - on foot or afloat - that makes you delve deeper, that evinces responses, that engenders 'negotiations and love songs'.

Forging east from Salford Junction, two overbridges called Troutpool (might be a character in a Terence Rattigan play) recall the pre-industrial landscape which predated the B&F's late 18th century completion. Between Troutpool and Erdington Hall bridges the canal glides claustrophobically beneath an overhanging works once belonging to Birlec, manufacturers of electric arc furnaces. Bromford Bridge (aka Birmingham) Race Course held meetings from 1894 to 1965. In 1915 the grandstand was set on fire by sufragettes. Lester Piggott rode two winners at the final meeting.

At Wood Lane Bridge there are BCN concrete posts, and beyond Brace Factory Bridge glimpses south to Fort Dunlop, the massive tyre factory dating from 1916. To transport the workforce to and from this new plant, the company operated a small fleet of passenger carrying narrowboats between Aston and Bromford until the neighbouring Tyburn Road was laid with tram tracks. Apparently the two and a half mile, lock-free journey took around half an hour and each boat could seat a hundred passengers.

Fort Dunlop is enjoying a fresh lease of life as an hotel and office space. Not so fortunate, though arguably of equal architectural value, the Art Deco Cincinnati Machine Company's premises below Minworth Top Lock have been demolished and ignominiously replaced by harmless, yet bland, new housing. It is difficult to comprehend why the imposing facade, at least, could not have been incorporated in this development like the Ovaltine factory at Kings Langley on the Grand Union Canal.

for details of facilities in Minworth turn to page 33

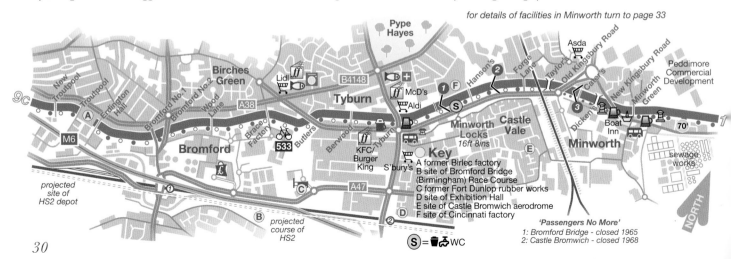

Key
A former Birlec factory
B site of Bromford Bridge (Birmingham) Race Course
C former Fort Dunlop rubber works
D site of Exhibition Hall
E site of Castle Bromwich aerodrome
F site of Cincinnati factory

'Passengers No More'
1: Bromford Bridge - closed 1965
2: Castle Bromwich - closed 1968

S = 🗑🚻 WC

In 1938, as Britain was belatedly arming for war, fields in the vicinity of Castle Bromwich, were occupied by a 'shadow' munition factory. During the next seven years over eleven thousand Spitfire fighter planes were built at the plant. In the 1960s a housing zone called Castle Vale replaced the factory and adjoining aerodrome. Five thousand homes in blocks of flats rising to sixteen floors, housing the population of a medium-sized town. Socially it wasn't a success, crime rates soared, and the tower blocks were subsequently demolished.

The trio of locks at Minworth lie alongside the busy A38 dual-carriageway. Goods trains rumble across the canal on a line linking Castle Bromwich with Walsall which lost its passenger services in 1965, though there are periodical calls for them to be reinstated. Castle Bromwich was the location of the British Industries Exhibition Hall, a forerunner of the NEC. The BI Fair was held over a fortnight, annually from 1920-60, and was quite something in its day.

Minworth Sewage Works is Severn Trent's largest treatment plant and disposes of the waste of over one and a half million West Midlanders. Narrowboats unloaded ash in the arm to the east of Minworth Green Bridge for use in the plant's filter beds. An 2ft gauge railway was employed in transporting dried sewage around the site. Land on the opposite bank of the canal is being swallowed up by the vast Peddimore development. Upwards of six thousand jobs are confidently expected of being created.

Stoppage at Minworth Middle

ANTI-CLOCKWISE Warwickshire Ringers, anxious not to overnight in Birmingham's bowels, so to speak, habitually moor no further west than Wiggins Hill Bridge, girding their loins for an eight hour stint at the tiller to reach the bucolic security of Catherine-de-Barnes (Map 7) the following day; and, of course, vice versa. Progress of the Peddimore Development Zone (Map 10) to the north west of Wiggins Hill Bridge may further emphasise the disparity between 'town and country' - we shall have to wait and see - but as if to celebrate leaving the West Midlands for Warwickshire, the towpath

promptly deteriorates, becoming narrower and muddier; though just about cyclable. Not the most charismatic of canals, the Birmingham & Fazeley nevertheless evinces a sort of sullen charm, though you sense its relative popularity lies in its importance as a link between the east and west midlands, together with the fact that it is part of two popular circular routes: the Warwickshire Ring, and the Black Country (aka Staffordshire) Ring. Incidentally, the B&F opened in 1789, and was engineered by John Smeaton, whose 'CV' included the third Eddystone lighthouse of 1759.

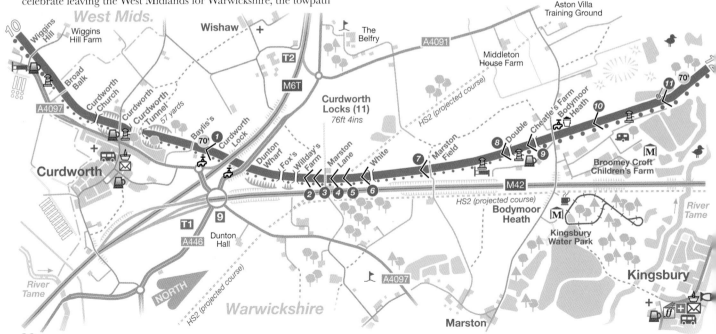

Couched in a wooded cutting, a short tunnel at Curdworth precedes a flight of eleven locks, single-gated top and tail, as per BCN custom, with which the B&F merged in 1794. Construction of the M6 Toll road necessitated repositioning of the top lock and replacement of the lock-keeper's house at Dunton Wharf.

Locks 2-5 come in a cluster, otherwise they are of sufficient distance apart to make indolent lock-workers think twice about walking between them. The western route of HS2, northwards from Birmingham to Manchester, is earmarked to cross the canal between locks 5 and 6. The controversially truncated eastern route will parallel the M42. Their trains will travel sixty-four times faster than your narrowboat; but who will be journeying, in the words of Robert Louis Stevenson, more hopefully?

Not far north from Dunton Wharf, along the A446 is the Belfry Hotel and its famous golf course, scene of several nail-biting Ryder Cup

Curdworth Tunnel

denouements. Another sporting association belongs to Bodymoor Heath where Aston Villa, the illustrious Birmingham football club, have their impressive training ground.

The bottom lock of the Curdworth flight is overlooked by a quartet of canal cottages. Life must be pleasant here if, as one supposes, the inhabitants find the isolation conducive. Skeins of geese rise into the wide skies from flooded gravel workings. Gravel has been extracted from the valley of the Tame since the 1930s. Originally by dredger, later by dragline. Nowadays conveyor belts carry the minerals to screening and washing plants where they are sorted into varying types of aggregates. The landscape might have been irrevocably scarred by such activities were it not for the imaginative creation of Kingsbury Water Park out of the abandoned gravel workings. Moorings are available above the bottom lock and it's but a short walk to the park's visitor centre.

Minworth Map 10
Eating & Drinking
BOAT INN - Old Kingsbury Road. Tel: 0121 257 4129. Canalside pub open from 7am daily, food served throughout. Caribbean Fridays. B76 9AE
CUTTLE BRIDGE INN - Kingsbury Road. Tel: 01675 475626. Canalside pub/motel. Breakfast from 7am (8am weekends), main menu from noon. B76 9DP
Shopping
Convenience stores. Large Asda supermarket to NW.
Connections
BUSES - X16 hourly to/from Birmingham/Tamworth.

Curdworth Map 11
Curdworth is one of the oldest settlements in this part of the world and derives its name from Crida, the first King of Mercia.
Eating & Drinking
WHITE HORSE - Kingsbury Road (adjacent Curdworth Bridge). Tel: 01675 470227. 'Vintage Inn'. Open from noon, food served throughout. B76 9DS
Shopping
Post Office stores in village on far side of A4097.
Connections
BUSES - 75 hourly to/from Sutton Coldfield/NEC.

Bodymoor Heath Map 11
Despite proximity of M42 (and impending HS2), still a remote community to east of Sutton Coldfield.
Eating & Drinking
DOG & DOUBLET - Dog Lane (canalside Cheatle's Farm Bridge). Tel: 01827 873907. Rambling Georgian pub with attractive interiors and garden with dovecot. Open daily from noon. Pub grub/Chinese. B76 9JD
OLD BARN CAFE - Kingsbury Water Park. Tel: 01827 874823. Open daily (from 10.30am) for breakfasts, coffees, lunches and afternoon tea. B76 9JB
continued on page 35:

WARWICKSHIRE gives way to Staffordshire as the Birmingham & Fazeley Canal, done with locks, ambles absentmindedly towards its junction with the Coventry Canal at Fazeley. A leafy half-mile's walk west of the canal from Fisher's Mill Bridge, Middleton Hall was the home of two eminent naturalists, Francis Willoughby and John Ray. Queen Elizabeth stayed here in 1567, her retinue lustily eating their way through sixty-nine beef cattle, one hundred and twenty-eight sheep, and two thousand chickens during the course of a week. In recent years the property has been painstakingly restored by the Middleton Hall Trust.

On the opposite bank of the canal, the Royal Society for the Protection of Birds acquired a large area of worked out gravel workings in 2007 and opened a nature reserve to human visitors four years later. These Middleton Lakes, as they have become known, play host to an increasingly wide range of flora and fauna. Bitterns are not unknown, and murmurations of up to ten thousand starlings have been sighted (and counted).

Now and again on a canal journey, one encounters an object decorated extravagantly beyond the usual tenets - however gracious - of 18th and 19th century civil engineering. Drayton Foot Bridge is one such example, and consists of two crenellated towers (encasing spiral staircases) which support a slender iron span: the kind of eccentric structure where the inner child feels compelled to engage in swashbuckling acts. The structure's ornate origins are likely to find their source at nearby Drayton Manor. No, not the contemporary theme park, but the 18th century mansion designed for the Prime Minister Robert Peel by Robert Smirke, the celebrated Greek Revival architect responsible for the British Museum and Covent Garden Theatre. Demolished in the mid-1920s, the house's last occupants were Peel's great grandson and his wife, Beatrice Lillie, a comedy actress once widely considered 'the funniest

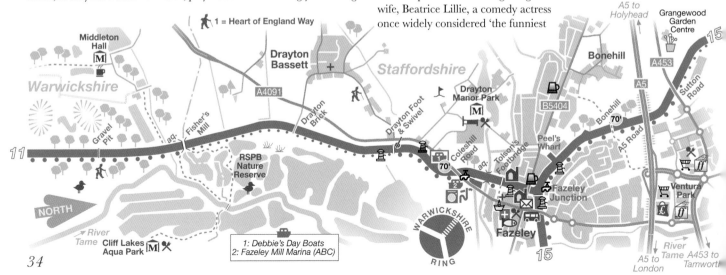

1 = Heart of England Way

Middleton Hall

Drayton Bassett

Staffordshire

Warwickshire

Gravel Pit

Fisher's Mill

Drayton Brick

RSPB Nature Reserve

Drayton Foot & Swivel

Drayton Manor Park

Coleshill Road

Tolson's Footbridge

Peel's Wharf

Bonehill

A5 to Holyhead

Grangewood Garden Centre

A453

A5

Sutton Road

B5404

70'

70'

A5 Road

Fazeley Junction

Ventura Park

NORTH

River Tame Cliff Lakes Aqua Park

1: Debbie's Day Boats
2: Fazeley Mill Marina (ABC)

WARWICKSHIRE RING

Fazeley

A5 to London

River Tame A453 to Tamworth

woman in the world'. The grounds were later used for speedway and greyhound racing, before being acquired by the entrepreneur George Bryan in 1949, and opened as a visitor attraction the following year.

Fazeley Junction, formerly one of the canal system's more lugubrious locations, has gradually smartened up its act in recent years. The Birmingham & Fazeley reached here in 1789, and the following year Sir Robert Peel (father of the Prime Minister) opened the mill by Tolson's Footbridge for cotton spinning and calico printing. A second mill, of five towering storeys overlooking the junction, was erected in 1883 for the weaving of haberdashery; corset ribbons being something of a speciality. This imposing mill has been smartly re-purposed as fifty-nine residential units, in a mix of apartments and town houses. A saw mill, overlooked by a lofty crane, and a converted United Methodist chapel add additional visual interest to the scene. BCN house No.261 (pictured here) presides over the meeting of the B&F and Coventry canals. 7-day visitor moorings on all three sides of the junction give opportunities for a breather.

---

continued from page 33:
Things to Do
BROOMEY CROFT CHILDREN'S FARM - Bodymoor Heath Lane. Tel: 01827 873844. Not so much a genetically-modified approach to child-rearing, more a fun day out for the family. Tractor rides, tea rooms and gift shop. 10am-4/5pm daily. B76 0EE
CLIFF LAKES AQUA PARK - Tamworth Road. Tel: 01827 230656. Watersports. Refreshments. B78 2DL
KINGSBURY WATER PARK - Bodymoor Heath Lane. Tel: 01827 872660. Over six hundred acres of waterside and woodland walks. Echills Wood Miniature Railway. Cycle hire, cafe and gift shop, Moorings above Bottom Lock. B76 9JB
MIDDLETON HALL (Map 12 - access from Fisher's Mill Bridge) Tel: 01827 283095. Open Wed-Sun, Apr-Sep, 11am-4pm. Craft Centre Wed-Sun. Coffee Shop daily (ex Tue) 9.30am-4.30pm. B78 2AE
RSPB - Middleton Lakes. Tel: 01827 259454. B78 2AE

Fazeley
Maps 12/15

The present A5 may cock a snook at Fazeley, but that doesn't appear to have reduced the amount of road traffic at the busy crossroads. By contrast the canal seems blissfully quiet and remote. The handsome terracotta Parish Hall was erected to commemorate Queen Victoria's Diamond Jubilee.

Eating & Drinking
FAZELEY PARK - Atherstone Street. Tel: 01827 261718. Indian restaurant open from 5pm. B78 3RF
IVORY TUSK - Coleshill Street. Tel: 01827 285777. A *second* Indian restaurant, open from 5pm. B78 3RG
KUDOS - Coleshill Street. Tel: 01827 254777. A *third* Indian restaurant, open from 5.30pm. B78 3RB
Plus fish & chips, three pubs and two Chinese take-aways.

Shopping
There's a Tesco Express (with cash machine), pharmacy and post office (beside the petrol station) in the village centre. From Bonehill Bridge a footpath leads under the A5 to Ventura Park featuring Asda and Sainsbury's supermarkets, M&S et al, plus Nando's, Pizza Express, KFC, Costa, and McDonald's.

Things to Do
DRAYTON MANOR PARK - open daily Easter to October. Admission charge. Access on A4091 adjacent to Drayton footbridge. Tel: 01827 287979. Family theme park, 'Thomas Land', amusements, zoo, farm park, nature trail and woodland walk. B78 3TW

Connections
BUSES - Arriva 'Sapphire' 110 runs every 15 mins (30 mins Sun) to/from Tamworth, Sutton Coldfield and Birmingham. Additional services (16, 115/6) also run to/from Tamworth. Tel: 0871 200 2233.

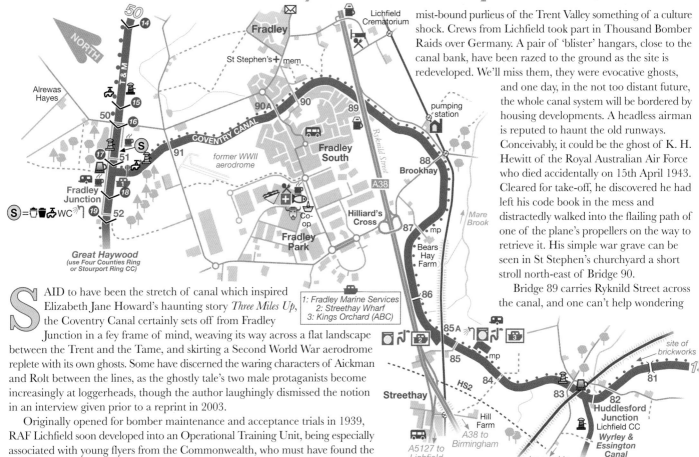

mist-bound purlieus of the Trent Valley something of a culture shock. Crews from Lichfield took part in Thousand Bomber Raids over Germany. A pair of 'blister' hangars, close to the canal bank, have been razed to the ground as the site is redeveloped. We'll miss them, they were evocative ghosts, and one day, in the not too distant future, the whole canal system will be bordered by housing developments. A headless airman is reputed to haunt the old runways. Conceivably, it could be the ghost of K. H. Hewitt of the Royal Australian Air Force who died accidentally on 15th April 1943. Cleared for take-off, he discovered he had left his code book in the mess and distractedly walked into the flailing path of one of the plane's propellers on the way to retrieve it. His simple war grave can be seen in St Stephen's churchyard a short stroll north-east of Bridge 90.

Bridge 89 carries Ryknild Street across the canal, and one can't help wondering

1: Fradley Marine Services
2: Streethay Wharf
3: Kings Orchard (ABC)

SAID to have been the stretch of canal which inspired Elizabeth Jane Howard's haunting story *Three Miles Up*, the Coventry Canal certainly sets off from Fradley Junction in a fey frame of mind, weaving its way across a flat landscape between the Trent and the Tame, and skirting a Second World War aerodrome replete with its own ghosts. Some have discerned the waring characters of Aickman and Rolt between the lines, as the ghostly tale's two male protagonists become increasingly at loggerheads, though the author laughingly dismissed the notion in an interview given prior to a reprint in 2003.

Originally opened for bomber maintenance and acceptance trials in 1939, RAF Lichfield soon developed into an Operational Training Unit, being especially associated with young flyers from the Commonwealth, who must have found the what the Romans would make of the modern A38 and the distribution hubs of Fradley Park which feed a constant stream of juggernauts onto it. Near Bridge 88 stands Fradley Pumping Station, a handsome assemblage of boiler houses and quaint employees' cottages with half-timbered gables belonging to the South Staffordshire Waterworks Company and dating from 1891. Did coal to fire the pumps come in by boat or train? Old maps show neither a dock, nor a siding off the adjoining railway, so perhaps it was simply shovelled ashore and carted across the road.

The South Staffordshire Railway briefly falls into company with the canal. Before that arch villan, Ernest Marples, stitched the railways up in the Sixties, it enabled the inhabitants of Walsall, Brownhills and Lichfield to journey north-eastwards without having to go south to Birmingham first. Nowadays it is used primarily for freight, weekend diversions, and as a means of getting 'Voyager' units to and from their maintenance depot at Barton (Map 49). The level crossing at Brookhay was once overlooked by a pretty little signal cabin and the crossing keeper's Tudoresque house, but they are long gone, though a path leads seductively through woodland reminiscent of one of David Hockney's East Riding watercolours. The property by Bridge 88 features a long narrow garden squeezed between the canal and the railway. By Bears Hay Farm a stone milepost quotes two and a half miles from Fradley and three to Whittington Brook.

Some of the buildings at Streethay Wharf's busy boatyard were originally malthouses, perhaps in connection with the nearby Trent Valley Brewery.

HS2, the controversial new railway between London, Birmingham, Crewe and Manchester is being constructed across land opposite Kings Orchard Marina. Counterintuitively, given the lie of the land, it will pass *beneath* both the West Coast Main Line and the A38.

The pair of redbrick cottages picturesquely overlooking Huddlesford Junction were provided for the respective toll collectors of the Coventry and Wyrley & Essington canal companies. A signpost points prophetically towards Ogley, anticipating restoration of the Wyrley & Essington Canal, abandoned in the mid-1950s before the canal system's leisure renaissance gathered momentum.

Enthusiastically championed by the Lichfield & Hatherton Canals Restoration Trust, reinstatement of seven miles of canal including four detours from the original route in response to post-abandonment developments, is aspired to. A Heritage Towpath Trail is being developed, fascilitating access to a number of points where progress has already been made, but the provision of expensive culverts beneath the A38, A51, Birmingham-Lichfield railway, and A5 remain major challenges. The LHCRT obviously mean business, if only they had a decimal point of HS2's budget at their disposal, progress could be markedly quicker.

Meanwhile, Lichfield Cruising Club employ the first half mile of the W&E as linear moorings. Barbara Jones - whose book *The Unsophisticated Arts* celebrated, amongst other topics, the Roses & Castles tradition of the canals - once painted a charming water-colour of Bridge 83.

Fradley Junction Maps 13/50
Eating & Drinking
THE SWAN - canalside, Fradley Junction. Tel: 01283 790330. This well known former boatmen's pub plays a leading role in the social life of Fradley Junction. Open from noon, food throughout daily. Everards & guest ales. Take-away food. DE13 7DN
LAUGHING DUCK - cafe located in part of the former maintenance yard buildings. Outdoor waterside tables. Tel: 01283 792508. DE13 7DN

KINGFISHER CAFE - cafe connected to holiday park. Tel: 01283 790407. DE13 7DN
FRADLEY FRYER - Tye Road. Tel: 01543 449291. New build fish & chip shop to SW of Bridge 90. Lunch and evening (from 4.45pm) daily ex Sun. WS13 8ST
BILASH SPICE - Tye Road. Tel: 01543 444637. Balti & Tandoori restaurant/take-away. WS13 8ST
Shopping
Co-op, Greggs, butcher, and pharmacy 10 mins walk from good informal moorings by Bridge 90.

Connections
BUSES - Midland Classic 12 hourly to/from Burton and Lichfield Mon-Sat from stops near Bridge 90. Tel: 0871 200 2233.

Huddlesford Map 13
Eating & Drinking
THE PLOUGH - Huddlesford Lane. Tel: 01543 432369. Comfortably furnished canalside pub open from 11am daily with food served throughout. WS13 8PY

14 COVENTRY CANAL Whittington & Hopwas 4½mls/0lks/1½hrs

NOT generally thought of as a beautiful canal, the Coventry nevertheless becomes almost picturesque in its wandering between Huddlesford and Fazeley; particularly as it glides through the brackeny woodlands of Hopwas, where red flags warn of military manoeuvres. Glibly we call this the Coventry Canal, but actually - and by now the presence of nameplates and not numbers on the bridges should have quickened your suspicions - the canal between Whittington and Fazeley was built by the Birmingham & Fazeley company. The Coventry Canal received its Act of Parliament in 1768, but seventeen years later it was nowhere near completion; primarily through periodic bouts of what we would now call cash-flow difficulties but also, historians suspect, because some of its directors with investments

in the Warwickshire coalfield were niggled by the thought that their through route, were it to be finished, would boost trade from the North Staffordshire pits at the expense of their own. In frustration the Trent & Mersey and Birmingham & Fazeley companies undertook to jointly build the canal between Fazeley and Fradley. The two met at Whittington Brook in 1790, at a point enterprisingly graced with a plaque provided by the local branch of the I. W. A. commemorating the bicentenary of the joining. At Whittington Bridge, Peel Farm (where s/c accommodation is available in an old barn) was once a public house known as the Peel Arms. When it was de-licenced by the Lichfield Brewery in 1937 the sale notice quoted adjoining land of 1 acre, 2 roods and 7 poles; 'more or less'.

Note how the bridge nameplates at Hademore are mis-, or perhaps more kindly, alternatively spelled. Nearby, a pair of ornate gateposts formed

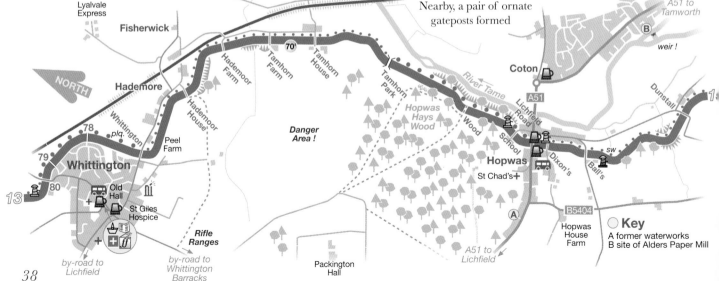

one of the entrances to Fisherwick Hall, a mansion once couched in a Capability Brown landscape, but demolished as long ago as 1818 to pay off the gambling debts of its profligate owner, the Marquess of Donegal.

Engine problems with his bi-plane forced the pioneer aviator, Claude Grahame-White, to land at Hademore on 23rd April 1910 whilst taking part in a London to Manchester challenge promoted by the *Daily Mail*. Enigmatic underground bunkers, on farmland to the north, belong to Lyalvale Express, manufacturers of shotgun cartridges. Gunfire also ricochets around the ancient woodland at Hopwas, part of Whittington Ranges - firing times are posted online. But fear not, the canal becomes so pretty that you could be forgiven thinking you were on the Monmouthshire & Brecon and that was the Usk glinting invitingly below you.

The canal curves endearingly through Hopwas. Lichfield Road Bridge bears the brunt of traffic on the A51, a main road linking Tamworth with Chester. To the west looms a one thousand foot high transmitting mast at Hints. Erected in 1961, it was a replacement for a tower half the height, erected five years earlier to broadcast the fledgeling ITV Channel.

Tamworth Waterworks Hopwas Pumping Station was built in 1879 to provide the town with a reliable source of water from a borehole in Hopwas Wood. Converted for domestic use, one of the properties is called 'Spruce' in homage to one of a pair of 50hp beam engines provided by Gimson & Co. of Leicester, itself named after one of the Tamworth Waterworks Company's board members. Happily, 'Spruce' was preserved, and can be admired - still chuckling merrily away to itself - at Forncett Industrial Steam Museum in Norfolk.

Across the Tame stood Alders Paper Mill, founded by Quakers in the late 18th century. Following closure in 1993, and subsequent demolition, the site was turned over to housing and there is sadly nothing left to see. Transport - raw materials in, finished products out - was provided by a branch line to the Trent Valley Railway. One of the firm's shunting locomotives (a Kilmarnock built Barclay saddle-tank dating from 1918) was fitted with a spark arresting chimney, a useful device, one imagines, in a paper-making environment. The odd appearance this lent the locomotive inspired the comical nickname: 'Guzzling Gertie'.

Whittington   Map 14

Whittington History Society's website is exemplary. From it we gleaned that Thomas Spencer, co-founder of M&S, lies buried in St Giles churchyard, having retired comparatively early from retailing and bought a farm in the neighbourhood. Another significant resident was the architect Samuel Lipscomb Seckham, developer of Park Town, Oxford, and erstwhile owner of Bletchley Park, Buckinghamshire, the WWII code-breaking centre, who dwelt at the Old Hall.

Eating & Drinking
BELL INN - Main Street. Tel: 01543 432377. Beamy village pub. Food lunchtimes and evenings from 6pm; 12-5pm Sun. Draught Bass, Pedigree etc. WS14 9JR
DOG INN - Main Street. Tel: 01543 432601. Comfortable pub offering a good choice of food weekday lunchtimes and evenings from 5pm. Sat 12-8pm, Sun 1-5pm. Up to four real ales. WS14 9JU
WHITTINGTON RUBY - Main Street. Tel: 01543 433397. Chinese takeaway, from 5pm. WS14 9JU

Shopping
Co-op store, pharmacy, and newsagent.

Things to Do
STAFFORDSHIRE REGIMENT MUSEUM - Whittington Barracks, Tamworth Road. Tel: 01543 434394. History of the Staffordshire Regiment from its formation in 1705 up to current incorporation in Mercian Regiment. Open daily 10am-4pm. Most easily accessed by catching 765 bus from village. WS14 9PY

Connections
BUSES - Arriva service 765 runs hourly Mon-Sat to/from Lichfield and Tamworth. Tel: 0871 200 2233.

Hopwas   Map 14

Points of interest include an 18th century river bridge, and a 19th century church in Arts & Crafts style.

Eating & Drinking
TAME OTTER - Lichfield Road. Tel: 01827 53361. Canalside (on towpath side) 'Vintage Inn' with an entertaining pun to its name. Open from noon daily, food served throughout. B78 3AF
RED LION - Lichfield Road Bridge. Tel: 01827 62514. Homely canalside (offside) pub with large garden and children's play area. Open daily from 10am for breakfasts and food throughout the day. B78 3AF

Connections
BUSES - Arriva service 765 runs hourly, daily to/from Lichfield and Tamworth. X65 provides an additional hourly service Mon-Sat. Tel: 0871 200 2233.

15 COVENTRY CANAL Glascote & Tamworth 5mls/2lks/2hrs

Key

A former bleach works
B former flour mill
C Old Mill
D Tolson's Mill
E site of paper/
  asbestos mill
F site of Reliant motor works
G site of S. E. Barlow's boatyard
H site of Samuel Barlow's boatyard
I course of Glascote Works Rly
J rems. of coly. basin

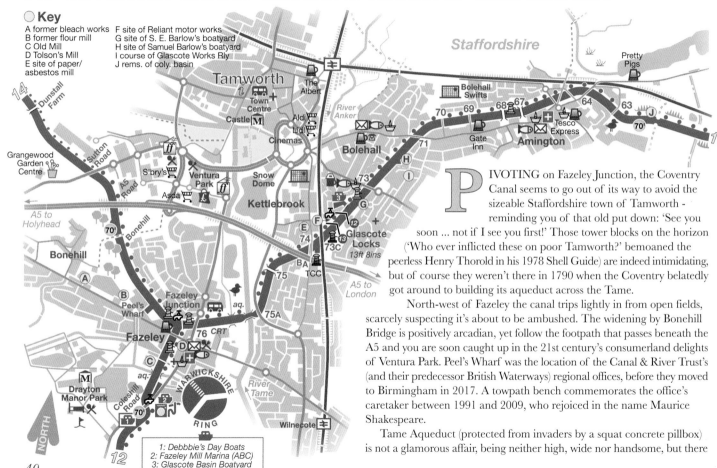

1: Debbie's Day Boats
2: Fazeley Mill Marina (ABC)
3: Glascote Basin Boatyard

PIVOTING on Fazeley Junction, the Coventry Canal seems to go out of its way to avoid the sizeable Staffordshire town of Tamworth - reminding you of that old put down: 'See you soon ... not if I see you first!' Those tower blocks on the horizon ('Who ever inflicted these on poor Tamworth?' bemoaned the peerless Henry Thorold in his 1978 Shell Guide) are indeed intimidating, but of course they weren't there in 1790 when the Coventry belatedly got around to building its aqueduct across the Tame.

North-west of Fazeley the canal trips lightly in from open fields, scarcely suspecting it's about to be ambushed. The widening by Bonehill Bridge is positively arcadian, yet follow the footpath that passes beneath the A5 and you are soon caught up in the 21st century's consumerland delights of Ventura Park. Peel's Wharf was the location of the Canal & River Trust's (and their predecessor British Waterways) regional offices, before they moved to Birmingham in 2017. A towpath bench commemorates the office's caretaker between 1991 and 2009, who rejoiced in the name Maurice Shakespeare.

Tame Aqueduct (protected from invaders by a squat concrete pillbox) is not a glamorous affair, being neither high, wide nor handsome, but there is always something of the intrigue of a conjuring trick where water crosses water. Steps down from the towpath facilitate a river level view.

Like a piggy bank, the two locks at Glascote (whose side-ponds are long disused) are slow to fill and fast to empty. Above the upper chamber the towpath rises to cross over an arm extending into the precincts of a former canal/railway interchange basin now known as Glascote Basin Boatyard. Up until its closure in 1998, the Reliant car factory overlooked Glascote Locks, and you could watch ungainly 3-wheeled Robins emerging in their undercoat from the depths of the works as you waited (interminably) for the locks to fill. At least the housing estate which took its place got called after another of Reliant's fondly remembered designs - Scimitar Park.

Glascote was the location for two famous canal carriers - Samuel Barlow and S. E. Barlow; the former (who also had a depot at Braunston - see Map 25) concerned with longer distance traffics, the latter specialising in short-haul work between the Warwickshire coalfield and the industrial centres of Birmingham and Coventry.

Predominantly suburban in appearance now, the look of the Coventry Canal hereabouts was very different in the past. In *Narrow Boat* L. T. C. Rolt describes meeting 'pitmen trudging home along the towpath, faces so blackened by coal dust and sweat that they grinned like coons at a seaside concert party'. Eighty, more politically correct and inclusive years later, the only clue to the area's coal mining past are the brick-lined remains of an interchange basin on the towpath side east of the winding hole near Bridge 63. Tamworth Golf Course has disappeared beneath new housing.

Tamworth   Map 15

A more historic and convivial town than the view from the canal would suggest. Between the eighth and tenth centuries Tamworth was the capital of the Kingdom of Mercia. King Offa lived here, then later Alfred the Great's daughter, whilst later still it became the residence of Athelstan. In the Middle Ages it belonged to the Marmion family made famous by Sir Walter Scott's eponymous novel.

Elsewhere, the castle, the imposing parish church, Thomas Guy almshouses, the delightful 18th century town hall and the Assembly Rooms all combine to create an interesting core of dignity to the town. A memorial in St Editha's Square (alongside the parish church) commemorates Colin Grazier who lost his life retrieving codebooks from a sinking U-boat, a selfless act which enabled Bletchley Park codebreakers to decipher the German's Enigma ciphers.

Eating & Drinking

THE ALBERT - Albert Road. Tel: 01827 767500. Stylish bar/restaurant near the railway station. Open from noon daily. B79 7JS

CHRISTOPHER'S - Aldergate. Tel: 01827 67676. Bistro housed within the Peel Hotel. B79 7DL
DAQUINO - Little Church Lane. Tel: 01827 65406. Little Italian restaurant open for lunch Thur-Sat, and dinner (from 6pm) Tue-Sat. B79 7AX
GATE INN - canalside Bridge 69. Tel: 01827 63189. Marston's pub with customer moorings. Food from noon throughout daily. B77 3BY

Shopping

The town centre is a brisk quarter of an hour's walk from the canal. The large indoor shopping mall known as The Ankerside dates from 1980 and exhibits all the hallmarks of its era. Market on Tue, Fri & Sat. Useful Co-op by Bridge 73.

Things to Do

TOURIST INFORMATION - Corporation Street. Tel: 01827 709581. Open 10am-4pm ex Sun. B79 7DN
TAMWORTH CASTLE & MUSEUM - Riverside. Tel: 01827 709626. Daily ex Mon, admission charge. Probably the original stronghold of Ethelfleda, daughter of Alfred the Great, but what remains is largely Norman outside and Jacobean in. B79 7NA

SNOWDOME - River Drive. Tel: 0344 800 0011. Real snow on an indoor ski slope. Great fun. Equipment hire and lessons for beginners. B79 7ND

Connections

BUSES - Arriva 'Sapphire' 110 runs every 15 mins (30 mins Sun) to/from Fazeley, Sutton Coldfield and Birmingham. Additional services (16, 115/6) also run to/from Fazeley. Tel: 0871 200 2233.
TRAINS - through trains to/from London, Birmingham and the North of England. Useful stopping services along the Trent Valley line for towpath walkers calling at Atherstone and Nuneaton. Tel: 0345 748 4950.
TAXIS - Acorn. Tel: 01827 63333.

Amington   Map 15

Formerly a coal mining and quarrying community, now part of suburban Tamworth. Good fish & chips near Bridge 67 - Tel: 01827 700183. The Pretty Pigs (Tel: 01827 63129 - B79 0ED) is a Crown Carvery near Bridge 64 which offers breakfasts from 8am and food throughout the day. Useful range of shops including: Tesco Express (with cash machine), Co-op and pharmacy; plus another pub called the Liberal House.

16 COVENTRY CANAL Alvecote & Polesworth 4½mls/0lks/1½hrs

YOU'D have to be singularly unimaginative not to respond to the multi-layered history jostling for your attention on this stretch of the Coventry Canal. The action starts immediately at Alvecote, where the marina invariably boasts a cluster of 'preserved' working boats in all their glory. The basin here was originally dug in 1873 to serve Tamworth (aka Alvecote) Colliery. In the early 1950s it was merged with the pits at Amington and Pooley Hall, but the shafts at Alvecote were abandoned soon afterwards. Years of mining provoked subsidence in the vicinity and permanent 'lakes' were formed by floodwater from the Anker. These expanses of water, known now as Alvecote Pools, form the basis of an attractive nature reserve administered by Warwickshire

Wildlife Trust. Kingfishers and egrets are commonplace, and up to a dozen varieties of dragonfly in Spring and Summer. As an attractive alternative to the towpath, you can follow the old 'Miners Path' through the reserve, imagining you're trudging home from a subterranean shift.

Set the dial on your time machine a little further back and you can recapture another era of history in the simple, yet highly atmospheric remains of Alvecote Priory, a Benedictine establishment dating from 1159 when it was built as an outpost to the priory at Great Malvern, Worcestershire. Moor here and rummage in the ruins, soaking up centuries of residual history from the stonework.

The M42 crosses the canal on Bridge 55A, and the East Midlands

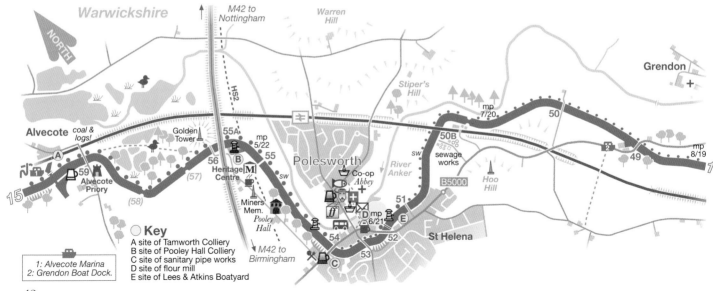

Key
A site of Tamworth Colliery
B site of Pooley Hall Colliery
C site of sanitary pipe works
D site of flour mill
E site of Lees & Atkins Boatyard

1: Alvecote Marina
2: Grendon Boat Dock.

extension of HS2 is destined to join it. Now employed as private moorings, the old basin where boats loaded coal from Pooley Hall pit stands close to the M42. Authentic eye-witness descriptions of loading here can be found in David Blagrove's *Bread Upon The Waters* and Tom Foxon's *Following the Trade*. The colliery closed in 1965, being notable as the first mine in the country to be provided with baths under the auspices of the Miner's Welfare Commission. The Duke of York (later George VI) opened these welcome facilities in 1924.

Alvecote Priory and Polesworth Abbey boast at least remnants of their former grandeur, but of the chapel which stood on Hoo Hill until Henry VIII's supression of the monasteries, the sole hint of its former existence is an obelisk erected to its memory. And that is not the only monument in the vicinity. On the ridge south-west of Bridge 55 is a memorial to the men of Pooley Hall Colliery who perished in the First World War; whilst on top of the mine's old spoil tip (rich in toadstools), overlooking Bridge 56, the Golden Tower of Leaves celebrates 'the alchemy of organic matter to become coal'. Moreover, these are just the tips, so to speak, of icebergs of history waiting to sink you emotionally at every bend in the canal.

Pooley Hall itself dates from 1509, and is possibly the oldest occupied building in Warwickshire. Winter is the best time to admire its battlements, for it is increasingly obscured by trees. In the 17th century it belonged to the Roman Catholic and Royalist, Aston Cockayne. More recently, Edwin Starr, the Tamla Motown soul singer best known for his rendition of the Norman Whitfield - Barrett Strong protest song *War* lived here. Far from Scotland, Belted Galloways graze Ankerside's meadows.

Poetry posts have been erected to sooth one's passage through Polesworth, renowned in working boat days for the boatyard of Messrs Lees & Atkins. The yard gained a reputation for the distinctive styling of its 'Roses & Castles' and was particularly favoured with the construction and repair of the boats of 'Number One' owner/operators. In a distant echo of such times, some interesting former working boats are sometimes encountered at Grendon Boat Dock near Bridge 49.

Alvecote   Map 16
'Samuel Barlow', the purpose-built pub at Alvecote Marina has been closed for some time, and its status is therefore uncertain. Coal and logs are available from Homefire by Bridge 59 - Tel: 01827 899441.

Polesworth   Map 16
An ancient settlement on the banks of the River Anker, Polesworth devoted itself to mining for many years, though you'd hardly know that now. A fine ten arch bridge dated 1776 spans the river and brings you to the narrow main street. A right turn at the top takes you past the Tudor-style Nethercote School and, a hundred yards beyond, another right leads beneath the 15th century Abbey gateway to the imposing, and largely Norman church of St Editha. In the graveyard you'll find an enigmatic mound and a suitably embellished gravestone commemorating Elizabeth Ward, an 18th century miner!

Eating & Drinking
BULL'S HEAD - Tamworth Road (Bridge 54). Tel: 01827 898990. *Good Beer Guide* listed local open from 11am. No food, but independently owned Little India restaurant upstairs - Tel: 01827 894112. B78 1JH *Other options include fish & chips, pubs and take-aways.*

Shopping
Shops across the river include Spar (with post office and ATM); Polesworth Toolbox (a charming hardware store) a small Co-op, and pharmacy. Smiths the butchers on Bridge Street sell award-winning sausages. Hambry's fishing tackle shop is just down from Bridge 54. Chester's antiquarian bookshop have moved from their old premises by Bridge 53 to a unit at Pooley Farm, but visitors are still welcome by appointment - Tel: 01827 894743.

Things to Do
POLESWORTH ABBEY - Tel: 01827 892340. In a more tourism-conscious setting, Polesworth Abbey would be more widely known, but in some respects that would spoil the surprise. Open Sun-Thur 9am-1pm, it repays close scrutiny, informing historically and imbuing spiritually. A highlight is a low-relief effigy of Osanna, an Abbess here in the 12th century. B78 1DU
POOLEY COUNTRY PARK - Tel: 01827 897438. Waymarked trails, plus heritage centre & tea room open weekends, bank hols and school hols. B78 1JA

Connections
BUSES - Arriva services 65 operates hourly, Mon-Sat to/from Tamworth, Atherstone and Nuneaton. TRAINS - a collector's item, one train per day *northbound* only. It leaves at 6.51am; don't be late! TAXIS - Polesworth Taxis. Tel: 01827 331133.

17 COVENTRY CANAL Atherstone 4mls/11lks/3½hrs

ELEVEN locks render the Atherstone flight neither too long to overstay its welcome, nor too short to fail to make an impression; both on your mind and on your muscles. A mix of rural and urban settings, moreover, adds to its character, ensuring that the chambers have a variety of backdrops which don't become repetitively monotonous; even if, in obtuse Coventry fashion, the locks take an inordinate amount of time to fill. Pass the time of day with the friendly 'vlockies'; note how many of the ground paddles seem to date from the First World War; or mourn the silting-up of the side-ponds which presumably speeded things up in the past. Solely Lock 6 retains this facility, though there are stern notices prohibiting its use.

Console yourselves with the Gothic silhouette of Merevale Hall up on the wooded bluff to the south-west, and the former

entrance to Baddesley Basin by Lock 7; once the despatch point for a considerable amount of coal traffic. The mineral railway down from Baddesley pit, was known locally as the 'Paddy Line', and was notable for employing a double-ended Beyer-Garratt locomotive named *William Francis*, now preserved at Bressingham, Diss.

Atherstone's strategic role in present day transport is emphasised by the huge warehouses and road distribution depots in the vicinity of the canal. Warehouses of an older disposition cluster around Lock 5 where Watling Street once crossed the canal. Adjoining woodland hides the site of a Second World War POW camp, the inmates of which built a huge grain silo beside the canal, for many years a landmark to rail, road and canal travellers alike, but demolished in 1988.

Top Lock was the northern terminus of the canal between 1771 and 1790, but apart from the

Key
A course of Baddesley Colliery Railway
B sites of hat works
C former wharf

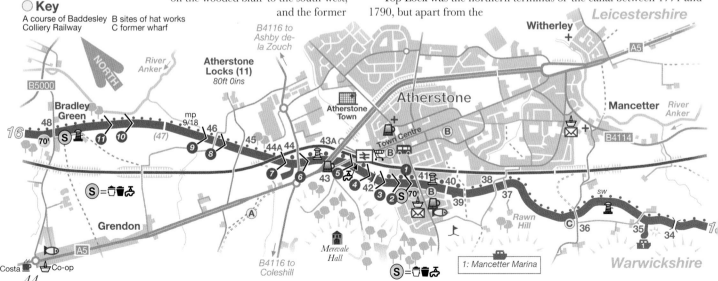

1: Mancetter Marina

44

lock-keeper's cottage most of its associated buildings were sadly demolished in the 1970s, and an arm spanned by a gracious hump-backed side-bridge disappeared beneath latterly-constructed dwellings to boot.

Wilson & Stafford's hat factory by Bridge 41 - a disconsolate facade of smashed windows - closed in 1999. They, along with Vero & Everitt whose site is now occupied by Aldi, were the last surviving firms of a proud tradition of hat makers associated with the town. Atherstone's suburbs are soon left astern and the canal curves pleasantly around Rawn Hill, a dome-shaped 'laccolith' in geological terms. Between Atherstone and

Hartshill lies the old Roman settlement of Mancetter, which many historians believe to have been the scene of Boadicea's (or Boudicca's if you're under sixty!) last battle with the Romans in AD60. Despite being considerably outnumbered, the Roman Legions, with the advantage of strict military training, overcame and slaughtered the wild, disorganised 'Iceni hordes'. The Roman chronicler, Tacitus, recorded that 80,000 Britons were killed. Boadicea poisoned herself rather than be taken prisoner, though her burial place has never been discovered. Up from Bridge 36, seasoned work boat operator, Andy Rothern, also farms a herd of Shorthorn cattle.

Atherstone   Map 17

A hundred miles up the Watling Street from London, in coaching days Atherstone must have been a stop travellers looked forward to. All along the main street are dignified, redbrick Georgian edifice's backed by a maze of alleyways and courtyards. The Atherstone Ball Game - an affair of not inconsiderable aggression - takes place each Shrove Tuesday on Long Street.

Eating & Drinking

ANGEL ALE HOUSE - Church Street. Tel: 0752 518 3056. Real ale pub open from 4pm weekdays and noon at weekends. CV9 IRN
CHAPEL HOUSE - Friar's Gate. Tel: 01827 718949. Intimate award-winning restaurant (with rooms) open for dinner (from 6.30pm) Thur-Sat. CV9 IEY
COSTA - Long Street. Tel: 01827 721676. Generic coffee shop open from 7am (9am Sun). CV9 IAU
KING'S HEAD - Old Watling Street (canalside Bridge 43). Tel: 01827 712078. 1950s tile-hung pub whose outdoor patio spills down to the canal bank. Daily from noon ex Mon. Customer moorings. CV9 2PA
THE LARDER - Long Street. Tel: 01827 717750. Retro 1940s cafe open 9am-4.30pm Mon-Sat. CV9 IAU
MAID OF THE MILL - Coleshill Road (adjacent Bridge 41). Tel: 01827 716157. Unspoilt local once frequented by the hat makers from next door. CV9 2AB

Shopping

The market is held on Tuesdays and Fridays, whilst there is a modicum of early closing on Thursdays. There are Co-op and Aldi supermarkets by the railway station, but there are also plenty of independent retailers: such as Masters & Son ("we bake throughout the day"); Bates Butchers, and Atherstone Toolbox.

Connections

BUSES - Arriva service 65 operates hourly, Mon-Sat to/from Tamworth, Polesworth, and Nuneaton. Stagecoach service 48A operates at 30 minute intervals (bi-hourly Sun) to/from Nuneaton and Coventry via Hartshill. Roberts service 7 runs three/four times a day (ex Sun) to Measham, offering the potential of an excursion to Twycross Zoo. TRAINS - hourly LNW service along Trent Valley. Tel: 0345 748 4950. The elaborately handsome Jacobean station building is now a veterinary centre. TAXIS - Atherstone Taxis. Tel: 01827 712427/8.

Hartshill   Map 18

Suburbanised hilltop village with ruined castle whose claim to fame is that Michael Drayton, the Poet Laureate, was born here in 1563. The village centre is best approached on foot via delightfully named Apple Pie Lane leading from Bridge 31 as opposed to Bridge

32, for the road has no pavement and is very busy. In any case the quieter road makes for a delightful walk in its own right, proffering a glimpse of Hartshill Grange, (not least its restored gazebo) former home of Nathaniel Newton, friend and associate of the Quakers' founder George Fox.

Eating & Drinking

THE ANCHOR - Mancetter Road (canalside Bridge 29). Tel: 0247 639 3444. Everards pub open from 4.30pm Mon & Tue, otherwise noon. CV10 0RT
MALT SHOVEL - village centre. Tel: 0247 639 2501. Cosy, friendly pub open from noon daily. CV10 0SS
STAG & PHEASANT - The Green. Tel: 0247 639 6352. Opens 4pm weekdays, noon weekends. CV10 0SW

Shopping

Small convenience store - useful if you're caught without supplies between Atherstone and Nuneaton. Dobbies Garden World (Tel: 01827 715511 - CV9 IRF) features an excellent farm food hall and cafe/restaurant as well as heaps of garden stuff, clothes and gifts - the only problem is reaching it on foot along busy roads without pavements from Bridge 32. A short hop on the bus might help!

Connections

BUSES - service 48A, see Atherstone entry.

18 COVENTRY CANAL Hartshill & Nuneaton 4½ mls/0lks/1½ hrs

BOATING this way, one drizzly September day, our voyage was enlivened by frequent encounters with working boats hurrying back from the (now sadly defunct) Shackerstone Festival as though still under orders with vital commodities to deliver. It was as if the clock had been turned back sixty years, and it was rewarding to see the canal, just for a moment or two, doing what it was dug for. Not that there is not plenty of passive evidence of that along this length in which quarrying, as opposed to coal mining, was the principal industry.

Waterway maintenance yards are invariably charming affairs and Hartshill is no exception. At the back of the yard stands a dignified, redbrick manager's house, but the best building of all is the arched dock of mostly blue brick, topped by an elegant clock-tower. Southwards towers a huge spoil tip left over from Jee's Quarry. Throw in a sewage plant, and

a works engaged in the noisome business of rendering animal parts, and you have all the makings of a classic industrial canalscape.

A fairly well waymarked 'Quarryman's Walk' adopts some of the towpath, together with neighbouring rights of way, to create a seven mile exploration of abandoned granite and quartzite quarries which once provided considerable trade for the canal. Roadstone was the predominant cargo, and a number of the quarrying companies, such as Jee's, Boon's and Judkins operated their own fleets, delivering that cumbersome commodity to often quite rural points around the canal system to save onward carriage. Spotting remnants of the old loading wharves is an exercise in melancholia. And as for the abandoned quarries themselves, deemed dangerous environments now, one longs for a bit of imagination

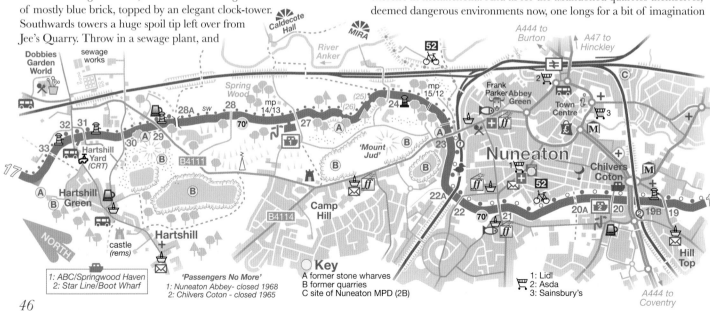

Key
A former stone wharves
B former quarries
C site of Nuneaton MPD (2B)

1: ABC/Springwood Haven
2: Star Line/Boot Wharf

'Passengers No More'
1: Nuneaton Abbey- closed 1968
2: Chilvers Coton - closed 1965

1: Lidl
2: Asda
3: Sainsbury's

to be employed. Surely they would be great locations for watersports and rock-climbing.

As indifferent to such lost opportunities as the powers that be, the canal winds almost idyllically between Atherstone and Nuneaton, like someone enjoying a new lease of life after being retired from the burden of manual labour. There are views east across the wide valley of the Anker to Caldecote Hall. Of Jacobean aspect, this particular version of the hall dates from 1880, though there have been various dwellings on the site. During the Civil War it belonged to Colonel William Purefoy, one of the signatories to Charles I's regicide. In Victorian times the hall was home to Dempster Heming who amassed and lost a number of fortunes and who is thought to have inspired the character of Harold Transome in George Eliot's *Felix Holt*.

Equally conspicuous on the eastern horizon are the redbrick headquarters of the Motor Industry Research Association's test track and proving ground which was opened in 1946 on the site of RAF Lindley. Between demolished bridges 25 and 26 an impressive telegraph pole, complete with cross-arms and insulators, remains intact, an isolated remnant of a network which once lined the canal.

But of all the landmarks hereabouts, it is 'Mount Jud' (late of Judkins quarry) which catches the eye, particularly at sunrise or sunset when it appears to assume the magic aura of an Egyptian pyramid; though, as far as we know, it doesn't contain the fabulous tomb of a pharaoh, just generations of sludge washed off quarried rock. Incidentally, if you think the height of the spoil heap is impressive, you should see the depth of the neighbouring holes quarrying left behind!

Nuneaton itself delivers an altogether different aspect to the canal as the countryside gives way to allotments and housing. The town centre lies the best part of a mile from the canal, but you can easily catch a bus from bridges 20 and 21 if that strikes you as too far to walk, whilst a five minute walk from Bridge 23 will bring you to the doorstep of Frank Parker's, one of the best butchers in this part of the world. Back on the canal, the Hargreaves Narrowboat Trust operate an electric trip-boat from Boot Wharf by Bridge 20.

Nuneaton   Map 18

Pork & stuffing batches are arguably Nuneaton's greatest contribution to civilisation ... though where else in the world would you find a statue of someone called 'George' wearing a dress? George Eliot (aka Mary Ann Evans) is the town's most famous resident, the celebrated 19th century authoress' demure likeness enhances Newdegate Square, inspiring newcomers to explore her *oeuvre* and its many local associations. Elsewhere Nuneaton, much damaged by bombing during the Second World War, is a not entirely displeasing mixture of pre-war and post-war architecture, and we were particularly impressed by the Corinthian columned Town Hall dating from 1932. There are gardens alongside the River Anker, which ducks and dives through the town in a manner reminiscent of the Stour at Kidderminster.

Eating & Drinking
HORSESHOES - Heath End Road (west of Bridge 20). Tel: 0247 638 2284. Everards pub. CV10 7JQ

Shopping
Asda and Sainsbury's supermarkets in the town centre 15 minutes walk to east of canal. Lidl on Queens Road 8 minutes east of Bridge 21. Sainsbury's Local just east of Bridge 21. Vibrant market held on Wednesdays and Saturdays. Ropewalk and Abbeygate (PO) shopping malls. The Kiosk on Newdegate Street is a popular venue for take-away Pork & Stuffing 'batches' and other sustaining items. Take-away batches are also a speciality of Frank Parker (established 1896) at their superb butcher's shop on Abbey Green, 4 minutes east of Bridge 23. They also do 'ready meals', and for carnivores to go by without sampling their sausage rolls would be a gross error of judgement.

Things to Do
MUSEUM & ART GALLERY - Riversley Park. Tel: 0247 637 6158. Open Tue-Sat 10.30-4.30 & Sun 2-4.30 pm. Permanent display devoted to George Eliot as well as other items of local history. Tearoom. CV11 5TU
NUNEATON HERITAGE CENTRE - Avenue Road, Chilvers Coton. Tel: 0247 632 5822. Open Tue 10am-4pm and Thur 10am-1pm. Local history. CV11 4LU

Connections
BUSES - Stagecoach service 48C runs at 10 minute intervals (half-hourly Suns) to/from Coventry via Bedworth. There are links with Hinckley (48L) and Stoke Golding (service 6), Snarestone and Measham (service 7) for Ashby Canal explorers.
TRAINS - services to/from Euston, the North, East Anglia, and Birmingham. Local trains to Coventry and Leamington via Bedworth. Tel: 0345 748 4950.

19 COVENTRY CANAL Marston & Hawkesbury 4½mls/0lks/1½hrs

GEORGE Eliot spent her youthful years in Chilvers Coton (Map 18) and it appears under the guise of 'Shepperton' in her early story *The Sad Fortunes of the Rev. Amos Barton*. She would presumably be sad to see suburbanisation of what was once a country parish. Griff Hollow was the inspiration for 'Red Deeps' in *Mill on the Floss*, and local buses carry the euphonious name on their destination blinds to this day. A footpath (initially dissuadingly muddy and narrow) runs through the hollows from Bridge 18, following more or less the course of the Griff Colliery Company's Canal, a six furlong branch running to an isolated basin linked to the pit head by a mineral railway. Brian Collings successfully evoked the rural atmosphere of the arm in a painting he did to illustrate the first edition of Tom Foxon's book *No. 1*. The old pit village of Bermuda was erected rapidly in just twelve weeks in 1893 to house miners at a recently sunk mine known firstly as New Winnings, but later Griff Clara. The name Bermuda was not invoked ironically, it paid homage to Sir Edward Newdigate, who had recently served as the other Bermuda's governor.

Snaking through deceptively open countryside, where quarrying still takes place, the Coventry Canal reaches Marston Junction. A pipe spanning the canal just before you get there more or less marks the former egress of the Arbury Canal which long ago linked the main canal with the estate of Arbury Hall, the seat of Sir Roger Newdigate (1719-1806) who built a small, yet quite complex, system of canals on his land including a unique '3 way lock'. This 'Canal of Communication' was constructed primarily to transport coal from shafts in the grounds of Arbury Hall, though there is some evidence that it was also used for decoration and pleasure.

Key
A site of Griff Quarry
B site of brick & tile works
C site of Charity Colliery
D site of Griffiths Boatyard
E site of Exhall Colliery

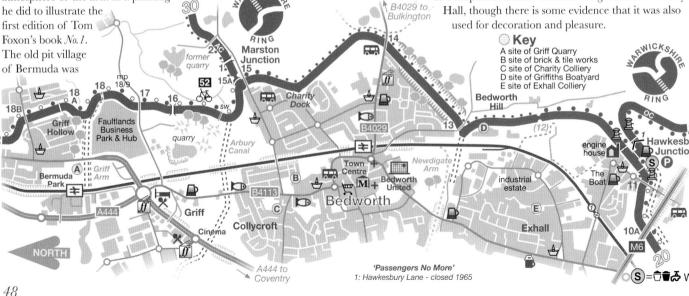

'Passengers No More'
1: Hawkesbury Lane - closed 1965

Located on the urban fringe of the old coal-mining town of Bedworth, Marston Junction forms an inauspicious point of departure for the Ashby Canal's lock-less, but inherently very beautiful, journey into the wilds of north-west Leicestershire. Make a pact to explore it one day if you haven't the time to detour immediately.

You may already be regretting your decision to remain steadfastly true to the Coventry Canal by the time you get to Charity Dock and its bizarre collections of mannequins. A famous and much revered boatyard despite appearances, the site was originally a loading wharf for the output of nearby Charity Colliery. Later it became the base of the Warwickshire Canal Carrying Company, whose distinctive black and white livery (not unlike the better known Shropshire Union fleet) led them to be nicknamed the 'Black Warwicks'. Certainly any artist attempting to capture the spirit of this neighbourhood back in its industrial heyday would require a good deal of burnt umber on their palette.

Skirting Bedworth, a deep cutting disguises the proximity of much urbanisation. By Bridge 13 at Bedworth Hill the Newdigate Arm branched off a short distance to an interchange basin connected by mineral railway to a colliery of the same name located a couple of miles to the west. John Griffiths, another canal carrying company of repute, had a boatyard at Black Bank Wharf on the offside just past the junction.

Memories are long on the canal network - that's part of their charm, isn't it? - and Hawkesbury Junction has been known to generations of canal users as "Sutton Stop" after one Richard Sutton, appointed toll clerk and wharfinger here in 1807. A gaunt blue-brick engine house loiters alongside the right-angled junction of the Coventry and Oxford canals, spanned by a particularly dignified cast iron roving bridge forged at the Britannia Foundry in Derby in 1837. The third, and perhaps most significant ingredient of this classic canal scene, is the Greyhound Inn, once much frequented by working boatmen and their kith and kin. Hawkesbury seems so inviolate now that it bears remembering that it wasn't the original junction between the two canals. Concerned that they would lose out on tolls, the Coventry insisted that the junction be made at Longford (Map 20) and so, from the opening of the Oxford in 1777 until common sense prevailed, quarter of a century later, the two canals ran side by side - as if dancing the Gay Gordons - for the best part of a mile.

Bedworth   Map 19

Historically 'home' to a number of canal boat families, Bedworth acts as a calming buffer-zone between its noisy neighbours Nuneaton and Coventry, and is not as 'depressing' as Pevsner sneeringly averred. Much redeveloped, it was formerly a centre for coal-mining, ribbon-weaving and hat-making. Victorian parish church by Bodley, but, architecturally, pride of place goes to the cloistered and clock-towered Chamberlain Almshouses. A Town Trail links Bedworth's salient landmarks: the War Memorial, Miners Welfare Park (where Coventry's trams once terminated), a winding wheel from Newdigate Colliery, the sculpture of a miner made out of scrap metal, weaver's houses, and churches of divers denominations. Marvellous stuff! Pearson 1 - 0 Pevsner.

Eating & Drinking

PRINCE OF WALES - Bulkington Road. Tel: 0793 522 5444. Welcoming local open from 10am daily with food served from noon throughout. CV12 9DT
THE GRIFF HOUSE - Coventry Road. Access from Bridge 17. Tel: 0247 634 3584. Beefeater restaurant/Premier Inn which, in its previous guise as a farmhouse, was the childhood home of Mary Ann Evans, alias George Eliot. CV10 7PJ
THE GRIFFIN INN - Coventry Road. Access from Bridge 17. Tel: 0247 631 1870. Marston's 'Rotisserie' pub open from noon daily. CV10 7PJ

Shopping

Excellent market held on Tue, Fri & Sat when the town hums! Good pedestrianised precinct notable for its butchers. Try Harry's bakery on Mill Street.

Things to Do

HERITAGE CENTRE - All Saints Square. Tel: 0247 661 9126. Open Tue & Fri 10.30am-1pm, Sat 10.30am-3.30pm. Delightful little museum devoted to Bedworth's lively history. Housed in one end of the almshouses. Postcards and local literature on sale. Admission free, donations deserved. CV12 8NR

Connections

BUSES - frequent services to/from Nuneaton and Coventry. Service 55 operates half-hourly Mon-Sat and hourly Sun from stops near Marston Junction. Service 56 operates half-hourly Mon-Sat and hourly Sun from Bridge 14 to the centre of Bedworth. TRAINS - West Midlands Trains approx hourly Mon-Sat service to/from Leamington, Coventry and Nuneaton. Tel: 0345 748 4950.

20 COVENTRY CANAL Coventry 4½mls/0lks/1½hrs

IT goes without saying, that the Coventry Canal's journey into and out of the city it was named after isn't most canallers' cup of tea, being far too urban for many dispositions. But when have the Canal Companions ever pandered to popular taste? Pearsons have always enjoyed exploring the Coventry Arm very much indeed, and attempt to do it full justice here, though 'Arm' is a misnomer, of course, for the route between Hawkesbury and Coventry belonged very much to the canal's main line.

Leaving Hawkesbury astern, the canal passes beneath the M6 to reach Longford, scene of the original junction between the Coventry and Oxford canals.

Between bridges 9 and 9A the River Sowe, a tributary of the Avon, is crossed. Hereabouts the first sod was cut in the construction of the canal in April 1768. Nearby, on the opposite side from the towpath now redeveloped as housing, was the wharf where boats loaded coal from Keresley Colliery, the last working mine in the area. Whilst some boats took coal away from the colliery wharf, others would arrive from more distant pits with coal for Foleshill gas works, the site of which is now occupied by a stadium previously known as the Richo Arena, but currently called the Coventry Building Society

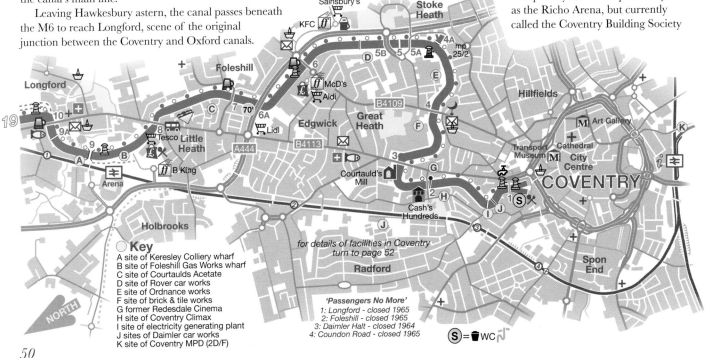

Key
A site of Keresley Colliery wharf
B site of Foleshill Gas Works wharf
C site of Courtaulds Acetate
D site of Rover car works
E site of Ordnance works
F site of brick & tile works
G former Redesdale Cinema
H site of Coventry Climax
I site of electricity generating plant
J sites of Daimler car works
K site of Coventry MPD (2D/F)

for details of facilities in Coventry turn to page 52

'Passengers No More'
1: Longford - closed 1965
2: Foleshill - closed 1965
3: Daimler Halt - closed 1964
4: Coundon Road - closed 1965

S = 🗑 WC

Arena. Coventry City Football Club play their home games here, as do Wasps Rugby. Beyond Bridge 8 (from which there is access to a sandwich bar humourously called - after the local habit of calling sandwiches and/or filled rolls 'batches' - 'Batch of the Day') the canal passes the site of Courtauld's former acetate works, redeveloped as housing. The old 'loop line' railway has been converted into the A444 running parallel to the canal for the next mile or so. Spanned by side-bridge 4A, Stoke Heath basin once belonged to the Co-op Dairy who operated their own fleet of working narrowboats. In later years it was the base of a hire fleet called Club Line.

The Foleshill Railway once accompanied the canal between bridges 5 and 3, serving a number of important factories en route. The line passed through the huge workshop of the Ordnance works which constructed fifteen inch naval guns during the Great War. At Bridge 4 a mosque occupies the site of a former tram depot. Between here and Bridge 3 the canal skirts terraced streets festooned with telephone wires and satellite receivers. Courtauld's clock-towered textile mill alongside Bridge 3 has been converted into apartments. The family originally came to England in the 18th century as Huguenot refugees.

By Bridge 2 stand the iconic 'Cash's Hundreds'. These are three-storey workers' terraced cottages which provided housing for Joseph Cash's workforce on the ground and first floors, and space for the individual weaver's looms on the top. A steam engine powered the looms via a network of overhead pulleys. There were to be a hundred dwellings - hence the name - but only forty-eight were ever erected. Passing beneath the bridge (from which there is no access to the outside world) you catch of glimpse

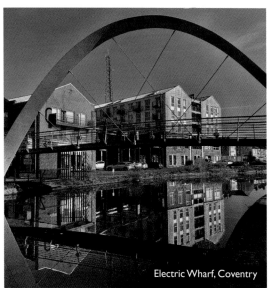
Electric Wharf, Coventry

on neighbouring Foleshill Road of the imposing Art Deco frontage of an unmistakable cinema. This was the Redesdale. Opened in 1933, it must have been an early victim of the post-war rush towards television, for it had shown its last film by 1956. Thereafter it changed hands on a number of occasions, reinventing itself as a rowdy venue for Irish show bands; a soul club hosted by Pete Waterman; and, latterly, surprisingly, a Sikh temple. On the offside bank of the canal stood the premises of Coventry Climax, perhaps best known as manufacturers of fork-lift trucks, though they also made pumps for Green Goddess fire engines, and many successful racing car engines.

Apartment blocks - the leitmotif of most inner city canals these days - line the canal, one sky blue gabled end managing to pay simultaneous lip service to both the local football club and the Coventry Canal Company. Much redeveloped, Electric Wharf marks the site of the city's original power station. Bridge 1 acts as an entrance arch into the twin terminal arms of Coventry Basin. For security reasons the towpath didn't pass beneath the bridge. Redeveloped in harmony with the original warehouses which still line its eastern side, the basin serves as an oasis of calm at the city's edge. A plaque recalls a photo-shoot for the 2 Tone band The Specials here in 1979; though you may be 'much too young' to remember them. A broad-bottomed statue of James ('Schemer') Brindley depicts the first genius of the Canal Age getting his bearings from an early edition of the *South Midlands Canal Companion*. The Riley Cars Archive Heritage Trust open their waterside doors to those of a motoring bent on Tuesdays and Wednesdays.

Hawkesbury

Maps 19 & 21

Famous canal community, hemmed in now by housing developments.

Eating & Drinking

THE GREYHOUND - canalside. Tel: 0247 636 3046. Classic canal pub which can become busy, both on account of its iconic location and its high reputation for freshly-cooked food served lunchtimes and evenings (from 5pm) and 12-7pm Suns. CV6 6DF
BOAT INN - Blackhorse Road, Exhall. Tel: 0247 636 5888. Cosy alternative to The Greyhound. CV66 6DL

Shopping

Small convenience store on Blackhorse Road easily accessed from footbridges 11A and 11B.

Connections

BUSES - NX bus 22 runs at 15 minute intervals (half-hourly Sun) to/from Coventry. Tel: 0871 200 2233.
TAXIS - Alpha. Tel: 0247 636 1111.

Coventry

Map 20

City of Culture status has raised the city's profile, and whilst the view from the footbridge spanning the inner ring road alongside the canal basin doesn't look promising, persevere and you will find yourself thawing. A four minute stroll down Bishop Street and The Burges, and soon you are in pedestrianised Broadgate, passing the time of day with Lady Godiva's equestrian statue and the amusing clock on the side of Broadgate House which, on the hour, opens to reveal Godiva making her naked ride, infamously overlooked by Peeping Tom. Inevitably - given the devastating events of 14th November 1940 - the bulk of Coventry's architecture is post war, though here and there are echoes of medieval Coventry: Bayley Lane and Spon Street being perhaps the best examples. With newly realised public open spaces like Millennium Place and University Square,

Coventry Basin Warehouses

one senses that Coventry is a city benefiting from an upwards trajectory; why, even 'wireless' trams are on the agenda. Furthermore, for those who relish a good literary association, let it not be forgotten that this was the city of Philip Larkin's youth. Culture indeed!

Eating & Drinking

OLD WINDMILL - Spon Street. Tel: 0247 625 1717. Mecca for real ale enthusiasts housed in 15th century town building on medieval Spon Street. Open from noon daily (ex Mon - 4pm). CV1 3BA
PLAYWRIGHTS CAFE - St Nicholas Street. (Canal Basin) Tel: 0247 767 0430. Open 8am-4pm daily ex Mon; 6pm Fridays. Extensive menu. CV1 4LY
TURMERIC GOLD - Spon Street. Tel: 0247 622 6603.

Award-winning Asian restaurant on medieval Spon Street. Open daily (ex Sun) from 5.30pm. CV1 3BB

Shopping

An excellent centre for shopping. Key areas include West Orchards, Cathedral Lanes and the long established precinct. The Indoor Market is one of the biggest of its kind in Europe. Crafts and antiques on Spon Street. En route the Arena Shopping Park features a large Tesco Extra and M&S, accessible via a footpath from the visitor moorings adjoining Bridge 9. The terminal basin features Baltic and Portuguese food outlets. Tesco Express across the ring-road.

Things to Do

TOURIST INFORMATION - Station Square. Tel: 0247 697 7001. CV1 5QP
CATHEDRAL - Priory Street. Tel: 0247 652 1200. The ruins of Coventry's medieval cathedral, largely destroyed in the blitz of 14th November 1940, stand poignantly alongside Basil Spence's 1962 replacement which has become a Worldwide Centre for Reconciliation. Highlights include Graham Sutherland's tapestries and John Piper's windows. CV1 5AB
COVENTRY TRANSPORT MUSEUM - Millennium Place, less than 10 minutes walk from canal basin. Tel: 0247 623 4270. Shop and cafe. Open daily from 10am. Cars, motorbikes, buses etc. CV1 1JD
HERBERT ART GALLERY - Jordan Well. Tel: 0247 623 7521. Open from 10am daily (noon Sun) until 4pm. Permanent and travelling exhibitions. CV1 5QP

Connections

BUSES - services throughout the district. NX bus 22 runs at 15 minute intervals (half-hourly Sun) to/from Hawkesbury. Tel: 0871 200 2233.
TRAINS - frequent connections to other nodal points on the canals covered in this guide: Nuneaton, Rugby, Leamington and Birmingham. Tel: 0345 748 4950.
TAXIS - Central Taxis Tel: 0247 633 3333.

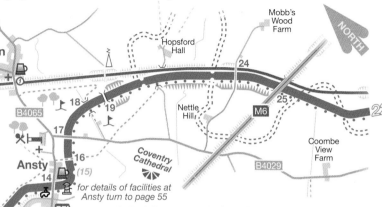

ASSUMING they have successfully negotiated the fiendish plumber's bend beneath, incidentally, one of the loveliest bridges on the canal system, smug boaters can look forward to the not inconsiderable charms of the Oxford Canal. Moreover, fifteen miles of lock-free cruising lie beyond the amusingly toylike stop lock which continues to separate the waters of the Coventry and Oxford canals long after the nationalisation of 1948 left them belonging to the same organisation. Still, it's little anomalies like this which make canal travel so enjoyable.

Beyond the stop lock, linear moorings on either side recall the long lines of working boats which would gather here in the past, awaiting orders, or queuing to discharge coal at Longford Power Station, known to generations of boating families as 'Coventry or Longford Light'. Marvellously atmospheric photographs of the neighbourhood in all its sooty glory can be found in Sonia Rolt's *A Canal People*. Rumours of a new marina on the site have yet to materialise.

for details of facilities at Ansty turn to page 55

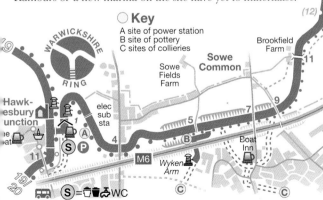

Key

A site of power station
B site of pottery
C sites of collieries

The Oxford Canal tentatively makes its way out into open country. Having emptied at 'The Light', working boats had to journey out past Bridge 5 to the entrance of the old Wyken Arm in order to turn. The long, straight cuttings between bridges 5 and 9 date from route shortenings undertaken between 1829 and 1834, which eliminated no less than fifteen miles between Hawkesbury and Braunston. As surveyed, Brindley's original route stretched the fifteen 'crow' miles between Coventry and Napton into a staggering forty-three miles of convoluted canal. Brindley didn't care. He felt that the more places his canal visited, the more influence and commerce one might accrue. No-one expected canal transport to be quick. Its benefits lay in convenience and reliability. Other generations' response to transport needs manifest themselves. Two motorways cross the canal, and for a while it is joined by the West Coast Main Line, which, as the Trent Valley Railway, had its first sod cut by Sir Robert Peel in his second term as Prime Minister in 1845; a bit of light relief from those pesky Corn Laws, perhaps.

Locks
1 Hawkesbury Stop Lock 0ft 6ins

'Passengers No More'
1: Shilton - closed 1957

22 OXFORD CANAL Brinklow & Easenhall 4½ mls/0 lks/1½ hrs

SLICING across the grain of the countryside, like someone cutting an appetising wedge of apple pie, the Oxford Canal revels in a rural landscape of shallow valleys and modest rises. Canal and railway share an embankment near Brinklow, scene of many well known photographs and paintings depicting narrowboats and steam trains in quaint juxtaposition; the tortoises and hares, respectively, of 19th century transport. Hamilton Ellis did a carriage print depicting the Francis Webb 2-4-0 *Precedent* roaring north on an express as a butty named *Sarah*, steered by a woman in a bonnet, passed more sedately southwards.

Stretton Stop was formerly a point at which tolls were taken. The scene here today is invariably busy and colourful. The old arm to Stretton Wharf is used for private moorings and as access to a boatyard. Some of the original buildings remain at the wharf which once featured a series of lime kilns. Back on the main line,

boaters should take care not to collide with the foot swing-bridge which links the towpath side with the boat-building sheds of Rose Narrowboats.

Bridge 30 carries the Fosse Way - the Roman Road which once linked Lincoln with Exeter - across the canal. Originally a twelve-arched aqueduct conveyed the canal over Smite Brook, but it was covered in by an embankment during the mid-nineteenth century improvements. Bridge 32 carries the 'modernised' towpath over the original route, retained as an arm to serve Brinklow. The depth of the 'new' cutting is considerable. It was the work of fledgling engineers Cubitt and Vignoles, both of whom were to make their reputations during the railway era. Global Warming appears to have re-watered the arm. The former Fellows Morton & Clayton steamer *Earl* had its back broken in 1930 and was ignominiously towed to a marshy grave on the edge of Brinklow where its skeleton remains, albeit officially out of bounds.

Grandiosely Italianate, the big redbrick mansion known as Town

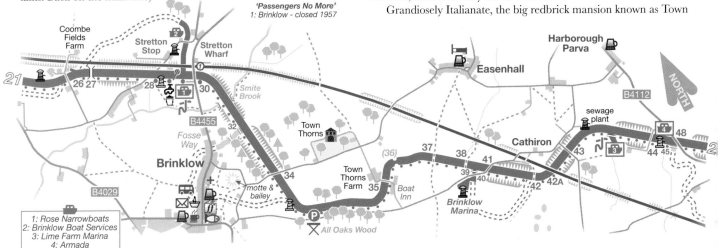

'Passengers No More'
1: Brinklow - closed 1957

Coombe Fields Farm

Stretton Stop

Stretton Wharf

Smite Brook

Harborough Parva

Easenhall

NORTH

B4112

sewage plant

21   26 27   28   30

B4455

32

Fosse Way

Brinklow

34

Town Thorns

Town Thorns Farm

35

(36)

37   38

39

40   42   42A

41

Cathiron

43   44 45

48

2

B4029

motte & bailey

Boat Inn

Brinklow Marina

1: Rose Narrowboats
2: Brinklow Boat Services
3: Lime Farm Marina
4: Armada

All Oaks Wood

Thorns was designed by Alfred Waterhouse for an American magistrate called Washington Jackson. Given that his curriculum vitae boasted Manchester's Town Hall and London's Natural History Museum, designs for provincial piles like this were probably dashed off on the back of his laundry list. During the Second World War the house provided sanctuary for children evacuated from Coventry. Now it is a care home. Sadly, the pretty lodge by Bridge 34 was gloomily boarded up when we last passed.

The canal threads its way aboreally through All Oaks Wood. Town Thorns Farm stands picturesquely on the canal bank, almost river-like at this point. Long ago, in the dense mists of canal time, the house on the opposite bank of the canal was a pub called the Boat Inn.

At intervals, other sections of the original route join and leave the canal beneath the spans of elegant cast-iron bridges made by the Horseley Iron Works Company of Tipton whose structures proliferate on the BCN. Fresh use of the Fennis Field Arm has been made to access Brinklow Marina. The towpaths of the old arms have vanished rendering them unexplorable even on foot, though here and there an ancient bridge remains stranded in the midst of some field or other.

Ansty   Map 21

Surrounded by motorways, Ansty lacks obvious interest, though the sequestered Victorian church boasts a mock medieval steeple. The hall is an hotel.

Eating & Drinking

BOAT INN - Shilton Lane, Potters Green (5 mins SW of Bridge 7. Tel: 0247 661 2191. Unspoilt local on long vanished loop of Oxford Canal. Food (ex Sun eve). Bass, Doom Bar & guests. CV2 2AB

ROSE & CASTLE - Main Road. Tel: 0247 661 2822. Open from noon daily, lunch and evening meals. Purity Mad Goose on tap. Large garden spilling down to the canal, but no direct access. CV7 9HZ

Connections

BUSES - Arriva 74 runs five times daily (ex Sun) to/from Coventry/Nuneaton. Tel: 0871 200 2233.

Brinklow   Map 22

Brinklow's agreeably wide main street is framed by an enjoyable miscellany of building styles and periods. At the edge of the village a pair of timber gates denote the location of a former wharf which lay on the old route of the canal. Past the Perpendicular church a footpath leads up to the motte & bailey outline of a Norman castle known affectionately by locals as 'The Tump', and worth scaling for a panorama of rural Warwickshire. Yes, Brinklow is one of the best villages to visit along the 'northern' section of the Oxford Canal, but do *beware* of the Fosse Way traffic which moves much faster than the Romans ever envisaged and more intimidatingly than their chariots.

Eating & Drinking

BULLS HEAD - Coventry Road (bear right at foot of Broad Street). Tel: 01788 221561. Well appointed pub offering accommodation. Food is served Wed-Fri lunch and evenings (from 5pm) and from noon at weekends - until 8pm Sat and 6pm Sun. CV23 0NE

PUMPKINS DELI - Broad Street. Tel: 01788 833094. Charming coffee shop and cafe offering a mouth-watering range of eat-in or take-away food. Open from 9.30am-3pm ex Sun. CV23 0LS

Two other pubs, a fish & chip shop (Tel: 01788 832766) and Chinese takeaway (Tel: 01788 833257).

Shopping

The boatyard shop stocks provisions, but in the village, about ten minutes pavemented walk from the canal, you'll find a post office stores.

Connections

BUSES - Nat Ex service 85A/B operates half-hourly Mon-Sat (Stagecoach on Sun) to/from Coventry and Rugby via Newbold-on-Avon. Tel: 0871 200 2233.

Easenhall   Map 22

Picturesque village reached by footpaths over or under the railway from bridges 37 & 38.

Eating & Drinking

GOLDEN LION - Main Street. Tel: 01788 833577. Comfortable 16th century inn which has been in the same family since 1931. Food Mon-Sat 11.30am-9pm, Sun 12-7pm. Accommodation. CV23 0JA

Newbold on Avon   Map 23

With its church, canal wharf, and access to the infant River Avon, Newbold is a pleasant enough suburb of Rugby - useful for the replenishment of stores.

Eating & Drinking

BARLEY MOW - Main Street. Tel: 01788 544174. Bar/restaurant food, pool, darts & skittles, patio and beer garden. Bath and laundry facilities available for boaters. Accommodation. CV21 1HW

Shopping

Co-op store/post office with cash machine.

Connections

BUSES - Nat Ex service 85A/B operates hourly Mon-Sat (Stagecoach on Sun) to/from Coventry and Rugby. Service 3 runs to/from Hillmorton via central Rugby half hourly ex Sun. Tel: 0871 200 2233.

DOING its level best to ignore the sizeable town on its banks, the Oxford Canal slips past Rugby on tree-lined embankments; prodigious earthworks dating from the 'cut-offs' of the 1830s. And to a marked degree, this subterfuge succeeds so well that some canal travellers (misguided folk, unequipped with Pearsons) have no idea that a town of seventy thousand souls - which bestowed its name upon one of the world's most sociable sports, and which can boast association with two of England's greatest poets - is going about the daily ruck and maul of life just beyond the towpath.

Newbold Tunnel illustrates the dramatic impact of Vignoles and Cubitt's improvements perfectly. The original tunnel - more or less at right-angles to the present one - was on one of the discursive loops which characterised the contour canal. Its bricked-up southern portal (with two 'eyes' left

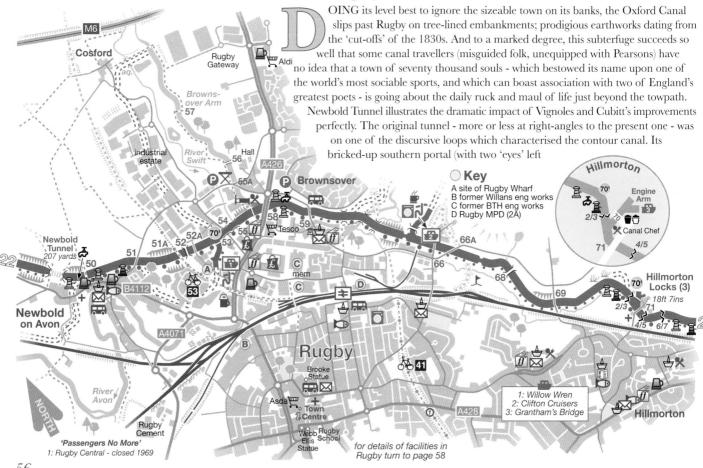

Key
A site of Rugby Wharf
B former Willans eng works
C former BTH eng works
D Rugby MPD (2A)

Hillmorton

Engine Arm

Canal Chef

Hillmorton Locks (3)
18ft 7ins

Hillmorton

Newbold Tunnel
207 yards

Newbold on Avon

Cosford

Rugby Gateway

Aldi

Brownsover Arm 57

River Swift

Hall

Brownsover

Tesco

mem

Rugby

Brooke Statue

Asda

Town Centre

Webb Ellis Statue

Rugby School

River Avon

1: Willow Wren
2: Clifton Cruisers
3: Grantham's Bridge

'Passengers No More'
1: Rugby Central - closed 1969

Rugby Cement

for details of facilities in Rugby turn to page 58

industrial estate

for bats to fly in and out) can be found at the rear of St Botolph's churchyard. The Newbold Arm was kept profitably in water to supply water troughs on the neighbouring railway; though not, apparently, until after nineteen years of tortuous negotiations between the Oxford Canal Company and the London & North Western Railway. Bookended by swarthy cuttings, the new tunnel opened in 1829. For a while it featured a light display, though it doesn't appear to have worked for some time: waiting for a contractor to replace a bulb, perhaps.

It was in the tunnel's western approach cutting that Robert Aickman and Elizabeth Jane Howard experienced a terrifying night upon a rudimentary hire boat in 1947. Overtaken by darkness on the return leg of a voyage from London to Fradley and back, they had moored 'not very sensibly' (Aickman admitted in *The River Runs Uphill*) and were awakened in the night by the sound of the saloon doors banging, when to their certain knowledge they had been bolted shut. On investigation they confirmed that it was impossible for the doors to move. Returning to bed, though understandably unable to sleep, they then heard a noise which Aickman described as 'resembling the sound of a mouse stealing about in straw'. Needless to say, there was no straw aboard the boat, and Aickman remained convinced that there was no mouse either, subsequently ascribing the noise to 'psychic or mediumistic powers' in his companion.

Loyal to the 300ft contour, the original route of the canal went wandering off a couple of miles to the north, looking for a point at which it could summon up the nerve to leap the River Swift. A footpath leads entertainingly (if muddily) along the old Brownsover Arm all the way to Cosford Aqueduct where, in a state of advanced decay, it still spans the Swift. The improvements of the 1830s involved a sequence of aqueducts and embankments across the valleys of the Swift and Avon which form a confluence just to the south.

There are lost railways to decipher as well. The Midland, London & North Western and Great Central all converged on Rugby, all crossed the canal, and were all abandoned in the nineteen-sixties. The LNWR Stamford line entered Rugby on a high, curving viaduct which still looms poignantly over the local golf course; waiting, misty-eyed, for the 6.25am from Market Harborough to puff across it. The Midland Counties Railway went as far as laying tracks down to a wharf established on one of the old sections of the canal, now used as a hire base. Bridge 51A carries its old route across the canal, converted into National Cycle Route 53. This provides the most romantic means of reaching the town centre on foot, highlight of which is the crossing of an eleven arch viaduct spanning the Avon, co-designed by Vignoles of all people. Rugby's eclectic skyline is panoramically presented for your appraisal: from Butterfield's soaring St Andrew's steeple to the Cape Canaveral-like outline of the Rugby Cement works.

If the canal tended to give Rugby the brush-off, the railways spawned the development of industry; particularly, in the early years of the 20th century, businesses specialising in machinery for the generation of electricity. Doyen of these was Willans & Robinson. The former cut his engineering teeth designing steam engines for river launches in Thames Ditton. In 1900 British Thomson-Houston opened a works between the railway and the canal, manufacturing electric motors, generators and turbines. Frank Whittle built his prototype jet engine on the premises in 1937. A memorial to employees of BTH who died in the two world wars stands by the rump of the works (now owned, as are Willans & Robinson's old works, by GE Energy) on Technology Drive.

The last of the lofty wireless masts - there were twelve of them, each 820ft high - belonging to Rugby Radio Station were demolished in 2007 and up to six thousand new homes are being built on the site. This new community is known as Houlton, the location of a receiving station in Maine, via which the first transatlantic telephone call was made on 7th January 1927. A substantial new bridge, numbered 66A, carries Houlton Way across the canal, a road destined to grow busier as the new suburb expands.

By road, Rugby and Hillmorton are inseparable. The canal, though, takes its time in travelling between the two, dallying in the fields before

continued from page 57:

a widening, fringed by reed beds, marks the course of yet another long lost loop. A group, known as the Old Mortonians, has aspirations of re-watering part of the canal's former course. A flight of three duplicated locks carry the canal up past the Oxford Canal Company's former workshops, framed by Bridge 70: Lock No.2 features rare iron gates; Lock 5 offers balance-beam-weary bottoms poetical solace.

Rugby
Map 23

Don't let its distance from the canal put you off. Rugby is an enjoyable town to visit. Its reputation is inextricably linked with its public school. Founded in 1567, it wasn't until Dr Arnold arrived on the scene in 1828 that the glory years ensued. Ever since, Rugby has held its place among the top schools in the country, and a steady stream of former pupils have gone on to make their mark on the world. Ironically, it was a boy casually flouting 'unwritten' rules who made the greatest gesture of all when, one day in 1823, to alleviate the boredom of a football match, he picked up the ball and ran with it, thereby founding the game of 'rugby'. A statue on the corner of Lawrence Sheriff Street and Dunchurch Road commemorates William Webb Ellis' defiant gesture, depicting him in full flight. There are also statues in the town of Thomas Hughes, former pupil and author of *Tom Brown's Schooldays*, and Rupert Brooke, son of a Rugby housemaster. Rugby School's past roll-call is particularly rich in such literary figures, and includes Matthew Arnold (son of the headmaster), 'Lewis Carroll', and Walter Savage Landor.

Eating & Drinking
BELL & BARGE - canalside Bridge 58. Tel: 01788 569466. Harvester restaurant/take-away. CV21 1RG
CAFE VIN CINQ - High Street. Tel: 01788 541304. Open Mon-Fri from 6pm and 5pm Sat. Self styled as 'a little sanctuary of Parisian heaven'. CV21 3BW
MERCHANTS INN - Little Church Street. Tel: 01788 571119. CAMRA'S *Good Beer Guide* holds this town centre pub in high esteem for its breweriana, comfort and range of real ales; food lunchtimes. CV21 3AW

ON THE ROCKS - Albert Street. Tel: 0782 141 6619. Meals 'table-cooked' on volcanic stone plates. Mon-Thur from 4pm, Fri & Sat from noon. CV21 2RS
PREZZO - Regent Street. Tel: 01788 550813. Reliable Italian chain. Open from noon daily. CV21 2QF
RUGBY TAP - St Matthews St. Tel: 0754 049 0377. Micropub and bottled beer shop. CV21 3BY
STEAM TURBINE - Barnaby Road (off Technology Drive). Tel: 01788 569612. Greene King 'Hungry Horse' bar/restaurant open from 10am. CV21 1GB

Shopping
Tesco stands conveniently adjacent to the canal, as do Marks & Spencer in the revamped Elliott's Field retail park, both accessed via Bridge 58. Otherwise all facilities, including a large Asda, are to be found in the town centre just over a mile south of Bridge 59 from whence bus service 4 operates at 12 minute (20 mins on Sun) intervals. Rugby is a comprehensive shopping centre without being overpowering, and in addition to the predictable chain stores there are a fair number of long established local retailers. Outdoor markets are held on Mondays, Fridays and Saturdays.

Things to Do
TOURIST INFORMATION - Rugby Art Gallery and Museum. Tel: 01788 533217. CV21 3BZ
RUGBY ART GALLERY & MUSEUM - Little Elborow Street. Tel: 01788 533201. Rugby's showpiece cultural attraction. Modern art, the Tripontium Collection of Roman artefacts, and social history objects relating to the town. Open daily ex Mon. CV21 3BZ
WEBB ELLIS MUSEUM - St Matthews Street. Tel: 01788 567777. Place of pilgrimage for lovers of the oval ball game. Mon-Sat, 9am-5pm. CV21 3BY

Connections
BUSES - Stagecoach service D2 links Rugby with Braunston bi-hourly Mon-Sat; service 3 runs half-hourly between Newbold and Hillmorton via Rugby town centre; service 4 operates at 12 minute intervals from Brownsover to Rugby. NatEx service 85A/B runs between Rugby and Coventry via Brinklow hourly Mon-Sat, bi-hourly Sun. Tel: 0871 200 2233.
TRAINS - station half a mile south of Bridge 59. Avanti services to/from Euston and Birmingham. Useful LNW services hourly to/from Nuneaton, Atherstone and Tamworth. Tel: 0345 748 4950.
TAXIS - People Express. Tel: 01788 546666.

Hillmorton
Maps 23/4

Rugby suburb with remnants of village green on A428. St John the Baptist's dates from the 13th century and stands near the canal but is invariably locked.

Eating & Drinking
THE BELL - High Street. Tel: 01788 544465. Pub less than 10 minutes walk west of Bridge 73. CV21 4HD.
CANAL CHEF - canalside at Hillmorton. Tel: 01788 567600. Charming cafe fronted by motor *Badsey* and butty *Angel*. Open daily Mar-Oct, 9am-6pm. CV21 4PP
EXOTICA - Lower Street, Hillmorton. Tel: 01788 551584. Bengal cuisine, daily (ex Mon) from 5.30pm. CV21 4NU
WATERSIDE - Bridge 73. Tel: 01788 561401. Formerly the Royal Oak, this Greene King pub opens from 11.30am daily, food served throughout. CV21 4PW

Shopping
Convenience stores and post office. Tony's Trains model railway outlet, Studios 4/5, Hillmorton Locks.

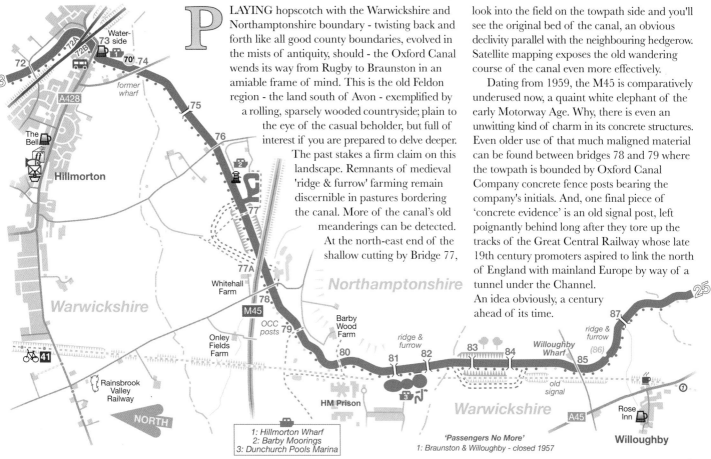

PLAYING hopscotch with the Warwickshire and Northamptonshire boundary - twisting back and forth like all good county boundaries, evolved in the mists of antiquity, should - the Oxford Canal wends its way from Rugby to Braunston in an amiable frame of mind. This is the old Feldon region - the land south of Avon - exemplified by a rolling, sparsely wooded countryside; plain to the eye of the casual beholder, but full of interest if you are prepared to delve deeper.

The past stakes a firm claim on this landscape. Remnants of medieval 'ridge & furrow' farming remain discernible in pastures bordering the canal. More of the canal's old meanderings can be detected. At the north-east end of the shallow cutting by Bridge 77,

look into the field on the towpath side and you'll see the original bed of the canal, an obvious declivity parallel with the neighbouring hedgerow. Satellite mapping exposes the old wandering course of the canal even more effectively.

Dating from 1959, the M45 is comparatively underused now, a quaint white elephant of the early Motorway Age. Why, there is even an unwitting kind of charm in its concrete structures. Even older use of that much maligned material can be found between bridges 78 and 79 where the towpath is bounded by Oxford Canal Company concrete fence posts bearing the company's initials. And, one final piece of 'concrete evidence' is an old signal post, left poignantly behind long after they tore up the tracks of the Great Central Railway whose late 19th century promoters aspired to link the north of England with mainland Europe by way of a tunnel under the Channel.
An idea obviously, a century ahead of its time.

Map labels:

Waterside
former wharf
A428
The Bell
Hillmorton
Whitehall Farm
Onley Fields Farm
Rainsbrook Valley Railway
NORTH
Warwickshire
Northamptonshire
Barby Wood Farm
OCC posts
M45
HM Prison
ridge & furrow
Willoughby Wharf
old signal
Warwickshire
A45
Rose Inn
Willoughby

1: Hillmorton Wharf
2: Barby Moorings
3: Dunchurch Pools Marina

'Passengers No More'
1: Braunston & Willoughby - closed 1957

JOURNEYING along the Oxford Canal, or around the Warwickshire Ring, there is no strict need to call at Braunston at all. Yet, for anyone with more than a passing interest in canal lore and legend, to miss Braunston would be tantamount to visiting Canterbury and not going to see the cathedral. For Braunston symbolises the magnetism of the Midland canals, and is a point of pilgrimage which has captured the imagination of waterway writers, artists and photographers more than almost any other canal location.

The triangular junction, with its twin Horseley Iron Works towpath bridges, was not the original meeting point of the Oxford and Grand Junction canals, but dates from the improvements of the 1830s. Prior to that, the Oxford had meandered extravagantly between Braunston and Wolfhampcote, and the junction was in the vicinity of where the marina is today. With the completion of the Grand Junction and Oxford routes, Braunston became the equivalent of one of those out of the way railway junctions of the succeeding transport era - another Melton Constable or Evercreech, where the importance of the junction far transcended the size of the neighbouring community. In this case, Braunston village remained demurely aloof on its ridge, letting canalside Braunston hustle and bustle its way through two centuries of water transport.

Map labels

26

Braunston Tunnel
2042 yards

by-road to A361

A45 to Daventry

1: Braunston Marina
2: Braunston Boats
3: Union Canal Carriers

Braunston Locks
35ft 6ins

Admiral Nelson

Boat Shop

5 6
4
3
4
3
2
1

Braunston

Northamptonshire   *Warwickshire*

Bush Hill 539ft

Old Olive Bush

Flecknoe

Nethercote

St Peter's

70'

91

Braunston Junction

93 95

Hall

97

Wolfhampcote

98

70'

99 100

101

102 1

94

Midland Chandlers

89

90

WARWICKSHIRE RING

88

River Leam

by-road to Barby

ridge & furrow

ridge & furrow

A45 to Coventry

24

'Passengers No More'
1: Braunston - closed 1958

NORTH

Braunston inset

Braunston

3

A45

2 2

Stop House

1

MAIN STREET

70'

91

93

90 (S)

94

(S) = ♨ WC

Many of the fabled names of canal history went about their business here at one time or another: Pickfords in the early days; then Fellows, Morton & Clayton, whose steamers traded up from London and transhipped into horse-drawn narrowboats at this point. Down the years the roll-call lengthened: Nursers, boatbuilders, and painters of arguably the most sublime 'Roses & Castles' ever seen on the system; Samuel Barlow, coal carriers whose boats were always in the most pristine of condition; and, towards the end, Willow Wren and Blue Line, who kept canal carrying defiantly afloat into the era of the juggernaut.

But the working boats have gone, and with them, inevitably, something of Braunston's old magic. Nevertheless, this is still a flourishing canal centre, home to a hire fleet and a large marina based on former reservoirs, as well as numerous canal-based industries from boatbuilders to suppliers of traditional boater's wear. Wander along the towpath and you'll see new boats being built, old ones restored, and a regular stream of traffic up and down the locks, and it only takes the aroma of a charcoal stove, the beat of a Bolinder, or the rattle of the ratchets in the twilight of an autumn afternoon for the old days to be almost tangibly evoked. Six wide beam locks carry the Grand Union up to the western portal of Braunston Tunnel: a worthwhile detour even if you're not heading that way.

The five mile section between Braunston and Napton is interesting scenically and historically. It is a thoroughly remote length of canal; the countryside falling flatly away to the north-west, but climbing abruptly to a notable ridge in the opposite direction. There are ghosts and echoes everywhere: reedy old loops; abandoned railways; lost villages; and, at Wolfhampcote, the splendidly isolated medieval church of St Peter, cared for by those paragons, the Churches Conservation Trust. Apparently John Betjeman and John Piper, on a visit circa 1960, stumbled into the vault, characteristically succumbing to a fit of giggles.

When the Grand Union Canal was formed in 1929, there remained a gap between its former Grand Junction (London-Braunston) and Warwick & Napton constituents which belonged to the Oxford Canal. Knowing a good thing when they saw it, the Oxford company kindly allowed the Grand Union to pick up the tab for a programme of dredging and concrete banking, at the same time continuing to extract tolls from them until Nationalisation.

Braunston Map 25

Village Braunston demurely straddles its ridge, four hundred feet up on the slopes of the Northamptonshire uplands. Enclosed fields, still bearing the pattern of ridge & furrow, distil the spirit of the Middle Ages. Sauntering along the High Street from the village green to the tall crockett-spired church (last resting place of a number of working boat men and women) one encounters a mixture of stone and brick buildings, including a sail-less windmill and a 17th century manor house. At the foot of a long hill the A45 crosses the canal. This was the Chester turnpike road which became part of Telford's route from London to Holyhead. Now, handsome modern flats overlook the marina, and Braunston must be as busy and as populated as never before.

Eating & Drinking

ADMIRAL NELSON - canalside Bridge 4. Tel: 01788 891900. Refurbished canalside inn. Restaurant and bar meals, attractive garden. NN11 7HJ

THE BOAT HOUSE - canalside Bridge 91. Tel: 01788 891734. Marston's 'Two for One' family pub with customer moorings. NN11 7HB

MIDDLEMORE FARM - Hidcote Way (above Braunston Tunnel - see Map 26). Tel: 01327 706708. Marton's pub. Food from noon daily. NN11 8AE

OLD OLIVE BUSH - Flecknoe. Tel: 01788 891134. Charming village pub idyllically approached on foot from Braunston via Wolfhampcote or by mooring in the vicinity of bridges 101 or 102. CV23 8AT

OLD PLOUGH - High Street. Tel: 01788 878126. Food served lunch and evening (ex Sun eve). NN11 7HS

YOUR CAFE - High Street. Community cafe. Gifts, teas, ice creams and homemade cakes. NN11 7HR

Shopping

Post office stores - open from 6am to 7.30pm (6pm Sun) - who advertise that they are happy to deliver to your boat (Tel: 01788 890334), and an enterprising butcher who additionally deals in hot pies and filled rolls and who also makes his own chutneys and sauces. Fred & Carol Barnes' Boat Shop (Tel: 01788 891310) opens from 8am-8pm throughout the summer season and deals in just about everything from gifts to groceries and friendly local knowledge.

Connections

BUSES - Stagecoach service D2 operates bi-hourly Mon-Sat to Rugby and Daventry. Tel: 0871 200 2233.

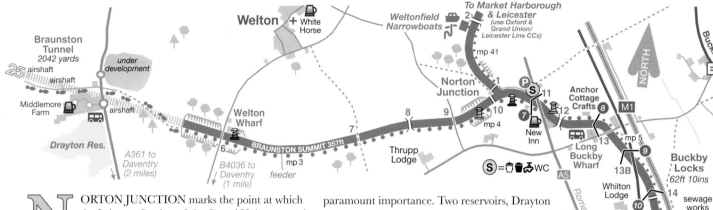

Welton + White Horse

Weltonfield Narrowboats

To Market Harborough & Leicester (use Oxford & Grand Union/ Leicester Line CCs)

Braunston Tunnel 2042 yards

under development

airshaft

airshaft

Middlemore Farm

airshaft

Drayton Res.

A361 to Daventry (2 miles)

B4036 to Daventry (1 mile)

feeder

Welton Wharf

BRAUNSTON SUMMIT 357ft

mp 3

mp 41

Norton Junction

mp 4

Thrupp Lodge

New Inn

Anchor Cottage Crafts

M1

NORTH

Long Buckby

Long Buckby Wharf

A5

S = cup/bin/tap/WC

Buckby Locks 62ft 10ins

Whilton Lodge

sewage works

Roman Road

chandlery & provisions

Whilton Marina

Saywards

mp 6

Smiths 16

Watling St.

Muscott Hill 18

Heart of the Shires

ORTON JUNCTION marks the point at which the Leicester Section of the Grand Union network diverges from the main London-Birmingham line and heads off on its lonely cross country hike towards the famous locks at Foxton. The picturesque little toll house which overlooks the junction was the base, for many years, of Commander Fielding of the Salvation Army. In the Fifties he and his wife ran the mission boats *Salvo* and *Aster*, cruising around the canal system, ministering to the needs of the working boat families.

West of Norton Junction the Braunston Summit (one of three between London and Birmingham) essays its short, partially subterranean course between the lock flights at Braunston and Buckby. The scenery hereabouts is typical of the Northamptonshire Uplands. To the south can be seen the spire of Daventry's parish church, to the north, Welton's tower

With a summit pound barely three miles long, the provision of an adequate water supply was (and remains) of

paramount importance. Two reservoirs, Drayton and Daventry (great names for a pair of zany private detectives), go some way to meeting this need, whilst there are also pumps at the foot of each flight which help by returning water to the summit. Daventry District Council have a pipe dream for a brand new canal arm to provide a fresh focus for tourism in the town.

Braunston Tunnel is the seventh longest currently navigable. There is no towpath through it, but narrowboats can pass inside. Until the mid Thirties a steam tug service hauled unpowered boats through the tunnel. The brickwork was extensively repaired and replaced in 1979 and again between 1985-8, but somehow the soot from the tugs still clings to the older lining. Walkers make their way over the top of the tunnel by way of the old horse path, an enjoyable adventure in its own right, albeit in the process of being compromised by a new housing development.

South of Norton Junction lie Buckby Locks. Buckby is known throughout the waterways as the home of the 'Buckby Can'. These metal water carriers, adorned with 'roses & castles', were an essential piece of the boat families' inventory, because their boats were not equipped with water tanks and running water from a tap. Watling Street crosses the canal at Long Buckby Wharf and here the towpath changes sides.

For a couple of miles the canal is in close proximity to the M1 motorway and correspondingly loses much of its inherent peace and quiet. The ghosts in this landscape must be severely disturbed, but ghosts there must be, for the Roman settlement of Bannaventa stood adjacent to what is now Whilton Marina, and the medieval village of Muscott lay to the east of Bridge 18.

Buckby Wharf — Map 26
The New Inn (Tel: 01327 844747 - NN6 7PW) by Buckby Top Lock opens from noon daily and is popular with motorists and boaters alike. A few hundred yards down the towpath stands Anchor Cottage Crafts (Tel: 01327 842140 - NN6 7PP) a charming little canal shop.
Connections
BUSES - Stagecoach service D4 operates approx half a dozen times Mon-Fri to/from Daventry and Long Buckby Mon-Sat. Tel: 0871 200 2233.
TRAINS - Long Buckby station lies a mile to the east of Buckby Wharf and is served by trains between Northampton and Birmingham. Tel: 0345 748 4950.

Whilton — Map 26
Canalside community at the foot of Buckby Locks. Whilton Locks Garden Village features a restaurant. Small selection of provisions & cafe at Whilton Marina. Saywards Fruit & Veg open Fri-Sun. Tel: 01327 843391.

Muscott — Map 26
HEART OF THE SHIRES - west of Bridge 18. Tel: 01327 349508. Shopping 'village' of specialist outlets (including a tea room and a deli) housed in what was a Victorian 'model' farm. Open 10am-5pm daily. NN7 4LB

Weedon Bec — Map 27
Legend has it that Weedon's cornfields were being raped by flocks of geese until St Werburgh brought one of their number back to life, hence the shape of the weather vane on St Peter's ochre-coloured church,

in the shadow of the canal embankment. One of the graves marks the resting place of Alice Old who lived long enough in the 17th Century to be ruled over by seven sovereigns. Down from Bridge 24 you'll come upon a cornucopia of antique shops, but the quieter core of Weedon lies to the west, well away from the A5, where the former military depot may be seen.
Eating & Drinking
THE CROSSROADS - Watling Street. Tel: 01327 340354. Chef & Brewer pub/restaurant/hotel open from 11am daily (noon Sun). Food from noon. NN7 4BX
GRANNY'S CAFE - Church Street. Tel: 01327 349378. Cosy daytime eatery from 7am (8am Sun). NN7 4PL
HEART OF ENGLAND - High Street. Tel: 01327 340335. This imposing Marston's 'Two for One' pub/restaurant/hotel was originally constructed in the 18th century as a farmhouse. NN7 4QD
THE NARROWBOAT - Watling Street. Tel: 01327 340333. Charles Wells pub offering food and motel style accommodation alongside Bridge 26. NN7 4RZ
THE PLUME OF FEATHERS - Market Square. Tel: 01327 340978. Village-centre local. NN7 4QU
WEEDON HOUSE - High Street. Tel: 01327 349388. Chinese takeaway. NN7 4QD
Shopping
The village shops are located west of the canal and ideally - not to say idyllically - reached from the offside visitor moorings on the embankment, down steps and through the churchyard. The shops include a 'One-

Stop' convenience store (open 6am-10pm daily), pharmacy. Tesco Express at crossroads. In the old army depot are antiques and book outlets.
Things to Do
THE DEPOT - Weedon Bec. Tel: 01327 341303/226812. Fascinating insight into the history of Weedon's military depot. Open Wed 10am-4pm, Thur-Sat 10am-1pm, Sun 11am-3pm. NN7 4PS
Connections
BUSES - Stagecoach services D1/D2/D3 provide frequent links with Northampton and Daventry.

Nether Heyford — Map 27
Village with sizeable green. Nice parish church of St Peter & St Paul tucked away to rear of houses.
Eating & Drinking
FORESTERS ARMS - The Green. Tel: 01327 340729. Village local. NN7 3LE
OLDE SUN - Middle Street. Tel: 01327 340164. Charming pub characterised by enamelled advertisements and vintage machinery. NN7 3LL
Shopping
One-Stop convenience store (inc PO) open 6am-10pm daily, and butcher called Heyford Meats.
Connections
BUSES - Stagecoach service D3 operates hourly Mon-Sat (bi-hourly Sun) to/from Northampton and Daventry (via Weedon). Tel: 0871 200 2233.

27 GRAND UNION CANAL Weedon 5mls/0lks/2hrs

WHEN Napoleon was busy acquiring as much of Europe as he could early in the 19th century, the Government got out a map of England and looked for somewhere safe to hide King George III. Their eye fell upon the tiny Northamptonshire village of Weedon Bec which, not entirely coincidentally, had just been linked to London with the completion of William Jessop's Grand Junction Canal. Here they built barracks and a Royal Pavilion. A canal arm led off the main line, entering the barracks through a portcullis. It was obviously intended that Weedon would be defended to the last. Happily, Bonaparte met his match elsewhere, and the King never needed to use his splendid pavilion. But the barracks remained in use right up until the end of National Service in 1960, and on occasions, troops were carried by canal boat from here to trouble spots and ports of embarkation. Various cargoes were delivered by boat - from gunpowder to uniforms. When the London & Birmingham Railway was opened in 1838, a sliding bridge - like the one still in use on the Stainforth & Keadby Canal in Yorkshire - preserved access to the depot from the canal's main line. Sensitively being redeveloped as workshops, offices and retail outlets (antiques, books etc), The Depot features an excellent visitor centre which it would be a missed opportunity not to go and enjoy.

A fifteen mile pound separates the lock flights at Buckby and Stoke Bruerne. To maintain this horizontality, the canal accommodates the undulations of the countryside: wrapping itself around the sinuous valley of the upper Nene, and crossing the river by way of a high embankment at Weedon.

The Nene, one of England's most unsung, yet delightful rivers, rises near the village of Badby to the south-west of Daventry and flows into The Wash, a hundred and ten miles downstream. It is navigable between Northampton and Peterborough, as described in *Pearson's Canal Companion: Leicester Line and River Nene.* Meanwhile, back on the canal, look out for the high silos of Heygates flour mill as you curve past Nether Heyford. Furnace Wharf, by Bridge 32, recalls the existence of iron furnaces and brickfields in the vicinity during the 19th Century.

Map labels: Nether Heyford, High House 29, 70', Furnace Wharf 32, 70', 28 Standing Barn, Bridge 32 Supplies (Fred Tarry), 27 Flore Lane, R. Nene, Nene Way, mp 11, mp 10, Rugby Boat Sales Stowe Hill W'shop, 26 Stowe Hill, Watling Street, A5, 70', 25 Weedon Bec, Church Stowe, Weedon Wharf, Weedon Bec, 24, 23A, Weedon (csd 1958), 23, The Depot, A45 to Coventry, A45 to Northampton, Tesco Express, mp 9, mp 8, 22 Watling Street, 21 Brockhall Road, The Dial House, A5, mp 7, 19 Diamond, M1, 26, NORTH, course of Weedon & Leamington railway

for details of facilities at Weedon Bec and Nether Heyford turn back to page 63

64

THE landscape pitches and rolls like an ocean swell as mileposts count the distance to or from Braunston. Their initials - G. J. C. Co. - are *initially* mystifying ... shouldn't that J be a U? But this canal was built as the Grand Junction, the name Grand Union only coming into play in the 1930s following a series of amalgamations on the route between London and Birmingham. One doesn't think of the Grand Union as a pretty canal - it is too businesslike and muscular for that - but its remote journeying across the Shires has the reposeful quality of a postprandial stroll after a Sunday roast. At least that's how it feels for today's pleasure boaters, doubtless the working boatmen of the past were too preoccupied with 'getting 'em ahead' to pay homage to the countryside's charm. But if the neighbouring trains emphasise the modern urge to be elsewhere, the canal acclimatizes you kindly to each new view. The passengers in those sleek Avanti Pendolinos may be alighting at Euston before you get to Gayton, but people who go to great lengths to save time usually end up by having to kill it. Incidentally, the lack of freight trains doesn't mean that the M1 has finally robbed all commercial activity from the canal and the railway, it's simply that most of the goods goes the long way round through Northampton. 'Banbury Lane' - which links Banbury with Northampton - was once a drover's road, but its origins may go back to prehistoric times. In the heyday of the canal there was a wharf and tavern here. The buildings - three storeys with an attic - are typical of the architectural style of the Grand Junction

for details of facilities at Bugbrooke turn to page 67

Bugbrooke

company, and similar structures can be seen at many wharves along this section of the canal. As trade evaporated, most of the canal pubs lost their licences and were converted into private residences, a trend still sadly echoed to this day. As part of a scheme to eradicate level crossings on the upgraded West Coast Main Line railway, a new canal bridge was added alongside the original bridge number 43. Similarly, the footpath which crosses the canal at Bridge 38 has been expensively provided with a footbridge over the railway. Goodness knows how it comes to be so heavily graffitied in these rural climes. At Gayton Junction the Northampton Arm branches off from the main line and commences its whirlwind descent to the River Nene.

To Northampton (use Oxford & Grand Union CC)
ABC Boat Hire
Gayton Marina
Turnover 47
Grand Junction Boat Co
WC
mp 16
Gayton Junction
Blisworth Marina
46 Nightingales
45 Wright's Lane
East's 44
Banbury Lane 43 — mp 15 — 43A
Evans 42
Banbury Lane
Eykyn Arms
Gayton

Skew 41 — mp 14
40
38 Rudkins
34   35
Heyford Fields Marina   mp 13   36   70'   Bugbrooke Marina
Bugbrooke Wharf
mp 12
33
NORTH
↓ by-roads to A5 Watling Street

29 GRAND UNION CANAL Stoke Bruerne 4mls/2lks/2hrs

BLISWORTH and Stoke Bruerne are contrasting canalside communities separated by the third* longest presently navigable tunnel in Britain. The first attempt at a tunnel, commenced in 1793, was abandoned three years later due to instabilities in the ground. In the meantime cargoes were being transhipped across the hill; firstly by horse and cart, subsequently via a tramway employing L-shaped rails. A second attempt at tunnelling, on a different alignment, was successfully opened in 1805, its completion confirming the fulfilment of the Grand Junction Canal.

Blisworth Tunnel's dimensions permitted narrowboats to pass inside, but no towpath was provided. At the outset boats were poled through, rather in the manner of Oxford punts, but this practice was apparently abandoned in favour of the more traditional art of 'legging', though with, not surprisingly, a considerable number of fatalities. The canal company provided registered leggers who wore brass arm bands proclaiming their role. Later, as traffic increased, a steam tug service was provided, and although this was withdrawn as long ago as 1936, there is still a reek and an aroma of soot and steam to be savoured within the tunnel's confines. Bridge 50 is known as Candle Bridge, recalling that in far off days the lady who lived in a nearby cottage sold tallow candles to the leggers.

In the late 1970s, in common with many other impressive canal structures, Blisworth Tunnel was feeling its age, and suffering from a backlog of indifferent maintenance. Its lining deteriorated to such an extent that it became necessary to close the tunnel for four years, effectively severing the canals of the Midlands from those of the South-East. £4 million was spent on relining the bore, and the tunnel re-opened in 1984.

The Grand Union skirts Blisworth, passing beneath the A43 and the West Coast Main Line in the process. This area was once riddled with iron stone quarries linked by tramway to loading stages along the canal bank, much of the stone being carried the comparatively short distance by boat to Hunsbury Hill Furnaces on the Northampton Arm. Blisworth railway station was the junction for the Stratford & Midland Junction Railway as well as the line from Blisworth to Peterborough which used, picturesquely, to accompany much of the course of the River Nene.

Blisworth Mill, a handsome brick building once used as a depot by the Grand Union Canal Carrying Company - but now, perhaps inevitably, converted into housing - overlooks Bridge 51. Blisworth Tunnel's northern portal is built from blue brick. Half an hour after entering the tunnel you can compare this with the redbrick of the southern portal. Here, two small buildings provide reminders of the canal's working days: one was used as

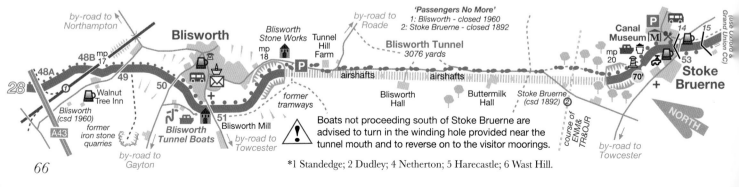

*1 Standedge; 2 Dudley; 4 Netherton; 5 Harecastle; 6 Wast Hill.

a bunkering and maintenance shed for the tunnel tugs; the other a stable.

Where Blisworth dreams, Stoke Bruerne bristles, both with boaters and tourists, the latter attracted here primarily by the village's Canal Museum. Steerers should handle their craft with consideration and courtesy, keeping a special eye open for the trip boats which ply between the winding hole and the top lock. As the cutting recedes, the canal narrows through the site of Rectory Bridge, then widens as it reaches the wharf and associated buildings which, taken as a whole, make Stoke Bruerne such a cherished canal location. A three-storey, stone built mill dominates the wharf. Once it ground corn with machinery driven by steam, now it houses the museum, first opened to the inquisitive public as long ago as 1963. A basin for boats delivering coal to the mill lay behind where the tall poplar trees now stand, and all trace has vanished of a roving bridge which carried the towpath over the entrance to this dock. A row of stone cottages originally provided for millworkers - but later used by canal employees - separates the mill from a brick house of Georgian style. This was for many years a shop catering for the needs of boating families. But in the twilight days of commercial carrying it was the home of Stoke's favourite daughter, Sister Mary Ward, a lady of high ideals and humility, who took it upon herself to look after the boat people in sickness and in health until her retirement in 1962. Buildings on the west bank of the canal include the wharfinger's office and house where the late canal author and water transport campaigner, David Blagrove lived. His book, *Bread Upon the Waters*, paints a vivid description of life on the Grand Union Canal towards the end of commercial carrying in the 1960s. The house now belongs to the Morleys, who run a small craft shop/chandlery adjoining the pub. All part of the charm and enduring fascination of Stoke Bruerne, covered more fully in *Pearson's Oxford & Grand Union Canal Companion*.

Bugbrooke   Map 28

Once upon a time Bugbrooke was known as a centre for ladder-making. Handsome church. Heygates Bugbrooke Mill, a mile to the north on the banks of the Nene, produces flour and animal feeds.

Eating & Drinking
BAKERS ARMS - High Street. Tel: 01604 832954. Homely village local. No food Mons. NN7 3PG
VILLAGE TAKEAWAY - Great Lane. Tel: 01604 831000. Burgers, kebabs, wraps and desserts. Open Tue-Sat 4-9pm. Local delivery service (min £16). NN7 3PE
THE WHARF - Cornhill Lane (Bridge 36). Tel: 01604 832585. Purpose-built canalside pub offering bar and restaurant food. Large waterside garden. NN7 3QB

Shopping
Convenience store 6am-8pm ex Sun (6.30am-4pm).

Connections
BUSES - Stagecoach service D3 operates hourly Mon-Sat (bi-hourly Sun) to/from Northampton and Daventry (via Weedon). Tel: 0871 200 2233.

Blisworth   Map 29

Church and Baptist chapel dominate the view from the canal, and there are some fine looking stone buildings, reminders of the village's significance as a centre of quarrying. On the road which runs across the hill, in parallel to the canal's subterranean course, stands a handsome building bearing the inscription: 'Blisworth Stone Works'.

Eating & Drinking
WALNUT TREE INN - Station Road. Tel: 01604 859551. Former 19th century station hotel smartly refurbished. Bar and restaurant food, real ales and B&B. NN7 3DS
ROYAL OAK - Chapel Lane. Tel: 01604 858723. Village 'local' offering eat-in/take-away food. NN7 3BU

Shopping
General store and post office in main street of village.

Connections
BUSES - Stagecoach service 88 to/from Northampton and Towcester bi-hourly Mon-Sat. . Tel: 0871 200 2233.

Stoke Bruerne   Map 29

Stoke Bruerne transcends its popularity, attracting the kind of crowds which many a theme park would envy, whilst remaining largely 'unspoilt'.

Eating & Drinking
THE BOAT INN - canalside above top lock. Tel: 01604 862428. Thatched 'local' popular with visitors and villagers alike which has been run by the same family since 1877. Regular *Good Beer Guide* entry. Northamptonshire skittles. Restaurant with view over canal to mill and museum. Bistro, breakfasts (from 9am), basic provisions. NN12 7SB
SPICE OF BRUERNE - canalside Indian restaurant, also offering take-away service and free delivery within 4 miles radius. Tel: 01604 863330 - NN12 7SE

Things to Do
THE CANAL MUSEUM - Tel: 01604 862229. Open daily mid Feb to mid Dec. Shop and Cafe. Admission charge. Interesting collection of authentic and well-displayed artefacts. NN12 7SE

WHAT a little treasure 'The Ashby' is. A dozen times we've researched it down the years. Yet it never fails to captivate; throwing up fresh perspectives every time we renew its acquaintance. Pinteresque is the epithet which springs most readily to mind when seeking to encapsulate its atmosphere. A journey along this lockless, and almost entirely rural waterway is akin to attending a performance of one of Harold's plays: nothing much appears to happen, but the effect is profound.

The Ashby Canal leaves the Coventry Canal at Marston Junction on the outskirts of Bedworth. A milepost by roving bridge 15A implies that there are thirty miles to explore, and indeed if you are walking or cycling there are. But boaters - pending further restoration - have just over twenty-two miles at their disposal. These mileposts, incidentally, are replicas of those erected by the Midland Railway who acquired the canal in 1846.

The canal narrows at the site of a former stop lock, originally built - as was the whole canal - to broad beam dimensions. The aroma of horse dung emanates from a neighbouring stable, evoking olfactory echoes of horse-drawn boats. On the offside, what is now a ragworty pocket of wasteland was once occupied by a lock-keeper's house memorably photographed (along with an old lady and a bucket) by Eric de Mare in his landmark 1950 book, published by the Architectural Press, *The Canals of England*.

The canal gains momentum, loyal to a 303ft contour which its original engineer, Robert Whitworth, adroitly surveyed in 1781. A sequence of stone-built overbridges ensues, each bearing characteristic number plates. Bridge 2 looks authentically hump-backed, but at one time it carried a mineral line from a granite quarry, which lay to the north, to an interchange with the main line railway at Marston Jabbett; not just any old railway, but

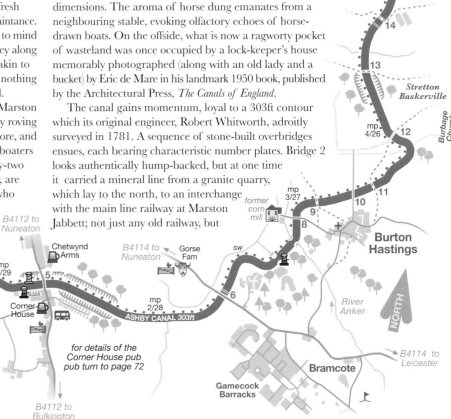

for details of the Corner House pub
pub turn to page 72

A London-bound express crosses the Ashby Canal by Bridge 4

the West Coast Main Line linking London Euston with Crewe and Glasgow.

There are designated visitor moorings just short of Bridge 5. Mooring is less formally controlled than on, for example, the Shropshire Union Canal, but there are plenty of opportunities, especially if you've had the foresight to bring clips easily attached to the Armco piling which predominates. A lengthy cutting, overlooked on the offside by static homes made whimsically individualistic by their owners, ushers the canal towards its two mile point, and you soon begin to sense that you're in the middle of nowhere ... which, when all is said and done, is rather a nice place to be!

Bridge 6 carries a B-road which offers an intrinsically more bucolic means of driving between Nuneaton and Leicester than the M69; indeed, beyond Sapcote it adopts the course of the Fosse Way. A farm shop and butchery lie quarter of a mile west of Bridge 6, but the traffic is fast and there's no pavement. At the top of a small hill to the east stand Gamecock Barracks, an extensive Ministry of Defence facility which can trace its origins back to a Second World War aerodrome. Beyond the bridge the canal used to be overlooked by Bramcote Hospital, a tuberculosis sanitorium, but this has been demolished and the site redeveloped for housing, though a small NHS respite care facility remains.

The next overbridge is numbered '8', and there appears to be no historic evidence of a Bridge 7. Perhaps the number related to the largely invisible aqueduct which carries the canal across the River Anker, employed at one time to power Burton Mill alongside Bridge 8. A lane leads up to the isolated village of Burton Hastings. St Botolph's church is the cynosure of interest here, and highly picturesque. A sundial dated 1867 exhorts one to 'seize the day'. Old maps show the presence of a smithy in the village, but these days it appears every bit as deserted as Stretton Baskerville, a lost village east of the canal, rendered obsolete by the field enclosures of the 16th century, unhedged again in the 20th. Man's more modern imprint is in the form of a plethora of electricity pylons. To the east the slender spire of Burbage church is a prominent landmark. Into this open landscape, winds blow malevolently unchecked from Putin's Urals.

69

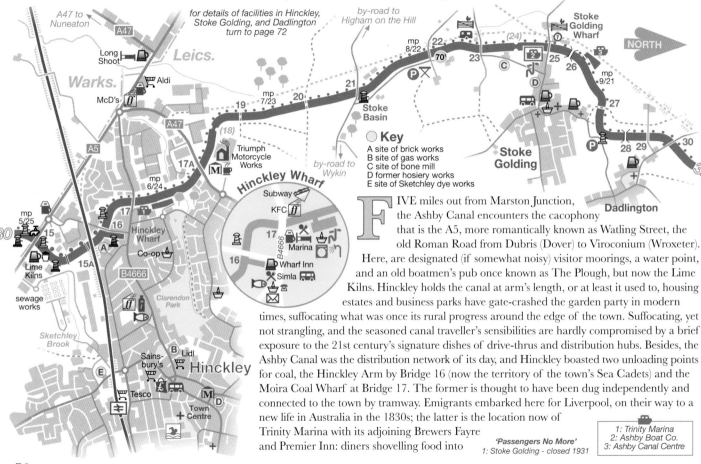

A47 to Nuneaton

for details of facilities in Hinckley, Stoke Golding, and Dadlington turn to page 72

by-road to Higham on the Hill

Stoke Golding Wharf

NORTH

Leics.

Long Shoot

Aldi

Warks.

McD's

A47

A5

Triumph Motorcycle Works

mp 8/22

mp 7/23

Stoke Basin

Stoke Golding

Dadlington

Hinckley Wharf

mp 6/24

17A

mp 5/25

15

16

17

Hinckley Wharf

Co-op

A

Lime Kilns

15A

B4666

sewage works

Clarendon Park

Sketchley Brook

Sainsbury's

Lidl

Hinckley

Tesco

Town Centre

Subway

KFC

17

Marina

16

Wharf Inn

Simla

Key
A site of brick works
B site of gas works
C site of bone mill
D former hosiery works
E site of Sketchley dye works

by-road to Wykin

FIVE miles out from Marston Junction, the Ashby Canal encounters the cacophony that is the A5, more romantically known as Watling Street, the old Roman Road from Dubris (Dover) to Viroconium (Wroxeter). Here, are designated (if somewhat noisy) visitor moorings, a water point, and an old boatmen's pub once known as The Plough, but now the Lime Kilns. Hinckley holds the canal at arm's length, or at least it used to, housing estates and business parks have gate-crashed the garden party in modern times, suffocating what was once its rural progress around the edge of the town. Suffocating, yet not strangling, and the seasoned canal traveller's sensibilities are hardly compromised by a brief exposure to the 21st century's signature dishes of drive-thrus and distribution hubs. Besides, the Ashby Canal was the distribution network of its day, and Hinckley boasted two unloading points for coal, the Hinckley Arm by Bridge 16 (now the territory of the town's Sea Cadets) and the Moira Coal Wharf at Bridge 17. The former is thought to have been dug independently and connected to the town by tramway. Emigrants embarked here for Liverpool, on their way to a new life in Australia in the 1830s; the latter is the location now of Trinity Marina with its adjoining Brewers Fayre and Premier Inn: diners shovelling food into

'Passengers No More'
1: Stoke Golding - closed 1931

1: Trinity Marina
2: Ashby Boat Co.
3: Ashby Canal Centre

Stoke Basin (*no sign of Cicely!*)

time. The purpose of the main line was exactly that of the Ashby Canal - to carry coal. Most of this coal was heading for London and the south-east, and the loop line had no part to play in this traffic. It was mothballed in 1875 though not formally abandoned until 1914. You might profit from a peep at Stoke Golding's old station by Bridge 25. Characteristic of the chalet-like style of the joint line, it is now in use as a dwelling, as is the old station master's house, whilst the goods shed has been incorporated into a small business park.

Stoke Golding Wharf is home to the Ashby Boat Company, a well-established hire boat operator, whose handsome cream & red liveried boats are encountered throughout the area covered by this guide. Follow Station Road up towards the centre of the village and you'll come upon an old hosiery works converted into apartments. These were the premises of Halls, manufacturers of socks; not least 35 million pairs shipped out to the front during the First World War. Known now as HJ Socks in deference to the original owner 'Honest John' Hall, they moved to Coventry Road, Hinckley in 1977, though whilst they can still lay claim to the title of the UK's largest purveyor of branded socks, production has emigrated overseas.

their mouths where their uncouth predecessors shovelled coal. Until 1953, Hinckley Urban District Council were tasked with monitoring the sanitary standards of boats based on the Ashby Canal. The luxuriously appointed craft berthed in the marina are unlikely to cause such concerns.

Evading the grasp of Triumph's motorcycle factory and a giant Tesco warehouse, the canal re-establishes its unspoilt credentials, twisting past the hilltop settlements of Higham on the Hill, Stoke Golding and Dadlington; wandering from church spire to church spire like some doddery enthusiast of box pews and carved lecterns. For a while the canal shares the journey with an abandoned railway, one which holds the peculiar claim of never having carried a train. The line was stillborn out of an uneasy alliance between the Midland and London & North Western railway companies. They shared construction costs between Ashby and Nuneaton, and this loop was built between Stoke Golding and Hinckley at the same

Stoke Golding Wharf

Hinckley
Map 31

Lock-wheeler's childhood in Hinckley lies farther back in time than the Victorian age was when he lived here in the 1950s. Indeed, the little hosiery town he was so familar with then had more in common with the 19th century than the 21st. Perambulating its streets today proved largely an excercise in alienation. It wasn't so much a matter of popping into the Hinckley & District Museum for a quick look around, but rather the inherent sense of belonging it engendered ... as an exhibit. Knitting frames were being worked in Hinckley in the 1640s, but it was during the 20th century that the hosiery trade was at its height. In 1959, over five thousand of the town's population were members of the National Union of Hosiery Workers. One of the best known firms were Atkins Brothers. Their flagship 'Art Deco' High Cross works on Regent Street derived its name from the meeting place of the Watling Street and Fosse Way four miles south-east of Hinckley. The company's older, Victorian works on Lower Bond Street has become a gallery and centre for creative businesses. Though not a native, the town's most celebrated son, Joseph Hansom, was a feted architect and inventor of the eponymous horse-drawn predecessor to the taxi. Many a Sherlock Holmes mystery might have gone unsolved but for a Hansom cab within hailing distance.

Eating & Drinking

CORNER HOUSE - Nuneaton Road, Bulkington (near Bridge 5, Map 30). Tel: 0247 638 6159. Marston's 'all-day' pub offering a wide choice of food. CV12 9SB
LIME KILNS - Watling Street (canalside Bridge 15). Tel: 01455 631158. Buswells Brewery home brew pub with canalside garden. Open 12-3pm and 5.30-11pm Mon-Fri, and from noon weekends. Food 12-2pm and 6-8.30pm Mon-Sat and 12-2pm Sun. LE10 3ED

THE MARINA - Tel: 01455 636493. Canalside Brewers Fayre restaurant. Premier Inn adjacent. LE10 0NB
SIMLA - Hinckley Wharf. Tel: 01455 633955. Highly regarded Indian restaurant & take-away occupying former wharf house. Opens 5.30pm. LE10 0NQ

Shopping

Trinity Marina sells basic provisions (and offers laundry facilities) but it isn't far to a bustling convenience store on Coventry Road (easily reached from bridges 16 or 17) which boasts a cash machine and does a roaring trade in freshly filled 'batches' between 7am and 2.30pm Mon-Sat - Tel: 01455 637130. The town centre is good for shopping but the less agile may prefer to get there by bus from stops near the canal. Markets on Mon, Fri and Sat; plus 4th Suns May-Sep.

Things to Do

ATKINS BUILDING - Lower Bond Street. Tel: 01455 247070. Art gallery and exhibition centre (with Hansom cab) housed in old hosiery works. LE10 1QU
HINCKLEY & DISTRICT MUSEUM - Lower Bond Street, town centre. Tel: 01455 251218. Open Easter to October Sats & Mons 10am-4pm. Local history displays in a 17th century thatched cottage once used by frame knitters. Tea room & shop. LE10 1QU
TRIUMPH FACTORY VISITOR EXPERIENCE - Normandy Way (Bridge 17A). Tel: 01455 453088. 10am-4.30pm Wed-Sun. Fascinating exhibitions of motorcycling development. Cafe & shop. LE10 3BZ

Connections

BUSES - useful (Mon-Sat) links along the Ashby Canal corridor with Stoke Golding (No.6) and Market Bosworth (No.159). Frequent services (10/48) from stops adjacent Bridge 17 into Hinckley.

TRAINS - connections with Nuneaton and Leicester etc from station 1 mile east of canal.

TAXIS - A1. Tel: 01455 615161.

Stoke Golding
Map 31

A Blue Plaque on Station Road commemorates Crown Hill where King Henry VII was crowned on 22nd August 1485. The imposing 13th century parish church of St Margaret of Antioch has the air of a small cathedral, and coffee is served by charming ladies on Wednesday mornings. Apparently the steeple was dismantled for the duration of the Second World War so that it wouldn't impede flights from RAF Lindley.

Eating & Drinking

GEORGE & DRAGON - Station Road. Tel: 01455 213268. Good Beer Guide listed Church End Brewery pub. Closed Mon. Lunches Tue-Sat. CV13 6EZ
THREE HORSE SHOES - High Street. Tel: 01455 212263. Village centre pub incorporating an Indian restaurant. From 5.30pm (1pm Sun). CV13 6HE
THE WHITE SWAN - High Street. Tel: 01455 212313. Village local offering Leicester-brewed Everards ales. Food served Wed-Sun lunchtimes and Tue-Sat evenings from 6.30pm. CV13 6HE

Shopping

Shopping facilities include a small convenience store stocking newspapers and a moderate range of provisions. Spinneybank Farm Shop at Bridge 23 (Tel: 01455 212445) is well attuned to the needs of boaters. Another farm shop called Tomlinson's (Tel: 01455 212199) lies west of Bridge 25.

Connections

BUSES - Service 6 runs hourly, Mon-Sat to/from Hinckley and Nuneaton. Tel: 0871 200 2233.

Dadlington
Map 31

Eating & Drinking

DOG & HEDGEHOG. Tel: 01455 213151. Comfortable country pub. Open from noon daily. Lunches daily, dinner from 5.30pm Mon-Sat. CV13 6JB

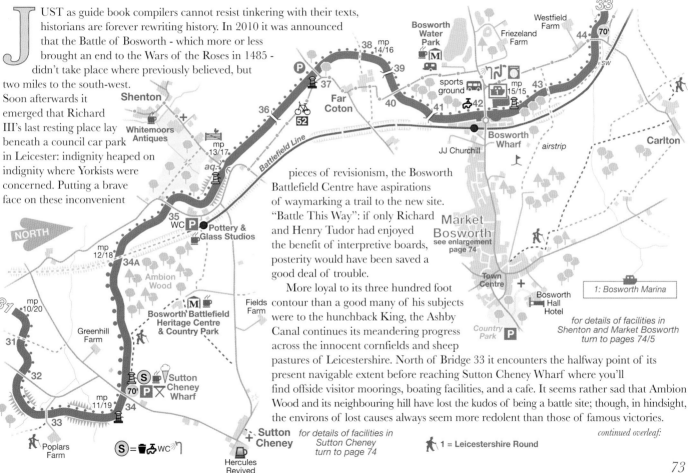

JUST as guide book compilers cannot resist tinkering with their texts, historians are forever rewriting history. In 2010 it was announced that the Battle of Bosworth - which more or less brought an end to the Wars of the Roses in 1485 - didn't take place where previously believed, but two miles to the south-west. Soon afterwards it emerged that Richard III's last resting place lay beneath a council car park in Leicester: indignity heaped on indignity where Yorkists were concerned. Putting a brave face on these inconvenient pieces of revisionism, the Bosworth Battlefield Centre have aspirations of waymarking a trail to the new site. "Battle This Way": if only Richard and Henry Tudor had enjoyed the benefit of interpretive boards, posterity would have been saved a good deal of trouble.

More loyal to its three hundred foot contour than a good many of his subjects were to the hunchback King, the Ashby Canal continues its meandering progress across the innocent cornfields and sheep pastures of Leicestershire. North of Bridge 33 it encounters the halfway point of its present navigable extent before reaching Sutton Cheney Wharf where you'll find offside visitor moorings, boating facilities, and a cafe. It seems rather sad that Ambion Wood and its neighbouring hill have lost the kudos of being a battle site; though, in hindsight, the environs of lost causes always seem more redolent than those of famous victories.

continued overleaf:

Shenton
Whitemoors Antiques
mp 13/17
aq.
Far Coton
36
52
mp 14/16
38
37
39
40
41
42
43
44
70'
sw
Bosworth Water Park
Friezeland Farm
Westfield Farm
sports ground
mp 15/15
JJ Churchill
Bosworth Wharf
airstrip
Carlton
Market Bosworth
see enlargement page 74
Town Centre
Bosworth Hall Hotel
Country Park
1: Bosworth Marina

for details of facilities in Shenton and Market Bosworth turn to pages 74/5

35
WC
Pottery & Glass Studios
NORTH
mp 12/18
34A
Ambion Wood
Bosworth Battlefield Heritage Centre & Country Park
Fields Farm
Greenhill Farm
mp 10/20
31
31
32
mp 11/19
34
33
Poplars Farm
S = WC

Sutton Cheney *for details of facilities in Sutton Cheney turn to page 74*

Hercules Revived

Sutton Cheney Wharf
70'

1 = Leicestershire Round

continued from page 73:

The Battlefield Line is a preserved section of the Ashby & Nuneaton Joint Railway, originally closed to passenger trains as long ago as 1931, though retained for goods until 1970. On operating days the line's archaic steam engines and pensioned-off diesels trundle nostalgically up and down the five mile route between Shenton and Shackerstone, offering a tempting opportunity for one-way towpath walks. Steps by Shenton Aqueduct lead down to the charming little village of Shenton and Whitemoors Antiques Centre. For all its inherent air of remoteness, the Ashby Canal frequently throws up entertaining things to do.

An especially scenic length of canal ensues as it wriggles round the hilltop hamlet of Far Coton. The neighbouring farm boasts some fine Dutch gables. Seventy-three new homes are being constructed between the canal and the railway on the hitherto sylvan approach to Market Bosworth. Hedging their bets, the builders have taken their cue from two layers of history and risibly called the development King Richard's Wharf. The unlucky Plantagenet will be turning in his Leicester Cathedral grave of 2015. The original Bosworth Wharf lay fifteen miles from Marston Junction and here, in times gone by, stood a brick yard and a gas works. Nowadays there's a sports ground, marina, and more housing, erected in the quasi-warehouse vernacular style which canalside settings invariably inspire.

A large blue Canal & River Trust sign at Bridge 44 advises canal users that they are entering a Site of Special Scientific Interest. Traversing the canal at Easter, when cowslips and celandine were flourishing along the towpath, we couldn't help feeling that Nature herself was quite capable of reminding us of our responsibilities. And though it was officially the close season for coarse fishing, the herons which preceeded us unhurriedly from one undesignated beat to the next seemed equally inclined to cock a snook at superfluous signage.

Sutton Cheney Map 32

Sutton Cheney Wharf attracts many visitors by virtue of the access it provides to Bosworth Battlefield. There's a nice row of almshouses in the village itself.

Eating & Drinking

SUTTON WHARF - Tel: 01455 213838. Purpose built canalside cafe/bar purveying coffees, lunches and teas 9.30-4.30 daily. Ice creams from a boat! CV13 0AL
HERCULES REVIVED - Main Street. Tel: 01455 699336. Country pub open lunch & evening (from 6pm) Mon-Sat and Sun noon to 4pm. CV13 0AG

Things to Do

BOSWORTH BATTLEFIELD - Tel: 01455 290429. Access from the canal via footpath from Sutton Cheney Wharf, bridges 34A and 35, or Shenton Aqueduct. Visitor centre - admission charge. Re-enactments, interactive displays, history walks and falconry. Battlefield Trails open all year round, free access. Tithe Barn Cafeteria and gift shop. CV13 0AD

Market Bosworth Map 32

Not so much as a B-road ruffles 'Bosworth's inherent calm. From the top deck of a number 153, as it whisks you uphill from the wharf to the town centre,

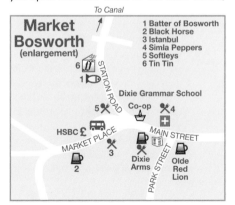

To Canal

Market Bosworth (enlargement)

1 Batter of Bosworth
2 Black Horse
3 Istanbul
4 Simla Peppers
5 Softleys
6 Tin Tin

STATION ROAD
Dixie Grammar School
Co-op
HSBC £
MARKET PLACE
MAIN STREET
PARK STREET
Dixie Arms
Olde Red Lion

keep your eyes peeled for Churchill's aerospace factory on the right hand side, relocated here after the Coventry Blitz. Their founder, Walter Churchill, was a WWII Spitfire ace who died defending Malta. His brother, Peter, was with the Special Operations Executive, and married Odette Sansom, infamously imprisoned and tortured by the Gestapo, as related in the 1950 film *Odette*, starring Anna Neagle, with Trevor Howard playing Peter Churchill.

And if, at first, from your omnibus eyrie, the little town appears overtly suburban, persevere. Redemption comes with the market place where - purloining a lyric of Alan Jay Lerner's - 'enchantment pours out of every door'. Dr Johnson taught at the imposing Tudor style Dixie Grammar School for a brief period, but looked back on his time here "with the strongest aversion". You are unlikely to concur. Eastwards lies Bosworth Country Park with its arboretum, lakes, wildflower meadow; scene of the Bosworth Show on the first Sunday in July.

Eating & Drinking

BATTER OF BOSWORTH - Station Road. Tel: 01455 290025. Delicious award-winning fish & chips, worth patronizing for the awful pun alone. CV13 0JS

BLACK HORSE - Market Place. Tel: 01455 290278. Gourmet fine-dining open Mon-Sat lunch and evening (from 6pm) and Sun lunch. CV13 OLF

ISTANBUL - Market Place. Tel: 01455 293162. Turkish restaurant open from noon daily. CV13 OLF

SIMLA PEPPERS - Main Street. Tel: 01455 293311. Indian restaurant (& t/a) open 5.30pm. CV13 0JN

SOFTLEYS - Market Place. Tel: 01455 290464. Attractive eating house serving lunches (Tue-Sun) and dinners (Tue-Sat) and accommodation. CV13 OLE

TIN TIN - Station Road. Tel: 01455 292828. Acclaimed Chinese take-away. CV13 0JS

Shopping

The last shops between this point and the canal's current terminus. There's a little market on Wednesdays, though it must be a pale shadow of the rollicking junkets of yore. A Co-op food store, and several antique/gift shops. HSBC bank. Farmers' Market 4th Sunday of the month. Basic provisions in marina shop. No Post Office!

Things to Do

BOSWORTH WATER PARK - west of Bosworth Wharf. Tel: 01455 291876. Fifty acre leisure park offering sailing, windsurfing, pedalos, canoeing and fishing opportunities with equipment available for hire. Cafe and bar - Tel: 01455 292685. CV13 6PD

Connections

BUSES - Arriva service 153 operates to/from Leicester hourly Mon-Sat starting from its terminus adjacent to Bosworth Wharf and thus provides a useful lift into town. Roberts service 159 operates hourly Mon-Sat to/from Hinckley in one direction

and Coalville in the other from the market place.
TAXIS - Bosworth Private Hire. Tel: 0774 268 1003.

Shenton   Map 32

Extremely pretty hamlet centred on a 17th century hall. Admiral Arbuthnot, who fought at Trafalgar, is remembered in the church. Small farm shop near aqueduct. Paul Young Ceramics (Tel: 0771 162 8337) and Station Glass (Tel: 01455 371978) are a pair of appealing craft studios located at the railway station.

Things to Do

WHITEMOORS - Mill Lane. Tel: 01455 212250. Appealing gallimaufry of antique and craft outlets (open daily from 10am) about just over ten minutes walk from the canal aqueduct. S/h book section worth investigating. Tea rooms (with lovely stream-side garden) where lunches are served daily. CV13 6BZ

Congerstone   Map 33

St Mary's church was restored in 1834 by Earl Howe of Gopsall Hall. Pevsner deemed the wide chancel 'extraordinary', and admired the box pews and Kempe

glass. On the by-road to Sibson there's a gibbet, erected in 1801 to contain the remains of John Massey who had battered his wife to death by Bilstone Mill. His skeleton leered down on passers-by for over twenty years.

Eating & Drinking

HORSE & JOCKEY - Bosworth Road (easily reached from Bridge 47 moorings). Tel: 01827 881220. Splendid gastro-pub open for dinner Mon (from 6pm), lunch and dinner Tue-Sat, and Sun lunch. CV13 6LY

Shackerstone   Map 33

The festival, which ran annually between 1994 and 2019, is, alas, no more, but Shackerstone remains a pretty village 'lost' in the Leicestershire countryside. Spacious St Peter's contains a fine east window dedicated to local men killed in the Great War.

Eating & Drinking

HELP OUT MILL - Heather Lane (half a mile north of Bridge 53). Tel: 01530 260666. Fine dining in granary of former watermill on River Sence. Open Fri-Sun for lunch and dinner, booking essential. CV13 0BT

RISING SUN - Church Road. Tel: 01827 880215. Good Beer Guide listed pub offering Marston's, Taylor's Landlord and guest ales together with a good range of food served Wed-Fri lunch and evenings (from 6pm) and weekends from noon. CV13 6NN There's also a Victorian Tea Parlour open Wed, Sat & Sun at the preserved railway station.

Things to Do

BATTLEFIELD LINE - stations at Shackerstone, Market Bosworth and Shenton (pictured). Tel: 01827 880754. Operates weekends throughout the season and some weekdays in high summer. There's a delightful 'light railway' feel to this little line; Colonel Stephens - indomitable rescuer of many lost ferroequinological causes - would be in his element. CV13 6NW

Y OU can tell you're off the beaten track when BT have left the villages' traditional red telephone kiosks with working apparatus. Keep the secret to yourselves and they may survive at least a little longer. Moreover, up here in the *ultima Thule* of North West Leicestershire, this succession of prefixed '-stones' have nothing to do with Mick, Keith or the late, lamented Charlie, but rather the little, out in the sticks communities of 'Conger', 'Bil', 'Shacker' and 'Snare'.

More sleeping than rolling, the canal barely acknowledges their presence, after all they could hardly have provided much trade for what was primarily a coal carrying canal. Perversely, the coal mines which brought prosperity to the canal, caused, through subsidence, successive shortenings back from the original terminus: to Donisthorpe in 1944; Illott Wharf, near Measham, in 1957; and Snarestone in 1966. Working boatmen always referred to this as the 'Moira Cut'. A trip up the canal afforded a tempting opportunity for

boating families to obtain pottery ware now commonly known as 'Measham', but for the most part manufactured across the border in neighbouring South Derbyshire. Measham teapots, with their distinctive brown glaze and relief ornamentation, found a home in many a narrow boat cabin, often customised with the owner's or his boat's name. Twisting past Congerstone, the canal reaches Shackerstone where an aqueduct –

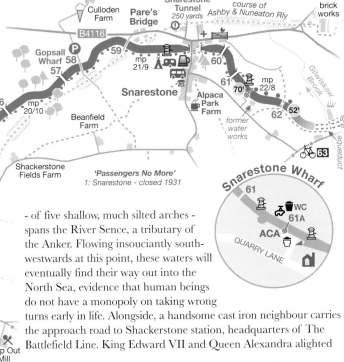

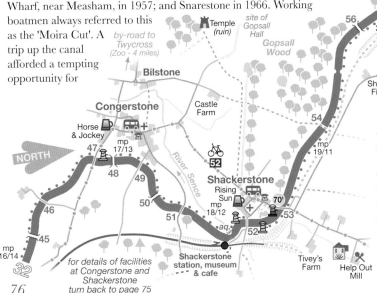

- of five shallow, much silted arches - spans the River Sence, a tributary of the Anker. Flowing insouciantly south-westwards at this point, these waters will eventually find their way out into the North Sea, evidence that human beings do not have a monopoly on taking wrong turns early in life. Alongside, a handsome cast iron neighbour carries the approach road to Shackerstone station, headquarters of The Battlefield Line. King Edward VII and Queen Alexandra alighted

for details of facilities at Congerstone and Shackerstone turn back to page 75

for details of facilities at Snarestone turn to page 80

here in 1902 en route to Gopsall Hall. Shackerstone was the junction for a long lost line which picturesquely skirted the northern fringe of Charnwood Forest on its way to Loughborough. The first two stations out from Shackerstone rejoiced in the titles of Heather & Ibstock and Hugglescote, but such bucolic nomenclature came down to earth with a bump at the next stop, which went by the utilitarian, and rather more realistic name of Coalville.

Between bridges 52 and 53 moored boats line both banks. There are glimpses (west) of a medieval motte and the remnants of fish ponds, but there is not a great deal known about the history of 'Shackerstone Castle'. Beyond Bridge 53 and a comparatively spacious winding hole, the canal penetrates the green peace of Gopsall Wood. George Frideric Handel stayed at Gopsall Hall as a guest of its wealthy owner, the librettist for *The Messiah*, Charles Jennens, and is said to have spent three weeks in August/September of 1741 composing his masterpiece in a temple in the grounds, the ruins of which can still be reached on foot from Bridge 54. Perhaps, forty years on, the libretto was ringing challengingly in Whitworth's ears when he surveyed the canal: 'Every valley shall be exalted and every mountain and hill made low.'

Regrettably, the hall - at one point owned by the Warings of furniture fame - was demolished in 1951. Death duties in those days were simply unaffordable, and brought about the demise of many a country mansion. Twenty years earlier it had bequeathed its name to one of the Great Western Railway's 'Hall' class locomotives, No.4999. Unfortunately, the engine's nameplates read *Gopsal Hall*, reputedly because the guide book which the company scoured for inspiration contained a number of typographical errors: something we strive hard to eliminate in Pearson's.

Little more than a car park for anglers now, Gopsall Wharf has a niche in the history of canal carrying. Following closure of Illott Wharf,. coal was brought in by lorry from mines once directly served by the canal. The last 'commercial' cargo left Gopsall Wharf aboard the Willow Wren pair *Redshank* and *Ara* for Croxley Paper Mill near Watford on 26th August 1970. Following that, domestic coal - pre-bagged for sale throughout the canal system - provided a viable cargo under the enthusiastic auspices of the Ashby Canal Association and its subsidiary, Ashby Canal Transport. The last pair of domestic coal boats loaded at Gopsall were *Corona* and *Actis* on 30th July 1980, headed for the Upper Thames.

At Pare's Bridge the Ashby & Nuneaton Railway crossed the canal on a substantial skew bridge whose girders are long gone, but whose abutments remain intact. Snarestone's station-master's house and neighbouring goods shed have found new leases of life as domestic accommodation. A tree-lined cutting leads to Snarestone itself. Local expert, Geoffrey E. Pursglove (*Ashby Canal - Past Present & Future*), suggests that Snarestone Tunnel might easily have been by-passed to the west, but we can be grateful that it introduces an element of drama on a canal infamous for its uneventfulness.

Beyond the tunnel are the remains of a boathouse which was once elaborately decorated in canal art by Lees & Atkins of Polesworth. Note the pair of ornamental, pineapple-topped, mooring posts. To the west lie Measham and its brick works. There is a long tradition of brick-making in the vicinity. Joseph Wilkes (1733-1805) produced double-sized bricks locally - somewhat vulgarly known as 'Wilkes Gobs' - both to speed up construction techniques and to reduce the effect of a brick tax in force at the time. Wilkes additionally had interests in coal mining and cattle breeding, and collaborated with Sir Robert Peel at Fazeley. He was pre-eminent amongst promoters of the Ashby Canal, whose modern-day supporters operate an information kiosk in the shadow of Snarestone's former waterworks, opened in 1892 to provide a water supply to Hinckley: indeed, the pumping engine's beams are prominently on display.

Beyond swing-bridge 61A (CRT Yale key required to open) a length of canal re-opened in 2015 continues as far as reconstructed Bridge 62, just after which there is a 52ft winding hole - as wide as the land available would permit. This length of canal is administered by the Ashby Canal Association as opposed to CRT. A Transport & Works Act - similar to the Acts of Parliament which originally authorised construction of the canal at the end of the 18th century - has been obtained to facilitate reconstruction of the canal between Snarestone and Measham.

34 ASHBY CANAL Measham & Moira 7mls/11k

ILLOT WHARF marked the head of navigation between 1957 and 1966. This is the next target for restoration, and it will involve reconstruction of an aqueduct which once spanned Gilwiskaw Brook, a tributary of the Mease. Pending further advance - a matter, inevitably, of funding - the Ashby Canal Association have commendably waymarked a footpath following the projected course the canal will take towards Measham; slightly different - as you will see from the map - to its original route. This initiative deserves praise. Measham was always accessible on foot by road, but this traffic-free alternative is far more enjoyable, and demonstrates a commitment to further progress.

Illott Wharf the loading point for coal mined at the neighbouring Measham and Minorca collieries. Samuel Barlows carried large tonnages of Measham Colliery's output from here to Longford Power Station (Map 21), often employing a motor hauling two butties on what was effectively

a lockless route. Indeed, working boat people are said to have referred to this as 'the maternity run' because of its comparatively easy nature. In 1960, however, the National Coal Board chose to transfer the source of paper mill coal away from the Ashby Canal in favour of mines situated along the Coventry Canal and the Ashby Canal quickly silted up. Following the closure of Pooley Hall Colliery (Map 16) in 1965 however, Willow Wren Canal Transport, fresh with a contract to supply Croxley Paper Mill with coal from Donisthorpe Colliery, commenced loading at Illott once more, the coal being brought by road from Donisthorpe. The resulting flow, though welcome, proved shortlived. The National Coal Board began mining under the canal and the likelihood of subsidence resulted in the canal being cut back to Snarestone. Measham and Minorca collieries merged in 1955 and continued production until 1986. Little evidence that they ever existed remains, though the area was surface-mined (not entirely

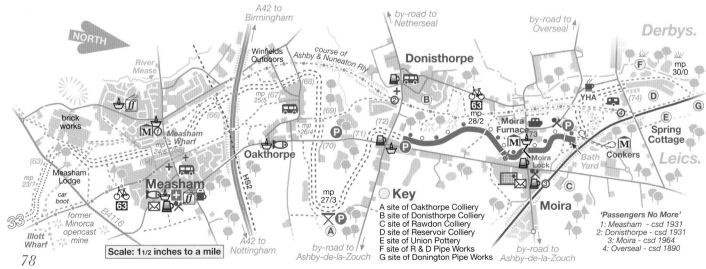

Key
A site of Oakthorpe Colliery
B site of Donisthorpe Colliery
C site of Rawdon Colliery
D site of Reservoir Colliery
E site of Union Pottery
F site of R & D Pipe Works
G site of Donington Pipe Works

'Passengers No More'
1: Measham - csd 1931
2: Donisthorpe - csd 1931
3: Moira - csd 1964
4: Overseal - csd 1890

Scale: 1½ inches to a mile

viably, nor without controversy) in recent times.

Exploration of the canal north of Measham is prosaically a more piecemeal experience. Sections of the canal have been filled-in and reverted to agricultural use. The Ashby & Nuneaton Joint Railway's trackbed, nowadays reasonably well-surfaced and designated the Ashby Woulds Heritage Trail and National Cycle Route 63, provides a less frustrating means of reaching the re-watered canal between Donisthorpe and Moira; though diehards will not easily be dissuaded from visiting isolated sections of towpath: such as at Oakthorpe where the long vanished Steam Mill Inn (*Bridge 69*) once catered for the prodigious thirsts of boaters; and the site of Oakthorpe Colliery where milepost 27/3 has been reinstated together with an interpretive board. From here, in the early days of the canal, a tramway once led through the town of Ashby-de-la-Zouch to limestone quarries in the neighbourhood of Ticknall, a link originally conceived as a canal which never materialised.

Historically, the coal which brought prosperity to the Ashby Canal ultimately became its downfall. By the early years of the 20th century subsidence was rife. A team of fifty men are said to have been employed raising banks and re-puddling the canal bed. There were major breaches in 1918 at Moira Furnace and in 1932 at Oakthorpe. A deviation had to be dug in the vicinity of Donisthorpe. Tensions arose between the colliery owners, and the railway company (Midland initially, then LMS, who by then owned the canal) regarding responsibility for maintenance and compensation claims. In places headroom was so restricted that empty boats required ballasting before being able to pass beneath overbridges. By the outbreak of the Second World War, as Geoffrey Pursglove succinctly puts it, 'The costs of maintaining the canal were out of all proportion to its usefulness'. Along with many others under their ownership, the London Midland & Scottish Railway considered closing the entire canal in 1944, but were thwarted by the Minister of War Transport who only consented to closure of the top two and a half miles, believing the canal still had a role to play in the carriage of coal under wartime conditions.

The best part of sixty years ensued before the canal was rewatered from Moira to Donisthorpe between 1999 and 2005, proving itself a popular amenity in the National Forest. One wishes there were boats on it - we live in a micro age, why not 'micro' canals? - but the canal snakes confidently enough towards Moira on a high embankment overlooked by freshly planted woodland. A far cry from the spoil heaps of the past. It is difficult to credit that Donisthorpe Colliery closed as relatively recently as 1990: though, given the issues experienced in energy sourcing these days, one can't help wondering if coal was an option prematurely discarded.

Moira Furnace is a remarkable survival from the beginning of the 19th Century. It was erected by the Earl of Moira in 1804 to smelt iron ore, but unfortunately its working life lasted merely eight years. The building, however, remained intact, and in recent years has been restored and opened to the public as a museum. A trip boat - appropriately named *Joseph Wilkes* - operates regularly from here down through Moira Lock to Conkers National Forest Visitor Centre. The need to build a lock when the canal was restored illustrates how subsidence had brought about changes to land levels over the years.

Bath Yard Basin marks the end of the rewatered section. The name derives from an attempt to create a spa resort in the neighbourhood, mineral water springs having been inadvertently discovered during sinking of a colliery shaft in 1805. A bath house and an hotel were erected, but oddly prospective customers appeared deterred by the presence of a coal mine on the doorstep. Subsequently the spa was moved to Ashby, the beneficial waters being conveyed thence in barrels by boat and tramway waggon.

Early in the canal's genesis there had been calls for it to connect at its north-eastern extremity with the Trent. These came to nought, but fresh proposals emerged in 1840 in the shape of a Burton & Moira Canal, involving two flights of locks and a tunnel at Gresley. These, though, were but the death throes of the canal age, soon the area would be criss-crossed by railways.

continued overleaf:

continued from page 79:

West of Bath Yard the bed of the canal has been overwhelmed by impenetrable woodland. Walkers determined to pursue the canal to its original terminus are advised to regain the Ashby Woulds Heritage Trail to reach an honourable conclusion in the vicinity of Spring Cottage. The canal hereabouts was infilled with colliery waste by the simple expedient of emptying the contents of railway wagons over the arches of the neighbouring railway viaduct, itself subsequently submerged. 19th century canal boatmen would be bewildered by the presence now of a Youth Hostel overlooking their old canal. The last few hundred yards of the canal, in water once again, lie alongside timber holiday lodges. The sanitary pipe works and colliery long gone. Lark song now; joggers, dog-walkers, reedbeds and a profound, post-industrial sense of lost endeavour.

Snarestone — Map 33

Back o' beyond village. Snarestone Lodge is Grade II listed. More chapel-like than church, squat, brick-built St Bartholomew's dates from 1752, and there's a plethora of cast iron grave 'stones' of interest.

Eating & Drinking

THE GLOBE - Main Street. Tel: 01530 272020. Roomy brick built pub above the tunnel. Food served Mon-Sat lunch and evenings (from 6pm) and Sunday lunches. Camping and caravanning. Elsan point. DE12 7DB

Shopping

Lodge Farm Shop on B4116. Tel: 01530 270690. Dreamy Cow ice cream made from contented Friesians at Culloden Farm - Tel: 01530 272000.

Things to Do

ALPACA PARK FARM - Main Street. Tel: 01530 271623. Charming family run farm with donkeys, goats, and chickens, but mostly alpacas. Tea room and wool shop open daily (ex Mon) 9am-4pm. DE12 7DB

Connections

BUSES - Roberts service 7 operates four times per day Mon-Sat to/from Measham, Atherstone and Nuneaton and provides a link with Twycross Zoo (Tel: 0844 474 1777 - CV9 3PX). Tel: 0871 200 2233.

Measham — Map 34

Sizeable north-west Leics village best known for bricks and car auctions. Derives its name from the River Mease which rises a couple of miles to the south-west at Appleby Magna, and flows into the Trent near Alrewas (Map 50). Horses Lane and Navigation Street hark back to the era of a working canal on its doorstep. Indeed the wharf's symmetrical warehouses, perched either side of the High Street, remain intact, though minus their loading arches at water level. The hoped for reappearance of a navigable canal on Measham's doorstep will be welcomed more, perhaps, than the advent of a high speed railway line from Birmingham. The parish church of St Laurence dates back to the 14th century and there is also a high, wide and handsome Weslyan chapel.

Eating & Drinking

Two fish & chip shops, a pub, an Indian restaurant/take-away, cafes and sandwich bar; almost too much choice for canal archaeologists and other, less definable, strayers up from Snarestone.

Shopping

Shops include Co-op and Tesco convenience stores, PO and a pharmacy for blistered towpath walkers.

Things to Do

MEASHAM MUSEUM - Mannings Terrace. Tel: 01530 271724. Open Tue 2-4pm and Sat 10am-12pm. Delightful local history displays housed in refurbished station building of distinctive character. Exhibits include various items of Measham Ware. An ice-breaker is displayed outside, together with a mosaic sundial in memory of local entrepreneur Joseph Wilkes. The neighbouring railway goods shed, previously used by a boatbuilding firm, now plays host to a company specialising in the use of motorcycle side-cars as funeral hearses.

Connections

BUSES - Midland Classic service 19/19A operates hourly Mon-Sat to/from Ashby de-la Zouch (well worth a visit) and Burton-on-Trent via Donisthorpe and Swadlincote. Roberts service 7 operates four times per day Mon-Sat to/from Atherstone via Snarestone and Shackerstone. Tel: 0871 200 2233.

Moira — Map 34

Gains its pretty (if not entirely representative name) from the Hastings family (see page 113) who held the Earldom of Moira in County Down, Ulster. Boosted by the burgeoning National Forest, (which has its headquarters at Bath Yard) this Moira is visibly and encouragingly recuperating from two centuries of industrial abuse. Facilities include two pubs, a Co-op convenience store, post office, bistro, and a YHA cafe.

Things to Do

CONKERS - Rawdon Road. Tel: 01283 216633. Family orientated visitor centre with both indoor and outdoor attractions. Narrow gauge railway links two sites. Open daily from 10am. Refreshments. DE12 6GA
MOIRA FURNACE - Furnace Lane. Tel: 01283 224667. Restored blast furnace, lime kilns, museum, woodland walks and boat trips. Tea rooms. DE12 6AT

Lock 20, Kingswood (Maps 6 & 40)

GALLERY

Winding at Bonehill (Map 15)

Turning onto the Ashby Canal at Marston Junction (Maps 19 & 30)

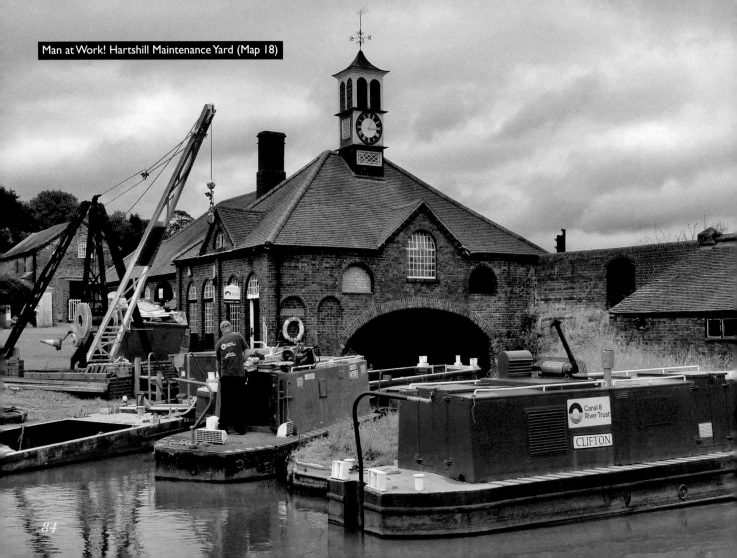

'Donkey Bend', the Ashby at Shenton (Map 32)

'Underneath the Arches', Hillmorton (Map 24)

Old Telegraph Pole, near Nuneaton (Map 18)

'I See No Ships': the Grand Union near Fosse Wharf (Map 3)

'Let's Stop for an Ice Cream!': Sutton Wharf on the Ashby Canal (Map 32)

93

OUR inland waterways, prized today as a leisure resource par excellence, might not have survived official indifference had two relative strangers not arranged to meet each other at Tardebigge just after the Second World War. Robert Aickman and L. T. C. Rolt (as they preferred to be known on their book jackets) went on to form the Inland Waterways Association, and though their relationship swiftly deteriorated to the point of outright enmity, it is no exaggeration to say that their initial encounter (and that of their respective spouses) paved the way for the canal network to be saved from almost certain extinction. A memorial to this historic event stands close to Tardebigge Top Lock, a pilgrimage not to be eschewed by anyone who derives the slightest pleasure from the canals to this day.

Coverage of the Worcester & Birmingham Canal in this Canal Companion runs from Tardebigge to Birmingham, primarily for the benefit of boaters setting out to do the Stratford Canal or Warwickshire Ring from one or other of the two large hire bases depicted on the accompanying map. The whole length of the canal between Worcester and Birmingham may be found more fully described in Pearson's Canal Companions to the Stourport Ring or Severn & Avon.

Lockless from Tardebigge to Birmingham, a series of tunnels provide alternative focal points for the canal traveller. Boaters become moles; walkers and claustrophobics have to take to the old horse paths across the tops, entertaining detours in their own right. Though much expanded, the village of Alvechurch barely deflects from the canal's dreamy progress, and there are panoramic views eastwards across Weatheroak Hill, crossed by the Roman's Ryknild Street, encountered elsewhere in this guide on its way between the Cotswolds and South Yorkshire.

A feeder comes in from Upper Bittell Reservoir beside an isolated canal employee's cottage near Bridge 66. The Lower Reservoir lies alongside the canal and is given a gorgeous wooded backdrop by the Lickey Hills, rising to over eight hundred feet.

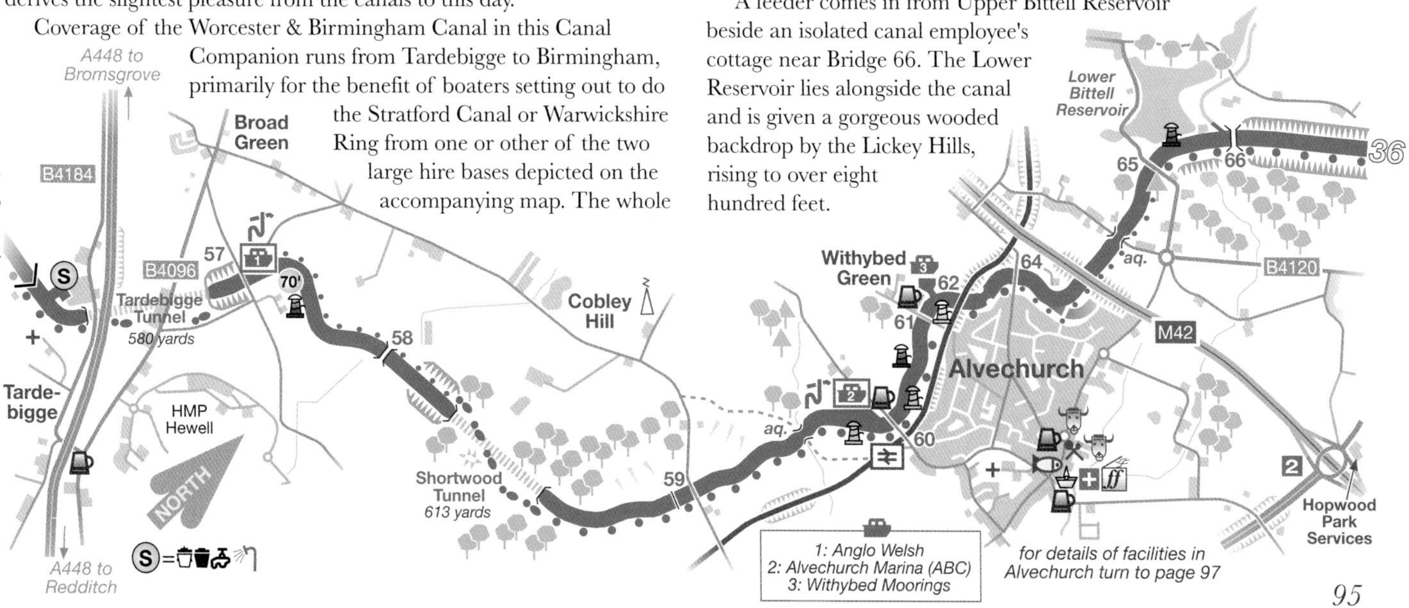

A448 to Bromsgrove

B4184

or Stourport Ring CC

Broad Green

B4096 57

Tardebigge Tunnel
580 yards

70'

Tardebigge

HMP Hewell

NORTH

Cobley Hill

58

Shortwood Tunnel
613 yards

59

A448 to Redditch

(S) = 🚽🗑️♻️🚿

Lower Bittell Reservoir

65   66   36

B4120

Withybed Green
3
62
61

64

M42

aq.

60

Alvechurch

aq.

Hopwood Park Services

2

1: Anglo Welsh
2: Alvechurch Marina (ABC)
3: Withybed Moorings

for details of facilities in Alvechurch turn to page 97

95

CURRENTLY the sixth longest navigable tunnel on the canal system, Wast Hill seems to separate theatrically the charming countryside of north-east Worcestershire from the urban sprawl of the West Midlands. It takes about half an hour to pass through, and don't be nervous if you see the headlight of another boat approaching, it is perfectly feasible to pass inside. Like all Worcester & Birmingham tunnels (except Edgbaston - Map 37), it has no towpath. The lads who led their boat horses across the tunnel top in the past would be flummoxed now to discover that half of their old route has been urbanised. Between the Fifties and Seventies, three large housing estates with the misleadingly bucolic names of Pool Farm, Primrose Hill and Hawkesley spread a brick and concrete stain over what had previously been farmland. Towpath walkers these days have to negotiate the third, follow the footprints and you won't go far wrong, it takes around three-quarters of an hour: slightly longer if you're tempted to stop for morale-boosting fish & chips.

On an historical note, look out for the semicircular brick-lined embrasures in the canal bank at either end of the tunnel - these are the remnants of the turning points for tugs which were once employed to haul unpowered craft through the tunnel.

A lengthy cutting leads eventually to King's Norton Junction where the Stratford Canal (described on Maps 38-43) sets off on its picturesque descent to the Avon. Currently under restoration, the old Junction House is backed by the soaring steeple of St Nicholas, the parish church of King's Norton, where the Rev W. Awdry of *Thomas the Tank Engine* fame was a curate during the Second World War. Astonishingly, Robert Aickman was his literary agent. A sizeable paper mill formerly overlooked the opposite bank and large quantities of coal were brought here by narrowboat from Black Country mines. A nebulous business centre occupies the site of King's Norton Metal Co., manufacturers of coins, medals and armaments. Lifford Wharf was an interchange point between canal and railway. Guest Keen & Nettlefold's screw factory continued in production until 1982, thereafter being split up into smaller units. Keep your eyes peeled for the intriguing WWII pillbox cunningly disguised as a factory chimney. Bournville engine shed closed in 1960.

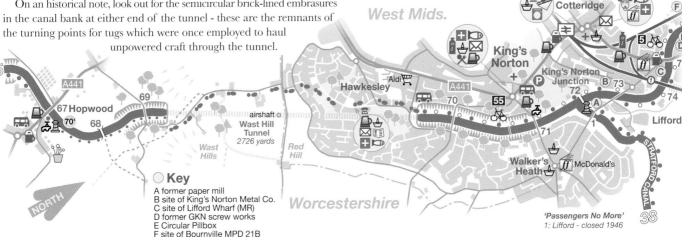

Key
A former paper mill
B site of King's Norton Metal Co.
C site of Lifford Wharf (MR)
D former GKN screw works
E Circular Pillbox
F site of Bournville MPD 21B

'Passengers No More'
1: Lifford - closed 1946

Alvechurch Map 35

Alvechurch is a pleasant Worcestershire village with some worthwhile facilities. Bit of a climb back, though!

Eating & Drinking

CAFE MORSO - The Square. Tel: 0121 306 0242. Stylish village centre cafe bar and lounge open 9am-5pm Mon-Sat and 10am-4pm Sun. B48 7LA
THE CROWN - Withybed Lane (canalside Bridge 61). Tel: 0121 445 2300. Open 11am, food lunchtimes Mon-Sat and evenings Wed-Sat. Sunday lunches bookable in advance only. B48 7PN
HOPWOOD HOUSE INN - Redditch Road (canalside Bridge 67 - Map 32). Tel: 0121 445 1716. Comfortably furnished Marston's 'Rotisserie' pub/restaurant open from noon. B48 7AB.
THE WEIGHBRIDGE - Scarfield Hill (canalside Bridge 60. Tel: 0121 445 5111. ABC owned pub housed in 'weighbridge' for a coal wharf in days gone by. Open 12-3pm and 7pm-11pm, food served. B48 7SQ
There is also a Chinese takeaway (Tel: 0121 447 8085) and an Indian restaurant (Tel: 0121 445 5583).

Shopping

Co-op, pharmacy, two butchers, and a nice deli called Gin & Pickles - Tel: 0121 445 6769.

Connections

TRAINS - half-hourly 'Cross-City' service to Redditch/Birmingham. Tel: 0345 748 4950.

King's Norton Maps 36/38

Arguably the most easily accessible facilities for canal travellers in this area. and it's only a short uphill walk to the centre, grouped about a pretty green.

Eating & Drinking

THE NAVIGATION - Wharf Road (Bridge 71). Tel: 0121 458 1652. Revitalized Wetherspoon pub open from 8am daily, food served throughout. B30 3LS

Shopping

Facilities include: a pharmacy, Spar shop, post office, newsagent, and off licence. Farmers Market 2nd Sats.

Cotteridge Map 36

Confusingly the location of King's Norton railway station. Shopping and fast food opportunities.

Shopping

COTTERIDGE WINES - 1825 Pershore Road. Tel: 0121 458 2839. Exceptional bottled beer shop. Open from noon, but ring to check closing time. B30 3DN

Connections

BUSES - the legendary 11A/11C outer circle buses cross the canal at Bridge 75 with stops nearby. 10 min interval (30 mins Sun) clockwise or anti-clockwise circumnavigation of Birmingham's suburbs, a 2 hour odyssey in its own right. Tel: 0871 200 2233.
TRAINS - 15 min interval 'Cross City' services (20 mins Sun) from King's Norton. Tel: 0345 748 4950.

Bournville Map 37

Bournville exists in a chocolatey paradise all its own, and which of us wouldn't want to do just that! Perambulating its arboreally nomenclatured streets, one quickly succumbs to the Cadbury vision. Use of a CRT 'facilities' Yale key provides access from the secure (if not, perversely, salubrious) offside moorings opposite Bournville railway station.

Shopping

Shops on Sycamore Road by The Green: convenience store, bookshop, butcher, pharmacy and bakery.

Things to Do

BOURNVILLE CARILLON - Linden Road. Tel: 0798 655 2770. 48 bells erected by George Cadbury in 1906 following an inspirational visit to Bruges. Performances on Saturdays at noon and 3pm throughout the year ex January. B30 1LB

CADBURY WORLD - Linden Road. Tel: 0121 393 6004. Self-guided tours 'choc-full of fun'. B30 2LU
SELLY MANOR - Maple Road. Tel: 0121 472 0199. A pair of medieval half-timbered buildings. Open from 10am daily Jun-Aug, Tue-Fri otherwise. B30 2AE

Connections

TRAINS - 'Cross City' line services every 15 mins.

Stirchley Map 37

Bournville Lane leads to Stirchley strung out along Pershore Road; a yang to Bournville's yin. Of note are the library and the public baths, the latter reconfigured as a community hub, though sadly sans pool.

Selly Oak Map 37

Studenty enclave on the A38 with a wide choice of shops and food/drink outlets. Battery Retail Park features a canalside Sainsbury's supermarket.

Edgbaston Map 37

Developed residentially for the well-to-do by the Gough-Calthorpe family from the opening years of the 19th century, Edgbaston is a garden suburb any city in the world would be proud to snuggle up to.

Things to Do

BARBER INSTITUTE - University of Birmingham. Tel: 0121 414 7333. Art gallery of international repute featuring works by Cezanne, Gainsborough, Magritte, Monet, Turner, Van Gogh etc. Open Tue-Sun 10am-5pm. Admission free. B15 2TS
LAPWORTH MUSEUM OF GEOLOGY - University of Birmingham. Tel: 0121 414 7294. Open 10am-5pm Mon-Fri and 12-5pm weekends. B15 2TT
WINTERBOURNE HOUSE - Edgbaston. Tel: 0121 414 3003. Captivating Arts & Crafts house erected 1903 for the industrialist John Nettlefold of GKN fame. Gardens inspired by Gertrude Jekyll. Open from 10.30am daily. Shop and tea room. B15 2RT

37 WORCESTER & BIRMINGHAM CANAL Edgbaston 4mls/0lks/1½hrs

NO canal approaches any city more politely than the W & B does Birmingham. Steerers should be handed their tea in an elegant cup and saucer. A mug would look out of place.

Bournville railway station lies alongside the canal by Bridge 77. Bournville's garden village owes its existence to the altruism of Quakers Richard and George Cadbury who built a chocolate factory on a greenfield site in the vicinity in 1879. The name Bournville dates from that time: Bourn relating to a local watercourse, whilst the rather fanciful suffix of 'ville' was deemed to have exotic Gallic overtones. Cadbury made great use of the canal, and later the railway. In 1911 they became the first operator to use motorised boats on the canals, and their sizeable fleet was signwritten in Cadbury house style of chocolate and maroon. A large wharf known as Bournville Waterside stood along the offside of the canal, being linked to

the works by the firm's private railway system which crossed the canal on Bridge 77A. Rather inevitably, all trace of the wharf has vanished under houses, but security ('anti-climb paint protected') fenced offside visitor moorings opposite the railway station provide boaters with the opportunity to visit Bournville. Stirchley, lying east of the canal, evokes a more commonplace atmosphere compared to its pulchritudinous neighbour.

Selly Oak has been significantly redeveloped, with a new Sainsbury's and a centre for the visually and aurally impaired amongst its focal points. Provision has been made - via a new undercroft - to safeguard the former Dudley No.2 (or Lapal) Canal, so that it may one day be fully restored. In March 2022 the West Midlands' Mayor, Andy Street, cut the first ceremonial sod of a widened expanse of water to facilitate entrance to the restored length of canal. Once upon a jollier time, Bridge 80 carried Birmingham's blue & cream liveried trams to Rednal,

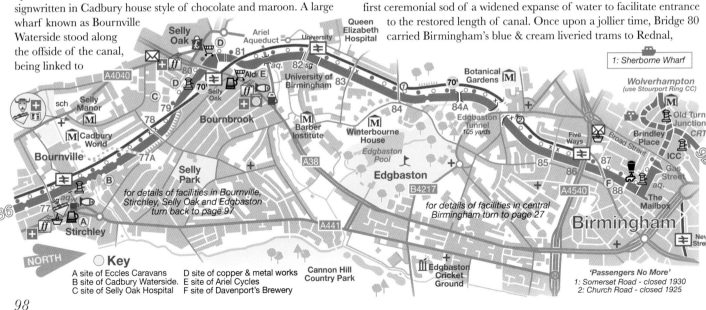

for details of facilities in Bournville, Stirchley, Selly Oak and Edgbaston turn back to page 97

for details of facilities in central Birmingham turn to page 27

1: Sherborne Wharf

Wolverhampton (use Stourport Ring CC)

● Key

A site of Eccles Caravans
B site of Cadbury Waterside.
C site of Selly Oak Hospital
D site of copper & metal works
E site of Ariel Cycles
F site of Davenport's Brewery

'Passengers No More'
1: Somerset Road - closed 1930
2: Church Road - closed 1925

'standing room only' with Lickey excursionists, so it deserves a bit of respect. Incidentally, the gates picked out in red enabled the Fire Brigade to lower their hoses down and avail themselves of canal water. Most of the city's overbridges sport similar, if less ornate red doors. Long since vanished are the massive premises of the Birmingham Battery & Metal Co. They didn't manufacture the sort of batteries which run out of power when you least need them to, but rather they 'battered' or hammered metal, steam locomotive boiler tubes being a speciality; which perhaps explains why they went out of business. Another significant employer in the vicinity was Ariel, makers initially of bicycles, but later motorcycles.

The old Birmingham West Suburban Railway dates from 1876 and is now the busy main line out of Birmingham to the south-west. When it opened in 1978, University station boasted four hundred thousand passengers per annum. Recently rebuilt, the figure now is in excess of three million. The canal skirts the University of Birmingham whose Italianate Chamberlain Tower, completed in 1909 and known as 'Old Joe' to its friends, stabs the sky. Viewed from the canal, you could be forgiven thinking you were looking at the skyline of Istanbul.

Edgbaston, redolent of its Test Match cricketing venue, is one of Birmingham's leafiest suburbs. Wealthy landowners were at pains to prevent the spread of industrialisation to its arboreal groves. Elegant stucco houses characterise the thoroughfares. Few, alas, lived in still, but employed as office accommodation for insurance brokers, solicitors, obscure affiliations, and focus groups. Schools and care/retirement homes proliferate, calibrating our lives from cradle to grave.

Anne Treneer, a Cornish author regrettably little read these days, taught at King Edward's (VI) High School for Girls (which moved out to Edgbaston in 1940) and in her book *A Stranger in the Midlands* described the towpath from Selly Oak to New Street as 'the best walk in Birmingham'. We see no reason to contradict her eighty years later, and certainly in terms of 'footfall', Edgbaston Tunnel must be one of the most walked (and cycled) through on the canal system: so 'cycled through', that the council have widened the towpath, thereby reducing navigable width in the process.

Bridge 87 was overlooked by Davenport's Brewery until its closure in 1989. They sold out to Greenall Whitley, so should have known the end was nigh. The site has been taken over by student accommodation. Davenports are fondly remembered for their cosy 'Beer at Home' television advertising campaigns of the Sixties and Seventies. On the towpath side lies the trackbed of the Midland Railway's branch to its extensive goods depot which tunnelled beneath the canal to terminate on Suffolk Street.

A right-angled bend (once less salubriously known as 'Salvage Turn') by The Mailbox leads to Worcester Bar and/or Gas Street Basin, the epitome - and for many the soul - of Birmingham's waterways. Work began on the Worcester & Birmingham Canal from the Birmingham end in 1794, but it was not until 1815 that the route was completed throughout. Fearful of its water supply disappearing down into the Severn, the Birmingham Canal Company at first refused to be directly linked with the newcomer, and so laborious transhipment of through traffic took place across an infamous divide known as the 'Worcester Bar'. Eventually, however, a stop lock was provided between the two waterways, affording the BCN some measure of protection, yet enabling through passage of boats.

It bears remembering, however, that the original terminal wharf of the Birmingham Canal lay to the east of Gas Street Basin, on a site unsympathetically occupied since the late 1960s by the Alpha Tower block, originally the home of Associated Television. It usurped the BCN's handsomely symmetrical offices on Suffolk Street, demolished in 1928. Fifty years later demolition controversially took its toll of much of the original Gas Street infrastructure as well, by which time the planners should have known better.

Beyond Broad Street, the canal penetrates the piazzas of Brindleyplace and the International Convention Centre. For once the hackneyed comparison about Birmingham having more canals than Venice seems apt. Culture and chronology collide as your boat eases its way past tourists queueing to get into the National Sea Life Centre; concert-goers sipping cocktails between Brahms and Beethoven in a Symphony Hall interval ; or punters waiting for the wrestling to start at Arena Birmingham.

THE STRATFORD UPON AVON CANAL, to give it its official, but bit of a mouthful title (for the first and last time in this guide) runs from King's Norton, on the south-western outskirts of Birmingham, to the Mecca that is William Shakespeare's birthplace on the banks of the River Avon, twenty-five and a half miles and fifty-six locks away. To boat along it represents one of the most satisfying means of attending a performance at the Royal Shakespeare Theatre, a point not lost on the three Yorkshire miners, Art, Ern and Abe in Peter Terson's fondly remembered television play of 1973, *Shakespeare or Bust*.

The Stratford Canal has not been without its own internal dramas down the years, various powers that be, at one time or another, having sought to abandon sections of it for reasons best known to themselves. Marvel that madness - of Hamletian proportions - can exist amongst those appointed in authority, before marvelling at the work done by unselfish groups and individuals to combat such malignant tumours.

The handsome junction house is being restored after a period of dereliction. No sooner have you put it astern, than the Stratford Canal is throwing up surprises. Just beyond Bridge 1 it narrows to pass beneath a curious 'guillotine' stop lock, officially numbered '1' in the fifty-six lock sequence: don't get the wrong idea, the rest will not be so labour-saving to negotiate.

The canal narrows at the site of Bridge 2, something of a *cause celebre* in the embryonic days of the Inland Waterways Association. It had been built as a lift bridge and, during the Second World War the Great Western Railway, who owned the canal at that time, clamped down the platform following damage by a lorry. Commercial traffic had ceased on the canal, but the IWA maintained that a right of navigation still applied. The GWR claimed that they would be only too happy to jack up the bridge to permit boats to pass as required, little realising that the IWA intended to organise as many boat passages as would be necessary to have the bridge fully repaired. Several campaign cruises ensued (as relived by L. T. C. Rolt in *Landscape With Canals* and Robert Aickman in *The River Runs Uphill*) but

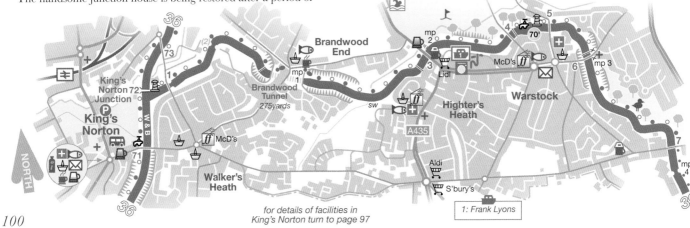

for details of facilities in
King's Norton turn to page 97

1: Frank Lyons

it was not until Nationalisation that a fully operable swing bridge was installed. Often erroneously referred to as Lifford Lane Bridge, Bridge 2 was, in fact, on Tunnel Lane.

A deep, wooded cutting leads to Brandwood Tunnel. Wool-gathering between sonnets, Shakespeare peers inscrutably down on approaching boats. Built without a towpath, horses were led over the top while boats were worked through by boatmen pulling on a handrail set into the tunnel lining. The horse path still provides walkers with a right of way and also offers access to some useful suburban facilities. Sometimes it's good to go 'over the top'. Mileposts, obligingly erected by the Stratford-on-Avon Canal Society, count the miles from King's Norton, though they are so diminutive that they are sometimes difficult to spot, especially in the summer months when

Guillotine Stop Lock, King's Norton

masked by undergrowth.

The accompanying map emphasises how built-up these south-western suburbs of Birmingham are, but the canal seems oblivious to the proximity of so many houses and people, retaining an aloof quality, like a recluse in a crowd. Occasionally, the boater's steady progress is interrupted by having to throttle down past boats moored at the bottom of gardens. The arm by Bridge 3 once served a group of limekilns. Adjacent to Bridge 5 stands the impressive facade of Yardley Wood bus garage, opened by Birmingham City Transport in 1938. How sad that the depot's current incumbents, National Express, no longer apply the city's traditional dark blackberry blue and clotted cream livery to their vehicles. Time was you could tell immediately where you were simply by the colour of the municipal bus fleet.

continued from page 102:

opened in 1821 to boost the summit's water levels. A feeder enters the canal from the reservoirs which lie to the south-west. These days they are a popular amenity, attracting ramblers, anglers, bird watchers and interpretive board collectors. The old engine house, to which narrowboats carried coal up the feeder until 1936, was covered in scaffolding on the occasion of our most recent visit, though with no suggestion of what fate might await it. Dixe Wills describes a visit to Earlswood (and its suitably diminutive station called simply The Lakes) in *Tiny Stations*.

Oak, alder, hazel and willow clothe the canal, creating a soothing, sylvan quality which, however beautiful, is apt to become soporific after a while. When you do catch glimpses of the surrounding countryside, it reminds you of the Home Counties, exuding an air of affluence epitomised by large detached houses, and horsey people, trotting down dappled lanes on dappled steeds. St Patrick's Church, by Bridge 17 at Salter Street, was built with money paid by the canal company in compensation for acquiring common land on which to build its reservoirs.

Near Bridge 19 the extensive miniature railways of the Birmingham Society of Model Engineers stand close to the canal - albeit masked from view by a cutting - and whilst essentially private, they do open their doors to the public on selected dates. The group was founded in 1936 and the site features tracks of varying gauges. Childrens birthday parties are a speciality - booking forms on the internet at: *birminghamsme.com*

The winding hole by Bridge 22 marks the site of a wharf once linked by tramway to the limestone quarries of Tanworth-in-Arden.

WHILST Shirley Drawbridge (No.8) may sound disconcertingly like some old flame you inadvertently bump into at a reunion, the only slightly less unnerving truth is that it's an electric lift bridge on a busyish by-road, necessitating the use of barriers, a control panel (accessed with a Canal & River Trust Yale key), and a mollifying way with motorists. Nearby a high embankment carries the canal above the River Cole, a twenty-five mile long tributary of the Tame. Wake Green Amateurs' precipitous football pitches defy opponents' calls for a level playing field.

The canal passes beneath the North Warwickshire railway line, opened belatedly in the Edwardian era by the Great Western Railway as an alternative route to Stratford and the West Country. Now it's a useful facility when planning one-way walks along the parallel Stratford Canal. The nearest railhead (echoing the despair felt by many a long-suffering commuter) rejoices in the name of Whitlock's End.

Billed as a 'village for the 21st century', anything less like a village than Dickens Heath would be difficult to imagine. Balconied apartments - which wouldn't look out of place in Fuerteventura - overlook the nonplussed canal. And whilst there are shops and restaurants in there (somewhere!) we would not advise you to go too far in search of them, lest you get irretrievably stranded in the future; and what true canal traveller could bear the thought of tha!

Cuttings and embankments provide variety. Earlswood Reservoirs were *continued back on page 101:*

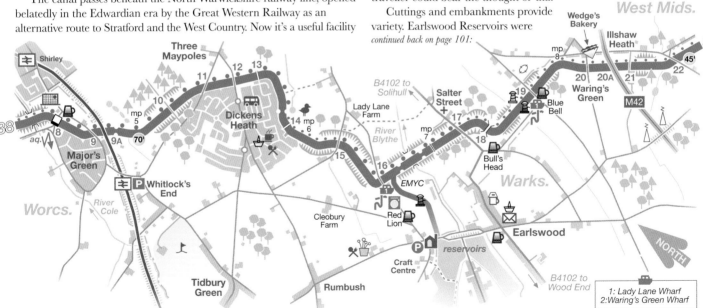

1: Lady Lane Wharf
2: Waring's Green Wharf

ESCAPING to Warwickshire from the West Midlands' wicked clutches, boaters are recommended to savour the last couple of miles of lock-free cruising before, quite literally, having to take the plunge down Lapworth Locks; twenty-five of the darned things in barely two miles: Alternatively, you can play for time, walking from the visitor moorings at Hockley Heath, southwards past an imposing Victorian Baptist church (built of blue lias), to the Nuthurst obelisk raised in 1749 by Thomas Archer - architect of St Philip's Cathedral in Birmingham - to modestly mark his elevation to the peerage.

Just to help you limber up, a pair of windlass-operated lift bridges precede the locks, which at least have the decency to start off spaced apart before taking it into their heads to abseil off Bridge 32. A winding-hole by Bridge 27 marks the temporary southern terminus of the canal between 1796 and 1800, a hiatus brought about by lack of capital. It actually took twenty-two years to complete the canal.

The summit alone cost as much as the budget for the whole canal. The engineer was Josiah Clowes, a somewhat shadowy figure in the annals of canal construction, who seems to have specialised in tunnels.

Alongside Lock 5 lies Lapworth Cricket Club's idyllic ground. They are members of the mellifluously named Cotswold Hills Cricket League, along with such poetically disposed elevens as Ashton under Hill, Chipping Camden and Kenilworth Wardens Thirds. Neville Cardus, John Arlott and Brian Johnston would have been in raptures.

Bridge 32 is the first, southbound travellers encounter, of the deceptively fragile cantilever design indigenous to the Stratford: cast iron arches leaping from brick abutments, the central gap being left to accommodate the towing line in horse boat days. Locks 8 - 14 represent the most dramatic section of Lapworth Locks, presenting a spectacular view irrespective of your direction of travel.

continued on page 104:

West Mids.

A3400 to Birmingham

Hockley Heath

Warks.

Packwood House

Wharf Tavern

Nuthurst

Top Lock

Lapworth

Lapworth Locks

Kingswood

Boot Inn

Canal Shop

Harborough Banks

Navigation

Kingswood Junction

footpath to Baddesley Clinton

1: Swallow Cruisers

A3400 to Stratford

for details of facilities in Hockley Heath and Kingswood/Lapworth turn to page 104

Locks 2-27 Lapworth Locks 158ft 6½ins

continued from page 103:

The pipe by Bridge 33 is a water main linking Tewkesbury with Coventry. Take a breather here and visit Briar Cottage Canal Shop.

Kingswood Junction never fails to captivate. Two reservoirs lie alongside the channel, which is bordered on the towpath side by a small coniferous wood incorporating an inconspicuous picnic site and car park. The lower of the two reservoirs has been adapted for long term moorings, the upper is used by anglers. Hail them with a hearty 'well done', for one senses they are only fishing for compliments.

Having become acquainted (not to say enraptured) with the canal's cantilevered bridges, Lock 22 introduces the first of the delightful barrel-roofed cottages which are a feature of the southern section of the Stratford Canal. A short branch canal was built between the Warwick & Birmingham Canal and the Stratford-on-Avon Canal in 1802. It became a bone of contention between the two companies, jealous of each other's traffics and water supplies. The original connection below Lock 21 was reinstated in 1996. These parallel canals inspire 'figure of eight' walks, and the proximity of Lapworth railway station makes it easy to arrive by public transport with an environmentally clear conscience.

The Stratford is no stranger to epoch making events. Until 1988 the section south of Kingswood belonged to the National Trust, under whose patronage it had been restored from dereliction and re-opened twenty-four years earlier. It was the first major canal restoration programme, and rightly occupies a celebrated niche in the post war redevelopment of the inland waterways for leisure use.

Earlswood   Map 39

Eating & Drinking
BLUE BELL - Warings Green Road (Bridge 19). Tel: 01564 702328. Canalside cider house with up to five real ales on tap. Food served from 9am. B94 6BP
BULL'S HEAD - Lime Kiln Lane. Access from Bridge 17. Tel: 01564 700368. Thwaites pub from 9.30am. Food throughout. B94 6BU

Illshaw Heath   Map 39

Wedge's wonderful bakery (Tel: 01564 702542 - B94 6RP) flourishes in its unlikely rural setting in the shadow of the M42. Fresh bread, sandwiches made to order, pies in profusion, mouthwatering cakes and puddings and a vegetable stall make it difficult for passing canaller's to resist. Outdoor tables beneath a canopy for immediate consumption.

Hockley Heath   Map 40

Commuterland strung out along what used to be the A34 between Southampton and Manchester. The War Memorial is poignantly inscribed: "The days short, the work great, their time passed like a shadow".

Eating & Drinking
WHARF TAVERN - canalside Bridge 25. Tel: 01564 782075. Canalside pub open noon daily. B94 6QT
There's also a fish & chip shop, Chinese takeaway, Indian restaurant, and Miller & Carter steak bar.

Shopping
Convenience store and post office on one side of Bridge 25, bakery and butcher on the other.

Connections
BUSES - Johnsons X20 links Hockley Heath hourly Mon-Sat (X50 Sun) with Birmingham, Henley-in-Arden and Stratford-on-Avon. Tel: 0871 200 2233.

Lapworth   Map 40

St Mary's church, reached by a field path from Bridge 30 or along the road from Bridge 29, is a gem, curiously equipped with a detached tower and a chantry atop an open archway. Inside there is a stained glass window dedicated to a victim of the First World War, and a memorial tablet by Eric Gill. The churchyard contains a tomb belonging to the Catesby family, of whom Robert Catesby was implicated in the Gunpowder Plot of 1605.

Eating & Drinking
THE BOOT - (adjacent Bridge 33). Tel: 01564 782464. Elegant country pub open lunchtime and dinner (from 6pm) daily ex Sun dinner. B93 0EB

Shopping
Village shop (which stocks Lashford Sausage Rolls) by railway bridge between the canals. Off licence/post office near Bridge 65 (Grand Union). Gifts, and canalia (plus home made cakes, and an array of potted plants) from the Briar Cottage canal shop by Bridge 33.

Things to Do
PACKWOOD HOUSE - Packwood Lane. Tel: 01564 782024. Sublime Tudor (National Trust) property remodelled by Graham Baron Ash (whose industrialist father was a director of Fellows Morton & Clayton) in the Twenties & Thirties. Famous for clipped yews resembling Sermon on the Mount. Open daily ex Winter Mons. Shop and cafe/restaurant. B94 6AT

Connections
TRAINS - approx bi-hourly Chiltern Railways service linking with Warwick, Leamington, Birmingham Moor Street/Snow Hill and Marylebone. Tel: 0345 748 4950.

41 | STRATFORD CANAL Lowsonford & Preston Bagot 4mls/14lks/4hrs

LIKE an already pretty teenager flowering into a great beauty, the Stratford Canal really comes into its own south of Kingswood. Woods border the canal, birdsong fills the air, the scent of wildflowers is intoxicating. If there are lovelier lengths of canal in England, you have blissfully mislaid their names. Toponymy does little to quell incipient ardour. Who would not fall in love with Lowsonford, Yarningale and Preston Bagot? Certainly Ernest Temple Thurston was smitten. In 1910 he pioneeringly hired a narrowboat known as *The Flower of Gloster*, the lugubrious services of its captain Eynsham Harry, and a horse called Fanny and set off on a journey of discovery described in an eponymous book which has remained a 'Desert Island' favourite of many canal lovers ever since. Temple Thurston described the Stratford Canal as being 'right out of the track of the world'; a sentiment it is still easy to share. He climbed the hillside to a farm at Yarningale for fresh milk, and Eynsham Harry bought beer from the wife of a lock-keeper. Not something, alas, you can readily do today.

Lock 25 is graced by another barrel-roofed cottage, home, for many years, of Doug Smith, celebrated cartographer of the canals, whose meticulously drawn 'Lockmaster' pen & ink maps of the system adorn many an enthusiast's wall. Doug was a ferroequinologist too, and relished the propinquity of both transport modes to his home. A wooden bench by Bridge 39 fittingly commemorates his contribution to the canals.

Briefly puncturing the spell, the M40 motorway vaults across the canal by means of a charmless concrete span, and then the bottom lock (No.27) of the Lapworth flight is reached; not that there is any real sense of hiatus before a sequence of individually numbered and, to all intents and purposes, unnamed locks ensues. Again, there are barrel-roofed cottages by locks 28 and 31, the latter available for holiday let under the auspices of the admirable Landmark Trust. An Antony (Angel of the North) Gormley sculpture briefly presided over the lock in 2015 to celebrate the Trust's 50th Anniversary. The design of these cottages is said to have resulted from the use of the same wooden frames employed in the construction of the brick road bridges which span the canal.

continued on page 106:

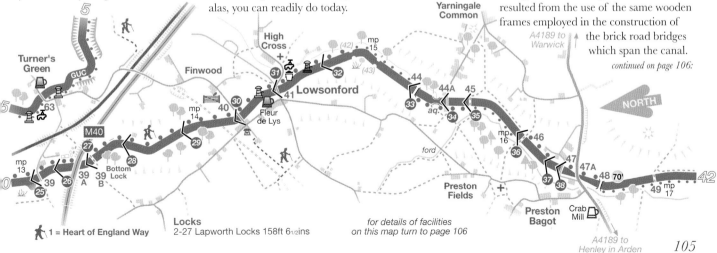

Locks
2-27 Lapworth Locks 158ft 6½ins

for details of facilities
on this map turn to page 106

🚶 1 = Heart of England Way

The abutments of an old railway bridge frame the canal near Lowsonford. The bridge carried a branchline to Henley-in-Arden, closed when the route was made obsolete by the opening of the North Warwickshire Railway. Legend has it that the track was despatched to The Front during the Great War but ended up at the bottom of the English Channel after the vessel carrying it was torpedoed. If, since Kingswood, the towpath seems comparatively busy, it may be because a loop of the Heart of England Way (a 102 mile waymarked trail from Stafford to the Cotswolds) appropriates it down to Bridge 40. It was on Lowsonford Bridge that Temple Thurston encountered a taciturn individual whose wife, it slowly emerged, had died the previous day, and whose body was lying at their nearby cottage, to which he could not bring himself to return. They had been married fifty-one years.

Narrowing at the sites of bridges 42 and 43 - probably simple lifting affairs connecting adjacent fields - the canal comes to Yarningale Aqueduct, the delightful baby of the Stratford's three cast iron aqueducts. The present girders date from 1834 and were supplied by the ubiquitous Horseley Iron Co. best known for its numerous side bridges on the BCN.

The barrel-roofed cottages by locks 34 and 37 have been incorporated into grander dwellings, and lost their innocence in the process. A public footpath ascends westwards from Bridge 46 to Preston Bagot's lonely little church where a brass memorial, dated 1637, marks the resting place of Elisabeth Randoll: five centuries in the blink of an eye!

Three years before Temple Thurston's travelogue was published, the Stratford Canal featured in the children's adventure story *True Tilda* by Arthur Quiller-Couch. 'Q' knew his waterways and took pains in the veracity of his landscapes:

Many locks encumber the descending levels of the Stratford-on-Avon Canal ... the boat glided deeper and deeper into a green pastoral country, parcelled out with hedgerows and lines of elms ... Very little traffic passed over these waters. In all the way to Preston Bagot our travellers met but three boats. One, at Lowsonford Lock, had a pair of donkeys to haul it ...

The elms and the donkeys may have vanished, and the canal's a tad busier, but the book is reasonably easily obtained via internet dealers and would undoubtedly enhance your journey.

Turner's Green   Map 41
Eating & Drinking
TOM O' THE WOOD - pub on GU, see page 17.

Lowsonford   Map 41
Eating & Drinking
FLEUR DE LYS - Lapworth Street, Lowsonford (access from either bridge 40 or 41. Tel: 01564 782431. Charming canalside country pub which once inspired a range of commercially produced pies and which can still boast eight varieties on the menu. Food served 10am-8.30pm daily. Greene King ales. B95 5HJ
Shopping
Finwood Hill Farm Shop (east of Bridge 40) open Tue & Sat 10am-5pm. (though a call may elicit them opening specially). They specialise in Dexter beef and Gloucester Old Spot pork. Tel: 0789 992 3075.

Preston Bagot   Map 41
CRAB MILL - *Status uncertain due to fire.*

Wootton Wawen   Map 42
Wootton Hall is a 17th century mansion which once belonged to Maria Fitzherbert, the *secret* wife of George IV. The parish church is of Saxon origin and considered one of Warwickshire's finest. A former paper mill has been converted into apartments. Compatriot and friend of Rachmaninov, the exiled composer, Nikolai Medtner (1880-1951) and his wife lived on the western outskirts of Wootton Wawen during the Second World War as guests of the pianist, Edna Iles and her parents. Inspired by the local countryside, Medtner's Third Piano Concerto was completed here and premiered at the Royal Albert Hall in 1944 under the baton of Sir Adrian Boult.

Eating & Drinking
VINEYARD 4 NAVIGATION INN - Stratford Road (canalside by the aqueduct). Tel: 01564 792676. Food lunch and evening (from 5pm) Tue-Sat and noon to 6pm Sun. Meeting place of SONACS. B95 6BZ
Shopping
Convenience store and post office.
Things to Do
YEW TREE FARM - Tel: 01564 792701. Barns and byres transformed into a 'contemporary shopping courtyard'. Farm shop & Cowshed Cafe. B95 6BY
Connections
BUSES - Johnsons X20 (X50 Sun bi-hourly) runs hourly to/from Birmingham via Hockley Heath and Stratford. Tel: 0871 200 2233.
TRAINS - West Midlands hourly service (ex Suns) to/from Birmingham and Stratford. Tel: 0345 748 4950.

AN almost (but not quite!) lock-free interlude affords boaters a welcome degree of relaxation: time to appreciate the nuanced landscapes of the Alne Valley and the canal's ethereal wanderings in the last vestiges of the old Forest of Arden. That odd looking cove on the towpath might be Jaques from *As You Like It*, 'sucking melancholy out of a song', or merely some passing guide book compiler self-consciously avoiding eye contact.

Wootton Wawen introduces a sense of humanity absent for much of the Stratford Canal's southern section, but it is more a sense of fragility that the village's aqueduct evinces in the face of thunderous traffic on the A3400. Seeking abandonment of the canal in 1958, in order to facilitate a number of road 'improvements', Warwickshire County Council wished to widen the road at this point and replace the aqueduct with a pipe to carry residual drainage.

Sixty years on, one can only be grateful they didn't get their myopic way.

Bearley (sometimes known as Odd for obvious reasons) Lock intervenes before Edstone (sometimes known as Bearley for equally obvious reasons) Aqueduct makes a dramatic appearance, spanning the North Warwickshire Railway, a by-road and a brook. Consisting of an iron trough resting on thirteen tapering piers, it is twenty-eight feet high and a hundred and fifty-eight yards long. Its sunken towpath offers walkers a strange, fish-eye lens view of passing boaters. Those with a highly-developed railway eye will notice an overgrown trackbed curving away from beneath the aqueduct across the countryside in a north-westerly direction. This was the Great Western Railway's Alcester branch, an ill-fated and relatively shortlived line which had its track lifted as an economy measure during the First World War, re-opened in 1923, then closed again at the beginning of the Second World War, apart from a cloak and dagger service operated for employees of a motor works evacuated from Coventry. A Heath Robinsonish arrangement of pipes and valves enabled steam locomotives on the branch to fill up with canal water directly beneath the aqueduct. Bearley station is useful for towpath walkers. Anne Treneer (Map 37) commuted from here to King Edward's High School for Girls in the 1930s.

Map labels:

Preston Hill Farm
50
51 mp 18
52
53
Yew Tree Farm
aq.
54
55 56
mp 19

Austy Manor
A3400

Bearley Cross Bearley

Bearley or Odd Lock
5ft 10ins
70'
39

mp 20
Edstone Aqueduct
57
58
70'
mp 21

Newnham

crse of Alcester Railway

Wootton Wawen
Wootton Pool
River Alne

Pennyford Hall

B4089 to Alcester

1: Anglo-Welsh
2: Hill Farm Marina

1 = Monarch's Way

NORTH

43

IN air travel parlance, the Stratford Canal commences a 'final descent' to its destination, and you are left praying your boat doesn't come down to earth with a bump. The little matter of seventeen locks, and you'll be relishing the running waters of the River Avon.

A winding hole on the outskirts of Wilmcote, together with the abutments of a former tramway bridge, mark the site of Greaves, Bull & Lakin's lime and cement works who operated a sizeable fleet of boats both here and at Stockton on the Warwick & Napton Canal (Map 2). Bridge 59 carries romantically named Featherbed Lane across the canal, but in 1958 Warwickshire County Council wanted to lower the road across the bed of the canal because the bridge was no longer capable of sustaining the amount of road traffic using it. Closure of the canal would surely have followed had the Stratford-on-Avon Canal Society not been able to produce two valid canoe licences, obtained a year earlier, thus demonstrating that the canal was still effectively being used for navigational purposes. As far as the Ministry of Transport was concerned, the County Council had to prove that the canal hadn't been used for at least three years. Their application to abandon the canal was denied, and thenceforth the Stratford Canal's fortunes were on an upward trajectory, as entertainingly described by Guy Johnson in *Save the Stratford Canal!*.

Nowadays, Wilmcote Locks are generally well kept and easy to operate, and a well-surfaced towpath makes them popular with walkers and cyclists. Yet it was these selfsame locks, their chambers 'leaking and crumbling', their gates 'flapping and jammed', that a youthful Robert Aickman encountered on a solitary walk in the 1930s, a chastening if eventually salutary experience which may, subconsciously, have been behind the iron will which did so much to foster the early advance of the campaign to save the whole of the inland waterways from the sort of threat the Stratford was under in the late Fifties.

Bridge 62A is known as Chaly Beate Bridge. Beneficial springs were apparently discovered at Bishopton in the 18th century, but it was not until 1837 that a group of Stratford entrepreneurs opened a spa here. Sadly for them, it failed to take off, though some of the associated buildings remain, not least Bishopton Lodge, an upmarket B&B these days, with a spring still bubbling in its basement, and bearing a blue plaque commemorating the fact that Bruce

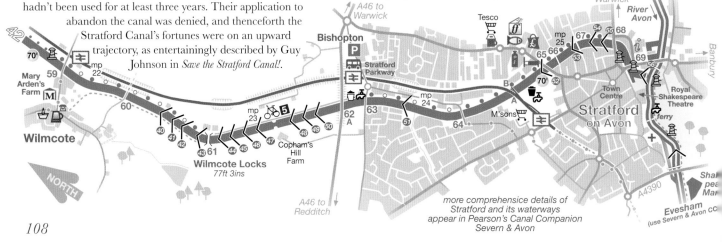

Bairnsfather, the First World War cartoonist, once lived there. Six weeks before becoming Queen, Princess Victoria opened the spa and overnighted at the Lodge.

Suddenly, the canal is ambushed by urban Stratford. You feel like you've been mugged by the modern day. This is not the atmosphere you anticipated, no warm Shakespearean embrace. Yet few towns of any size lack this paraphernalia now. Push on through and the Stratford of the tourist brochures will eventually emerge, all the more welcome for having persevered. And what is the Stratford Canal, if not a story of perseverance? Six years after its closure was miraculously witheld, the Queen Mother formally re-opened the canal on 11th July 1964. Full abandonment and filling in had been costed at around £119,000; restoration £42,000. It rarely happens, but for once the angels had defeated the philistines.

Through Bridge 69 the canal widens abruptly into Bancroft Basin, long ago a busy scene of transhipment between canal and river craft. Nowadays transactions are confined to the sale of ice cream, baguettes and artwork, but however frivolous, a sense of purpose remains intact. An entertaining spot to moor, assuming you are gregariously disposed and able to find a fishbone mooring. Usefully, the Avon Navigation and Canal & River trusts have conjoined in the provision of a floating information centre, somewhere to procure one or other organisations licences if you haven't already done so. Licences, you'll remember, are invaluable - after all, they Saved the Stratford Canal!

'All's Well That Ends Well', to coin a phrase.

Wilmcote   Map 43
The church may, or may not, be the work of Butterfield, the vicarage and school certainly are.
Eating & Drinking
MARY ARDEN INN - The Green. Tel: 01789 267030. Food and accommodation. Greene King. CV37 9XJ
Shopping
Convenience stores with PO 'outreach' service.
Things to Do
MARY ARDEN'S FARM - Tel: 01789 338535. Picturesque childhood home of Shakespeare's mother preserved as a working Tudor farm. Open daily from 10am. CV37 9UN
Connections
TRAINS - West Midlands services hourly to/from Stratford and Birmingham. Bi-hourly Chiltern service to/from Stratford and Leamington. Tel: 0345 748 4950.

Stratford-on-Avon   Map 43
That Stratford-on-Avon is second only to London in the esteem of foreign visitors, serves to emphasise the charisma surrounding Shakespeare. Without his omnipresence, one imagines Stratford's position in the league table of tourism would be academic. And yet, subtract the Shakespeare factor, and you are still left with an attractive town with a generous helping of good architecture, its setting enhanced by the proximity of the Avon; and there is a hair-down demeanour about the people in the streets which becomes infectious.
Eating & Drinking
BOATHOUSE - Swans Nest Lane. Tel: 01789 414960. Riverside restaurant, open from noon daily. CV37 7LS
CARLUCCIO'S - Waterside. Tel: 01789 335998. Italian cafe/restaurant/deli overlooking basin. CV37 6BA
LE BISTROT PIERRE - Swans Nest Lane. Tel: 01789 264804. Stylishly appointed French restaurant. CV37 7LT
ROOFTOP - Royal Shakespeare Theatre. Tel: 01789 403449. Open daily from 10.30am for lunch, drinks and dinner. CV37 6BB
SALT - Church Street. Tel: 01789 263566. Paul Foster's *Michelin Guide* listed restaurant. Lunches Wed-Sun, dinner (from 6.30pm) Wed-Sat. CV37 6HB
STRATFORD ALEHOUSE - Greenhill Street. Tel: 0774 680 7966. *Good Beer Guide* listed micropub open from 3pm Mon-Wed and from 1pm Thur-Sun. CV37 6LF

Shopping
The town bristles with quality shops engaged in the hectic business of emptying the bank accounts of visitors. But many of these shops have such character that you don't resent being plunged into the red.
Things to Do
TOURIST INFORMATION - Bridgefoot. Tel: 01789 264293. 9am-5pm (10am-4pm Suns). CV37 6GW
ROYAL SHAKESPEARE THEATRE - Waterside. Whatever else you do in Stratford, try to catch a performance at the RST. Tel: 01789 331111. CV37 6BB
SHAKESPEARE'S BIRTHPLACE - Henley Street. Tel: 01789 204016. S's childhood home. Additionally the custodians of four other properties in the district. CV37 6QW
CITY SIGHTSEEING - Open top bus tours providing a good introduction to the town. Tel: 01789 299123.
Connections
BUSES - Johnsons X20 runs hourly to B'ham via Wootton Wawen and Hockley Heath. Tel: 0871 200 2233.
TRAINS - half-hourly West Midlands services to Birmingham. Less frequent but useful direct link with London Marylebone by Chiltern. Tel: 0345 748 4950.

OKAY, okay; by no stretch of the imagination is Trent Lock, let alone the Trent & Mersey Canal, in the *south* midlands, but in the well known (not to say, much admired) Pearson spirit of public service they are included in this guide to facilitate circumnavigation of the Leicester Ring when used in conjunction with the *Leicester Line & R. Nene Canal Companion*. True, we did once cover the Leicester Ring in a single guide, but hardly anyone bought it, so you can regard having to buy *two* guides as a mild form of reprimand. Now read on ...

In *Downstream*, his almost entirely entertaining account of a journey by punt down the Trent, Tom Fort described Trent Lock as 'an uninteresting place opposite the mouth of the Soar'. But then travel writers are prone to unappreciative bouts of melancholy, the roots of which can normally be traced to vicissitudes beyond their control: a poor pint perhaps, or a reverse in the fortunes of their favourite football team.

Gainsaying Mr Fort, we happen to admire Trent Lock very much. Inland waterway 'crossroads' are rare beasts - though, oddly enough, three others feature in this guide - but it is not merely the multiplicity of routes which

makes this such an appealing location, it is the setting too, with Ratcliffe's increasingly less called upon octet of cooling towers overlooking a broad reach of the Trent where sailing dinghies tack to and fro, like something Sisley might have painted of the Seine.

On windy days, punching upstream to Sawley Locks can surprise boat engines more used to the serene waters of the canals, but it's an enjoyable experience in any weather, and you know you'll soon be on dry land again, so to speak. Sawley Locks are wide-beam, mechanised and duplicated and, more often than not, volunteer lockies will be on hand to help you through. Sawley Marina provides a wide range of boating facilities, whilst there are visitor moorings and water points on the towpath side. Upstream (journeying westwards, that is), the Trent has one more fling with you before you reach the Trent & Mersey Canal. It is bridged by the M1 motorway (on which the traffic often moves gratifyingly more slowly than you) and an impressively engineered pipeline which brings water supplies down from the Peak District to slake the thirst of Leicester folk.

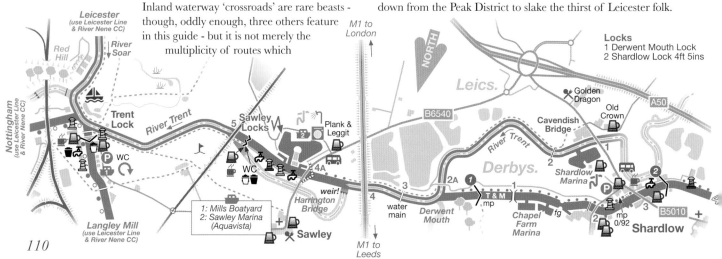

At Derwent Mouth (*not*, despite appearances, a waterway crossroads), the Trent goes off to Cavendish Bridge. But unless they've business at Shardlow Marina, boaters proceed to Derwent Mouth Lock where a milepost informs them they're 93¹/₂ miles from the other end of Brindley's famous Trent & Mersey Canal at Preston Brook near Runcorn in Cheshire.

Navigation from the Trent to the Mersey must have seemed like a proclamation for travel from the earth to the moon, but this was how the fledgling canal company advertised its purpose back in 1780. The words adorn the largest warehouse at Shardlow, the company's 'inland port', once known waggishly as "Rural Rotterdam". And Shardlow (unlike, regrettably, Preston Brook) has been fortunate enough to retain the greater part of its historic infrastructure. Pride of place goes to the handsome Clock Warehouse, now a popular pub, alongside Shardlow Lock. Like many of Shardlow's warehouses, it owes its survival to F. E. Stevens, an animal feed merchant, whose occupation of this, and several other canalside buildings, secured a use for them in the century which passed between the cessation of the local canal trade and a new era of refurbishment for leisure and commercial use. Look carefully, and you'll come across evidence of F. E. Stevens' use of Shardlow in faded signwriting on many a wall.

Forming the boundary between Derbyshire and Leicestershire, the original five-arched Cavendish Bridge, erected in 1771 at the site of Wilden Ferry, was swept away by the floods of 1947. Nine years passed before its rather less good-looking replacement was opened, so there must have been something of a tailback on what was then the A6, the most direct route in the pre-motorway age, from London to Manchester.

As for the Trent itself, navigation is unfeasible upstream of this point, though throughout most of the 18th century shallow-draughted river ketches were worked to and from Burton, being alternatively poled or hauled by rope from the bank by gangs of men. Locks were provided at King's Mills (Map 45) and Winshill (Map 48) to help in the control of sufficient depth, but in times of low rainfall craft would often be marooned or rely on the willingness of mill owners to open their sluices.

Trent Lock   Map 44
Isolated waterside community with two pubs and a cafe, further details of which are to be found in *Pearson's Canal Companion: Leicester Line & River Nene*.

Sawley   Map 44
Suburban sprawl to the south of Long Eaton, but nice church by the river. Harrington Bridge dates from 1788, but its masonry arches were replaced by steel girders following flood damage in 1904.
Eating & Drinking
LOCK KEEPERS REST/KATIE'S COFFEE SHOP - Sawley Locks. Tel: 0798 944 7337. NG10 3AD
PLANK & LEGGIT - Tamworth Road (adjacent marina). Tel: 0115 972 1515. NG10 3AD
Three other pubs and a tapas bar over the river bridge.
Connections
BUSES - Skylink services at 20 minute intervals to/from Nottingham (via Long Eaton railhead) and Loughborough via East Midlands Airport.

Shardlow   Map 44
Georgian village much quieter now that the A50 has siphoned off the traffic that used to plague its main street. Shardlow Hall was built in 1684 by Leonard Forsbrook from profits made on the river trade. There was once an orphanage in the village, foundlings being given the surname Shardlow.
Eating & Drinking
CLOCK WAREHOUSE - London Road (adjacent lock). Tel: 01332 650556. Revamped incarnation of Shardlow's most iconic warehouse. Marston's beers and a good choice of food. Open from noon daily. DE72 2GL
GOLDEN DRAGON - Cavendish Bridge. Tel: 01332 799158. Chinese restaurant/ta open lunch and evening (from 6pm) daily ex Sun/Mon lunch. DE72 2HN
TANDOORI NIGHTS - London Road. Tel: 01332 853383. Indian restaurant/ta open from 4.30pm daily. DE72 2GP *Six other pubs in and around the village!*
Shopping
Small convenience store a bit of a hike along the old A6, one mile west of the canal on Map 45.
Things to Do
HERITAGE CENTRE - Canalside, London Road. Open Easter to October, Sat & Sun noon to 5pm. Charming museum housed in Shardlow's oldest canal warehouse. The rise and fall of this inland port and the village's other activities are delightfully portrayed. Exhibits range from old boatbuilding tools to a mock-up narrowboat cabin. DE72 2GA.
Connections
BUSES - Skylink services run every 20 minutes, daily to Loughborough and Leicester (via East Midlands Airport) and Derby - Tel: 0871 200 2233.

THE canal sets purposefully out westwards, each mile counted by cast iron mileposts; some replicas, some original, manufactured in Stone, the T&M's headquarters, at the foundry of Rangeley & Dixon, hence the initials. Aggregates are extensively mined between bridges 4 and 7. Odd how jargon changes. Didn't these used to be known as gravel pits? Nowadays they are called quarries, something once more commonly associated with the extraction of stone from vertical faces.

Weston Grange, a handsome brick farmhouse, overlooks Bridge 7, then the canal passes beneath a hefty girder bridge carrying the old Midland Railway line between Sheet Stores (Long Eaton) and Stenson (Willington). Bereft of passenger services as long ago as 1930, even its goods trains appear to be dwindling, particularly given the dramatic decline in coal carried by rail. The canal, though, retains railway connections, for this is the jealously guarded beat of

Derby Railway Angling Club. Do they catch fishplates?

Weston Lock used to have Castle Donington power station for a backdrop, but in common with many of the Trent valley's old generating plants, it has been demolished. The lane from Bridge 8 provides easy access to Weston village in one direction, while the other way offers a peaceful walk down to the site of an old lock opposite King's Mills, a popular bathing spot until demolition of a weir in 1957 rendered such activities dangerous. Rummage in the undergrowth and you may discern the remains of the old lock. In the past there was a ferry here too, providing access

to mills on the Leicestershire bank of the Trent.

Passing well-mown lawns and Weston village's spired church, the canal glides through the tumbling woodland of Weston Cliffs. While construction of was proceeding eastwards, a wharf was erected here for the transfer of goods from barge to riverboat. Later it was used

Locks
3 Aston Lock 8ft 1in
4 Weston Lock 10ft 11ins

'Passengers No More'
1: Weston - closed 1930
2: Melbourne - closed 1930

○ **Key**
A site of wharf
B site of WWII bridging school
C site of military railway depot

Melbourne

King's Newton

Hardinge Arms

Bredon Hill

course of Derby & Ashby Railway

River Trent

East Midlands Airport

to King's Mills

mp 3/89

mp 4/88

Weston Cliffs

Tarasivka

mp 2/90

Weston Grange

Weston on Trent

Coopers Arms

11
11A
70'

mp 5/87

12

Shardlow Quarry

A50 to M1

mp 1/91

Aston on Trent

The Malt

White Hart

Dog & Duck

Shardlow

A50 to Stoke on Trent

for the transhipment of gypsum bound from Aston to King's Mills, whereupon, after being ground, the resultant plaster was despatched back up the canal for consignment via Swarkestone and the Derby Canal to a building merchant in Derby. In these days of the ubiquitous lorry, the labour-intensiveness of previous eras of transport is astonishing.

During the Second World War this dreamy riparian landscape was rudely awakened by the construction of an army camp at Weston Cliffs. It was built to house the army's railway engineers who operated the Melbourne and Ashby line as a military railway during the Second World War. The army camp also provided accommodation for soldiers attached to a Bridging School opened across the river at King's Newton. As part of their training they built a now vanished suspension bridge across the river to facilitate access between the camp and the school. The enigmatic remnants of a steam crane used by the bridge-makers remains beneath the cast-iron railway viaduct which now carries National Cycle Route 6 across the Trent near Bridge 11 (dated 1770). The trackbed of that line has been imaginatively resurfaced to create a traffic-free link between Derby and the handsome old market town of Melbourne.

Hardly had the railway engineers marched away, before the camp was commandeered to house Ukrainian refugees, a role it may sadly have to reprise in 2022. Several hundred arrived here to escape oppression in their homeland in 1944. Weston Rectory, visible on its low hilltop to the north of the canal, was used as a home for the centre's elderly residents, whilst parts of the camp were used by Ukrainian youth groups. A number of Ukrainian children were accommodated here following the Chernobyl nuclear disaster. The camp is known as Tarasivka and includes a tiny wooden chapel and a memorial to those who gave their lives for freedom in the Ukraine. A pub, originally named the Old Cliff Inn, is now a social club called Hospoda (Ukrainian for inn) where visitors are welcome on Sundays (12-4pm).

To the south, on the Leicestershire bank of the Trent, 'noises off' are likely to emanate from either Donington Park (heavy metal/motorsports) or East Midlands Airport at which a Ryanair jet appears to land or take off every thirty seconds throughout the day. Donington Hall was erected in Gothic style at the end of the 18th century for the Marquess of Hastings, who figured so prominently in the promotion of the Ashby Canal. The family's fortunes were ruined by the fourth marquess, Henry Rawdon-Hastings, pithily described by W. G. Hoskins in *Leicestershire - a Shell Guide* as 'a jackass of the first order'. Certainly he crammed a lot of debauchery into his 26 year lifespan, arguably the apotheosis of which was his elopement with a titled lady via the rear door of Marshall & Snelgrove's department store on London's Oxford Street in 1864. Ostensibly, she had been having a fitting for her wedding dress, while her husband-to-be waited, as it turned out, fruitlessly for her return via the establishment's front door.

Aston on Trent   Map 45

Suburbanised village whose gracious Georgian hall was once a mental hospital and is now apartments.
Eating & Drinking
MALT - The Green. Tel: 01332 799116. Half-timbered pub open from noon daily. DE72 2AA
Shopping
Convenience store and post office/newsagent.
Connections
BUSES - Notts & Derbys service 73 runs Mon-Sat, to/from Derby. Tel: 0871 200 2233.

Weston on Trent   Map 45

St Mary the Virgin tempted us but was locked!
Eating & Drinking
COOPERS ARMS - Weston Hall. Tel: 01332 690002. Bar/restaurant housed in 17th century mansion used by Cromwell as barracks. In WWI an escaped German prisoner hid here briefly before eventually making his way back to his homeland. Food lunchtime and evenings Mon-Sat, all day from noon Sun. DE72 2BJ
Connections
BUSES - service 73 as Aston-on-Trent.

Melbourne   Map 45

A small town of not inconsiderable charm and historical associations (i.e. Melbourne, Australia) pleasantly reached on foot (or by bicycle) along the old, resurfaced railway line from Bridge 11A. Viscount Melbourne (1779-1848) was Queen Victoria's mentor and twice Prime Minister. Melbourne Hall may be visited most afternoons in August, whilst its gardens are open to the public Wed, Sat, Sun & BHM Apr-Oct. Tel: 01332 862502. There are several pubs, cafes and restaurants; and a small Sainsbury's supermarket etc.

KEEPING itself to itself - as canals have a knack of doing, even in the least promising of circumstances - the Trent & Mersey skirts the southern fringes of Derby's ever expanding suburbs without letting on that a sizeable city lies just over the rim of the northern horizon. Even the A50 - shovelling traffic east to the M1 and west to the M6 - remains largely out of earshot, enabling the canal traveller to sustain a delusional sense of rustic well-being.

Bedevilled by traffic flows its medieval builders could never have envisaged, Swarkestone Bridge (or Causeway), wriggles its way across the Trent's broad valley. In 1745 this was the furthest south that Bonnie Prince Charlie's bedraggled army got in their attempt to capture the English throne. Historians have speculated that the Highlanders' morale dropped at the sight of the dull English midland landscape. Or as Ursula Fanthorpe memorably put it in her poem *At Swarkestone*: 'He turned back here. Anyone would.'

Just twenty-five years later the Trent & Mersey was being dug, and soon afterwards Swarkestone became the site of a junction with the Derby Canal, including a branch down to the river which only survived until around 1800. Overlooked by nationalisation in 1947, the Derby Canal was acrimoniously abandoned in 1964, though trade had ceased twenty years earlier. The company who owned the canal were no fools, being well aware that more money could be made from property deals than from running a publicly accessible navigation; a point not lost, towards the end of their existence, by the Canal & River Trust's nationalised predecessors, British Waterways.

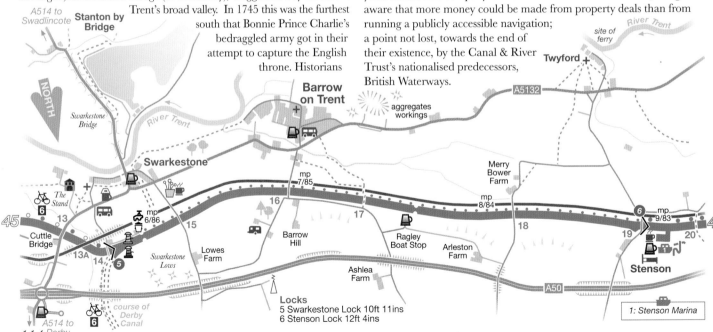

The old junction house remains intact, used, like the one at Huddlesford (Map 13), by a boat club. The Derby Canal's towpath has been resurfaced as part of National Cycle Route 6 and there are ambitious plans to restore at least part of the canal to navigation. Swarkestone Lows are the remains of a Bronze Age round barrow cemetery.

East of Bridge 16, a moving little memorial commemorates the tragic death of a teenage girl in 1978. Stenson is the Trent & Mersey's most westerly widebeam lock, though vessels of broader proportions may proceed to Willington, or Horninglow Wharf at Burton-on-Trent (Map 48) to turn.

Swarkestone   Map 46

There is a good view from the canal of The Stand, an intriguing 17th century pavilion surmounted by a picturesque pair of ogee domes which is thought to have been used as a grandstand for viewing bear-baiting or jousting, though more probably simply bowls. There was once a great mansion here belonging to the Harpurs, who decamped to Calke. The Landmark Trust has restored the pavilion as accommodation for just two occupants, who must be tolerant enough to accept a bathroom approached by way of the roof terrace! The Rolling Stones used The Stand for a photo-shoot in 1968.

Eating & Drinking
CREWE & HARPUR - Tel: 01332 700641. A well-appointed Marston's 'Rotisserie' inn and restaurant with accommodation. Open from noon. DE73 7JA

Connections
BUSES - Arriva service 2 runs half hourly (hourly Sun) to/from Derby and Melbourne. Tel: 0871 200 2233.

Twyford   Map 46

Since the chain ferry was irrevocably damaged by floodwater in 1963, Twyford has led a sequestered existence at the end of a cul-de-sac visited by few save for lovers and church crawlers; often, one suspects, one and the same. St Andrews' stained glass window was the gift of Sir William Towle, pioneer railway hotelier and caterer, who was born the son of the village's blacksmith in 1849. Trent

Adventure provide Canadian canoes for hire on the River Trent - Tel: 0787 675 1599. DE73 7HJ

Barrow-on-Trent   Map 46

Peaceful village on a bend of the Trent. Pinfold on the lane to the church: for straying cattle not parishioners.

Eating & Drinking
THE RAGLEY BOAT STOP - Deepdale Lane (between bridges 17 & 18, customer moorings with hook-up). Tel: 01332 703919. Food from noon daily. DE73 7FY

Stenson   Map 46

Eating & Drinking
STENSON LOCK COTTAGE - Tel: 0794 998 0884. Popular lockside cafe. Bacon butties! DE73 7HL
THE BUBBLE INN - Tel: 01283 703113. Open from 11am, food served Wed-Sun 11am-8pm. DE73 7HL

Mercia Marina   Map 47

An impressive cornucopia of boating facilities, eating & drinking establishments and retail outlets in the modern mould. Highlights include: The Boardwalk Bar & Dining, The Beetroot Tree Deli, and Lotus Indian Kitchen. There is also Willow Tree Cafe and small convenience store called Still Waters. Comprehensice range of boating accessories from Midland Chandlers.

Findern   Map 47

Eating & Drinking
NADEE - Heath Lane (Bridge 21) Tel: 01283 701333. Indian restaurant open Tue-Sat from 4pm; Sun from noon. DE65 6AR

Willington   Map 47

Hardly picturesque, and bedevilled by traffic, but a more than useful and popular watering-hole nonetheless. Inside St Michael's church, a plaque commemorates Morgan Maddox Morgan-Owen (1877-1950), Welsh international footballer, much decorated Great War hero, and Repton schoolmaster. Willington was the base of Blue Bus operations from 1922 until their garage burnt sadly down in 1976.

Eating & Drinking
BEVINGTONS - The Green. Tel: 01283 703321. Tea room and take-out. Open Tue-Sun. DE65 6BP
DRAGON - The Green. Tel: 01283 704795. Consistently good pub/restaurant which backs onto the canal and which opens daily from 8am. Good choice of (often local) real ales. DE65 6BP
WATERS EDGE - Castle Way (village centre). Tel: 01283 704444. Indian restaurant/take-away open from 5pm daily ex Mon. DE65 6BT
Two other pubs, fish & chips, and a Chinese take-away.

Shopping
Co-op store (with ATM) and post office. Betty's Farm sells self-service locally souced food from 7am daily.

Connections
BUSES - V3 'Villager' service runs hourly Mon-Sat (bi-hourly Sun) to/from Derby, Repton and Burton-on-Trent. Tel: 0871 200 2233.
TRAINS - fairly sparse Cross-Country services to/from Derby and Birmingham. Tel: 0345 748 4950.

WILLINGTON Power Station's five, three hundred feet high cooling towers have been a landmark in this part of the Trent Valley ever since they were erected in the late 1950s. The plant was decommissioned in 1999, yet their brooding presence has continued to define the local landscape. Plans for a new gas-fired power station and/or a housing development have stalled. Meanwhile a pair of peregrine falcons have nested on the lip of one of the towers for a number of years.

In contrast to the power station's fluctuating fortunes, Mercia Marina seems constantly on 'the up'. It is one of the few (though there is another successful example on Map 49) to have attracted retail development in addition to all the usual boater-focussed facilities, and has become a popular visitor attraction in its own right. The huge works to the north is Toyota's car plant, built on the site of Derby Municipal Airport.

Bridge 22A carries the former North Staffordshire Railway's line to Stoke-on-Trent and Crewe across the canal. The NSR bought out the T&M in 1847. Its rival the Midland Railway (both constituents of the LMS) had a transhipment basin where a green sward of grass is now in the centre of the village. Willington offers good visitor moorings and a rather better range of shops and pubs than its size might suggest.

Bordered by gravel pits - sorry, aggregates quarries - the canal threads its way between the railway and the A38 - in Roman times known as Ryknild Street. Egginton Wharf boasts a graceful Georgian wharfinger's house, and from Bridge 26 you can follow a lane, petering out into a path, to the confluence of the Dove with the Trent. A low-slung aqueduct, designed by Brindley in 1768, and sketched by J. M. W. Turner (with a horse hauling a boat across it) forty years later, carries the canal across the Dove, these days the boundary between Derbyshire and Staffordshire. Long ago retired from the responsibility of carrying road traffic, much of neighbouring Monk's Bridge dates from the late 18th century, though three of its four arches hint at its medieval origins.

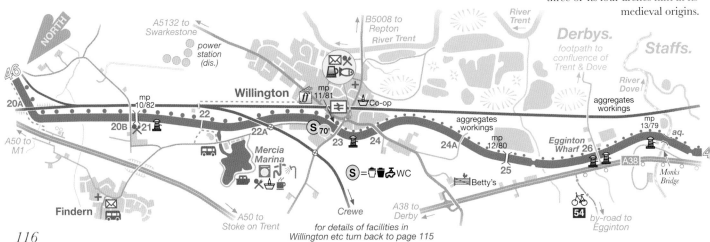

L IFE would have been a lot easier if the Trent & Mersey Canal had found its way through the middle of the town which could once justifiably claim to be the brewing capital of the world.

Unlike the railway which usurped it, the canal tiptoes tentatively around the town's north-western fringes, echoing the anonymity of the A38's 1960's by-pass. Curiously, there was no topographic impediment for such timidity. Walk into town from the canal to this day and you won't encounter any gradients, other than the man-made ones over the railway. Never mind, there are still days when the canal traveller can smell Burton before they can see it. And whilst the town centre is seldom less than a mile from the canal, that's no excuse for not making its further acquaintance.

Notwithstanding the (to some noses) aromatic smell of malt which hangs semi-permanently in the air, one thing which can't escape the notice of boaters and towpath walkers is the change of gauge that occurs abruptly at Dallow Lock. Hitherto, journeying westwards, they have been lulled into a wide-beam sense of false security, bringing rise to the mnemonic: 'west of Dallow the locks are narrow'. Back in the 1970s a widebeam hotel boat called *Tranquil Rose* made full use of the canal's bloated width beyond Burton, departing at regular intervals from Horninglow Wharf with excited explorers, anxious to experience the mysterious east. In earlier days it had been salt rather than would-be holidaymakers which was handled at Horninglow, and warehouses straddled the canal, creating

continued overleaf:

Key
A Rumenco
B Pirelli
C former elec. generating plant
D former maltings
E Bass Water Tower
F former grain warehouses
G Marmite/Bovril
H site of Burton MPD (17B/16F)

'Passengers No More'
1: Stretton & Clay Mills - closed 1949
2: Horninglow - closed 1949

for details of facilities in Burton turn to page 119

Map labels

A511 to Ashby
Winshill
Trent Bridge
weir
Bond End
Tesco
Town Centre
Lidl
Asda
Aldi
R. Trent
National Brewery Centre
Sainsbury's
Molson Coors Brewery
Claymills Pumping Station
Wetmore
sewage works
99
Lidl
F
TH
Shobnall Maltings
Morrisons
Burton on Trent
A
McD's
29A
Burton Albion FC
54
Shobnall
Marston's Brewery
33C
33E
McD's
mp 14/78
28
29
30
31
mp 18/77*
mp 15/77
32
32A
mp 16/76
33
mp 17/75
70'S
32B
Horninglow
Stretton
Sinai Park
1: Shobnall Marina
A511 to Tutbury
Locks
7 Dallow Lock 3ft 6ins
A38
B5017 to Uttoxeter

S = 🗑🍴♿WC
*incorrect mileage/location

continued from page 117:
the illusion of a tunnel.

But - in our excitement - we've raced ahead of ourselves, and there are cynosures aplenty along the Trent & Mersey's eastern approach to the town. From Bridge 29 there is access to Claymills Pumping Station. The high chimneyed, Italianate buildings were opened in 1885 to pump sewage from the town (rendered more than normally noxious by warm brewery effluent being discharged into the sewers) to a sewage 'farm' on Egginton Common. Four beam engines fuelled by five boilers combined to pump the sewage to eight hundred acres of filtration beds rotationally sewaged or farmed: a shed was erected to house eight steam-powered ploughing engines; they must have been a stirring sight. Long since replaced by its modern, far less charismatic neighbour, the Victorian pumping station has been painstakingly restored and regularly opens to the public.

Pirelli - the Italian company once as widely known for salacious calendars as tyres - have lent their name to Burton Albion Football Club's nearby stadium. Pirelli stand cheek by jowl with Rumenco, manufacturers of animal feed supplements, whose trading name derives from the fact that cows are ruminants and have four stomachs.

Carrying a road now, Bridge 31 was originally the North Staffordshire Railway's route in and out of town, the natural habitat of a well-loved push & pull shuttle to Tutbury nicknamed 'The Jinnie'. Just after six every weekday evening the 'York Beer' would puff across here, conveying Burton's finest ales to the hostelries and drinking dens of the north-east. The T&M milepost alongside the bridge is a bit of a puzzle. Notwithstanding that it's an R&D original, sequentially it should read 15 miles from Shardlow but clearly states 18. Neither is it in the correct position. Old large scale Ordnance Survey maps show it a quarter of a mile to the west.

Parallel to the canal, National Cycle Route 54 follows the course of the London & North Western Railway's Dallow Lane Branch, asphalted now and known as the Kingfisher Trail. It belonged to a uniquely dense network of railways which connected Burton's industrial premises, and mostly the breweries of course, to the main lines. Bass alone had sixteen miles of track and the town's road traffic was bedeviled by no less than thirty-two level

crossings. A charming glass-cased model of great verisimilitude, depicting the centre of Burton at the zenith of its railways and breweries, is on show at the National Brewery Centre.

Shorn of its warehouses, and shoulder-barged by the A38, Horninglow Basin feels rather lugubrious now, but it is usefully equipped with a sanitary station and remains the last turning point for wide-beam craft from the east. Forty-eight hour visitor moorings are signposted here with local shops and a fish & chip shop on hand, but the most salubrious Burton moorings lie beyond Dallow's narrow-beam lock on the offside adjoining Shobnall playing fields, scene of the IWA's 2022 National Festival.

It is at Shobnall - where a long established marina offers a wealth of facilities - that the canal traveller becomes most aware of Burton-on-Trent's stock in trade. When the canal opened in 1770, it brought a rapid decline in the use of the River Trent. To serve wharves previously established on the riverbank, however, a branch canal was built from Shobnall to Bond End. When the Birmingham & Derby Junction Railway was opened a drawbridge was provided to carry the line over this Bond End Canal. In 1846 a southbound train plunged into the canal because the bridge had been opened for the passage of a boat in the sadly erroneous belief that no train was due. The railways captured the bulk of beer transport from the canal, but at the end of the 18th century large volumes of ale were being carried along the Trent & Mersey for export via Hull to northern Europe, the Baltic and Russia, and via Liverpool to India and South America. Now, inevitably, beer goes out by road on elephantine juggernauts; you'll see plenty of them being loaded in the vicinity of Bridge 33C.

West of the canal stands Marston's twin-chimnied brewery, to the east the phalanxed silos of a modern maltings. The remaining girder of a railway bridge, stylishly advertises Marston's, and brings some colour to the scene. A common misapprehension is that Burton derives its excellence in brewing from Trent water. In fact the water used for brewing lies on beds of gypsum rock beneath the town and is pumped to the surface. The predominance of such stone made Burton a centre for the production of alabaster ornaments in the middle ages.

Burton-on-Trent Map 48

It is difficult to write dispassionately of one's home town - especially when it is not necessarily the home town of one's choice. Natives make poor guide book compilers. They cannot see the wood for the trees. Or, in this case, the beer for the bottling plants. Furthermore, in brewing terms, Burton is an Indian Pale shadow of its zenith, the town's economy revolving just as much around distribution these days: Boots, Waterstones and Holland & Barrett have huge warehouses adjoining the canal and the juggernaut is the favoured means of transport as opposed to the narrowboats or shock-absorbed railway vans of yore. So much traditional brewery infrastructure has 'Gone for a Burton' that Old Burtonians, returning from exile, are hard pressed to recognise their old stamping grounds. In any case, Burton is at its most beguiling in and around the washlands (or 'hays') which border the Trent. Perhaps it was always thus, for that is where the monks chose to erect their long vanished abbey, and where they started brewing beer. Liquid history.

Eating & Drinking
BREWERY TAP - National Brewery Centre, Horninglow Street. Tel: 01283 532880. Open Wed-Sun. Wide range of food. DE14 1NG
BURTON BRIDGE INN - mile south of Horninglow Wharf. Tel: 01283 536596. Worth the lengthy trek to sample the town's doyen micro-brewery. DE14 1SY
COOPERS TAVERN - Cross Street. Tel: 01283 567246. Cosy treasure owned now by Joule's. Turn right off Station Street on your way into the town. DE14 1E99
99 STATION STREET - Station Street. Tel: 01283 516859. Fine dining in an unlikely setting. DE14 1BT
There is easy access from the visitor moorings by pipe bridge 33D (along Third Avenue) to a plethora of eating establishments: Beefeater, Flaming Grill, McDonald's, Miller & Carter, Toby Carvery and Morrisons cafe.

Old brewery railway bridge, Shobnall

Shopping
The town centre is 15-20 minutes walk from the canal, though buses operate from both Horninglow and Shobnall. Market days Thur-Sat. The closest supermarket to the canal is Morrisons, accessed from pipe bridge 33D. Marston's Brewery Shop lies a tempting 250 yards west of Bridge 33.

Things to Do
NATIONAL BREWERY CENTRE - Horninglow Street (10 mins walk from Horninglow Wharf) Tel: 01283 532880. Open 10am-4/5pm daily, admission charge. 'Intoxicating' displays concerning the history of brewing. Tours include sample beer tastings. Shire horse and rail and road transport exhibits. DE14 1NG
CLAYMILLS PUMPING STATION - Meadow Lane, Stretton (5 minutes walk from Bridge 29). Tel: 01283 509929. Open Thur & Sat 10am-5pm for static viewing, and on steaming days - detectable by a pall of smoke over the surrounding countryside. DE13 0DA

Connections
BUSES - local services throughout the Trent Valley and South Derbyshire are mainly provided by the indigenous Midland Classic fleet in their distinctive scarlet and old gold livery. Tel: 01283 500228.
TRAINS - frequent Cross Country services to/from Birmingham, Derby etc. Tel: 0345 748 4950.
TAXIS - Station Taxis. Tel: 01283 532000.

Branston Map 49

Once a village (and the unlikely birthplace of a well known relish) now a continually expanding suburb; hardly pretty, but useful for its facilities reached via a subfusc pedestrian underpass beneath the A38.

Eating & Drinking
BRIDGE INN - canalside Bridge 34. Tel: 01283 564177. Marston's beers and predominantly Italian food, open from noon daily. Pleasant canalside garden. DE14 3EZ
PASCAL AT THE OLD VICARAGE - Main Street. Tel: 01283 533222. Fine dining. Lunches (Thur/Fri/Sun), dinners (Wed-Sat). DE14 3EX
RIVAJ - Main Street. Tel: 01283 536222. Indian restaurant/take-away. Open 5.30pm daily. DE14 3EY
Also fish & chips and Chinese take-away.

Shopping
Co-op convenience store and branch of Birds Bakery of Derby founded by three homecoming servicemen brothers - Frank, Thomas and Reginald - in 1919. Notable pork pies and caramel doughnuts.

Accomodation
LOCK HOUSE - Bed & Breakfast at Tatenhill Lock. Tel: 0779 175 1745. DE14 3HD

WHEN we first surveyed the Trent & Mersey, Burton-on-Trent more or less petered out in the vicinity of Marston's Brewery (Map 48) and open country ensued. Subsequently the tide of development on nominally 'greenfield' land has been relentless - one might go as far as saying remorseless - and there is little evidence that the stain will cease spreading anytime soon. Boaters used to relish the quasi-rural visitor moorings either side of Bridge 34 at Branston, but now those to the north - though still CRT designated - are compromised by houses and commercial premises. Preferable, then, are those to the south, between the Water Park and Burton Rugby Club's new stadium, if that is not too grandiose a term.

From Tatenhill ('Taytenhill' not 'Tat') Lock a path leads to the village of that name, tucked beneath the increasingly frayed hemline of the Needwood plateau, rising abruptly to over four hundred feet above sea level. In 1760 brothers Job and William Wyatt of Burton were awarded a Patent for a machine they had invented to manufacture iron screws. In 1776 they purchased a watermill at Tatenhill to further the process. The Forest of Needwood was one of the largest royal hunting grounds in the middle ages. St George's Park, England's centre of footballing excellence, lies three miles to the north-west.

The wharf at Barton Turn, presided over by a handsome canal company house, was provided for the villages of Barton and Walton, each a mile or so from the canal on opposite sides of the Trent. When the bridge across the river to Walton was damaged by floods in the 1947, the army were called in to erect a 'temporary' Bailey bridge -

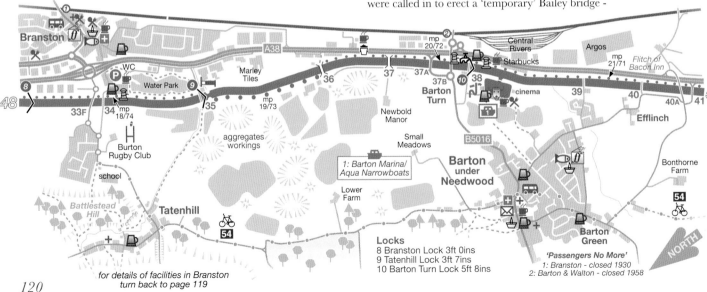

Locks
8 Branston Lock 3ft 0ins
9 Tatenhill Lock 3ft 7ins
10 Barton Turn Lock 5ft 8ins

'Passengers No More'
1: Branston - closed 1930
2: Barton & Walton - closed 1958

for details of facilities in Branston
turn back to page 119

so temporary that it has been in constant, and ever busier use for 75 years. Work, however, has begun on a replacement downstream, earmarked for opening in the Spring of 2023. Barton Marina (in common with Mercia, Map 47) has become a huge success, a honeypot for boaters and land-based visitors alike.

Central Rivers is a large railway maintenance depot, specialising in the care of the diesel units originally known as 'Voyagers', manufactured for the now defunct, and rather mourned, Virgin Trains. Business parks cluster along the A38 corridor. One wonders how it manages to absorb the increasing traffic they create. In 1939 L. T. C. Rolt wrote of 'all the tawdry ugliness which the motor-car has brought to the English road': goodness knows what he would make of the A38 today. A massive Argos distribution centre dwarfs the landscape unequivocally. Long before the A38 became the frenetically busy dual carriageway it is today, there was a wayside inn by Bridge 40 known as *The Flitch of Bacon*.

Tatenhill Lock

Barton-u-Needwood   Map 49

Mellifluously named but bloated village with good shopping facilities and several pubs approachable via footpath or B5016. Barton Marina attracts vast numbers of visitors, but the core of the village itself is still worth seeking out, not least the substantial parish church given to the village by its distinguished native, John Taylor, a 16th Century Master of the Rolls.

Eating & Drinking
APPLE TREE - Barton Marina. Tel: 01283 712332. Friendly deli and coffee shop with waterside tables. Try the excellent Staffordshire Oatcakes. DE13 8AS
BARTON TURN - Bridge 38. Tel: 01283 480682.

Cosy canalside Marston's pub with food. DE13 8EA
MARINA CAFE - Barton Marina. Tel: 01283 711666. Open daily 9am-3pm. DE13 8DZ
THAI MARINA - Barton Marina. Tel: 01283 329303. Stylish restaurant is open for lunch and dinner (from 5.30pm). Sunday buffet 12-3pm. DE13 8DZ
STARBUCKS - A38 Northbound (towpath side opp marina). Tel: 01283 716477. Coffee house. DE13 8EG
THE WATERFRONT - Barton Marina. Tel: 01283 711500. Popular bar/restaurant. DE13 8DZ

Shopping
BUTCHER BAKER - Barton Marina. Tel: 01283 711002. The name encompasses most of this

excellent outlet's activities, but it also offers fresh vegetables, deli items and basic provisions more than a little useful for boaters. DE13 8DZ
INDULGENCE - Barton Marina. Tel: 01283 716062. Italian wine/beer/coffees/pastries/gelato. DE13 8DZ
Barton Marina hosts a range of retail outlets. In the village there is a Co-op, post office, pharmacy and cycle shop.

Things to Do
RED CARPET - Barton Marina. Tel: 01283 716257. Cinema with cafe bar. DE13 8AS

Connections
BUSES - Midland Classic service 12 connects Barton with Lichfield and Burton. Tel: 0871 200 2233.

50 TRENT & MERSEY CANAL Alrewas & Fradley 3½mls/7lks/2½hrs

A S if eventually finding the A38's boorish behaviour too irritating to bear, the canal veers away to the west at Wychnor Lock, immediately assuming a quite different character as it negotiates a marshy, almost ethereal stretch of countryside, criss-crossed by drainage channels, or 'sitches', which thread their way through meadowlands to meet the Trent. The A38 is instantly forgotten, as the waterway puts you tantalisingly in touch with a past inhabited by eel-catchers, reed-cutters and sluice-keepers.

Wychnor Lock has a reputation for a fierce undertow. An arm extended in a south-easterly direction from here to Wychnor Forge which was in use until around 1800. Wychnor was the scene of a tradition - similar to the more famous one at Dunmow in Essex - whereby any man who could swear not to have wished to exchange his wife for another woman, at any time during the first year of his marriage, was entitled to a flitch of bacon from the Lord of the Manor. It may - or may not - surprise you to learn that the flitch was seldom successfully claimed: one notable exception being a sailor and his wife who rarely saw each other. Demurely perched above the canal, St Leonard's church dates back to the thirteenth century although the brick tower is a much later addition. There are some beautiful contemporary stained glass windows within. In sheep-grazed fields beside the church lies the pock-marked ground of a deserted medieval village.

Locks
11 Wychnor Lock 5ft 8ins
12 Alrewas Lock 5ft 8ins
13 Bagnall Lock 5ft 7ins
14 Common Lock 4ft 6ins
15 Hunts Lock 5ft 8ins
16 Keeper's Lock 6ft 10ins
17 Junction Lock 8ft 0ins

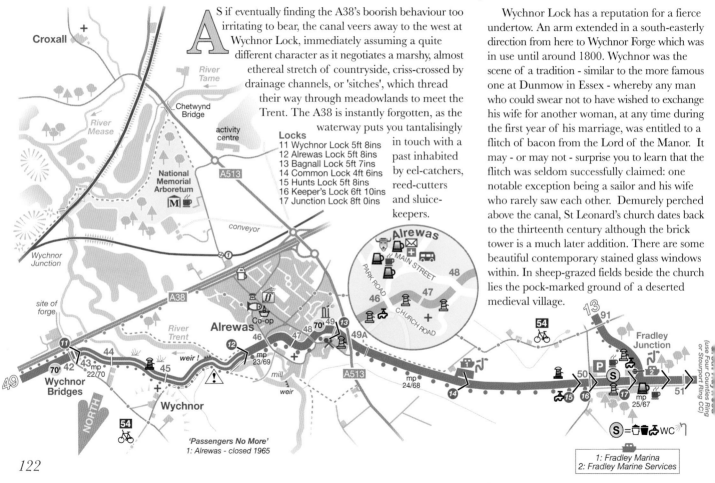

'Passengers No More'
1: Alrewas - closed 1965

S = 🚿🗑♿WC

1: Fradley Marina
2: Fradley Marine Services

Between Wychnor and Alrewas occurs one of those rare incidences of a canal merging with a river, in this case, of course, the Trent. Initially, the effect - where westbound, upstream boats are concerned - is minimal, but in the short section between the weir (where the river's main channel leaves the canal) and Alrewas Lock there are times when the strength of current precludes navigation, and signs at Wychnor Bridges and Alrewas inform boaters of this. Nevertheless, this is an exhilarating length of waterway, and it is good to feel the mercurial power of the river beneath your hull. A dreamlike sequence of metal side-bridges - each fastidiously bestowed with an alphabetical suffix - carries the towpath over a succession of reedy backwaters in a scene not unreminiscent of the Thames.

The mill race at Alrewas (alongside which there is a restful little civic amenity reached from Bridge 46) was used by boats to reach a flour mill. Converted into apartments now, within a gated community, its name appeared prominently on the roof, but had to be painted out during the Second World War to avoid becoming a landmark for the Luftwaffe. The gable end of a house alongside Bridge 48 is adorned with a delightful mural quoting the Water Rat from *The Wind in the Willows*. A cricket ground ensues, and you can't help but wonder how many 'towering sixes' have ended ignominiously up in the cut.

Between Alrewas and Fradley the canal crosses former common land, and the pancake flat nature of the adjoining fields engenders a distinct feeling of emptiness. Twenty-five miles from Shardlow the Trent & Mersey Canal reaches Fradley Junction, just about everybody's idea of a perfect canal community. Trade on this part of the T&M had more or less evaporated by the mid-Fifties, but British Waterways' maintenance yard continued to supply a sense of purpose to the scene, and the stables, warehouses and famous Swan Inn gradually attracted more and more sightseers by road. In the Seventies a hire fleet was based here, not inappropriately called Swan Line, and as the canals became more and more used for leisure, Fradley Junction enjoyed a renaissance from which it has never looked back.

Alrewas   Map 50

Thatched cottages counter-intuitively much further north than you'd expect. If you're entering the village from Bridge 46 along Post Office Road, keep your eyes peeled for the unintentionally amusing spelling of 'Coronation Square'.

Eating & Drinking

ALREWAS CANTONESE - Tel: 01283 790027. Chinese takeaway. DE13 7AE
ALREWAS FRYER - Tel: 01283 790432. Excellent fish & chips. Lunch and evenings Mon-Sat. DE13 7AE
BANK - Main Street. Tel: 0749 427 9220. Coffee house open 9am-4pm (10am-3pm Sun). DE13 7AE
THE CROWN - Post Office Road. Tel: 01283 791217. Re-opened after a period of closure. DE13 7BS
DELHI DIVAN - Kings Bromley Road (near Bagnall Lock). Tel: 01283 792743. Indian restaurant. DE13 7DB
GEORGE & DRAGON - Main Street. Tel: 01283 791476. Marston's, food, B&B. DE13 7AE
WILLIAM IV - William IV Road (near Bridge 46). Tel: 01283 791602. DE13 7AW

Shopping

The *piece de resistance* here is Peter Coates butcher's shop on Main Street (Tel: 01283 790205 - DE13 7AE) specialising in locally reared meats, boasting a wide choice of game, and also dealing in excellent pies, cheese, flour and vegetables. There is also a pharmacy (with post office) and Co-op store with cash machine.

Things to Do

NATIONAL MEMORIAL ARBORETUM - Croxall Road (approximately 1 mile south of Bridge 46, detailed instructions for canal travellers to reach the arboretum on foot are posted on the NMA website www.thenma.org.uk Tel: 01283 245100. The confluence of the Tame with the Trent provides an inspired location for an intensely moving hundred and fifty acre arboretum commemorating all those affected by wars. Twenty-five thousand trees have been planted and there are around four hundred memorials, pride of place going to the Armed Forces Memorial, landmarked by a gold-topped column. Two minute silence, Reveille and Last Post enacted daily at 11am. A land train provides transport (should you prefer not to walk). Shop, cafe and restaurant. DE13 7AR

Connections

BUSES - Midland Classic 12 hourly Mon-Sat to/from Burton (via Barton) and Lichfield (via Fradley and Streethay) Tel: 0871 200 2233.
TAXIS - Ambassador Cars. Tel: 01283 544700.

Fradley Junction   Maps 13/50
Turn back to page 37.

INFORMATION

This Guide

Pearson's Canal Companions are a long established, independently produced series of guide books devoted to the inland waterways and designed to appeal equally to boaters, walkers, cyclists and other, less readily pigeon-holed members of society. Considerable pride is taken to make these guides as up to date, accurate, entertaining and inspirational as possible. A good guide book should fulfil three functions: make you want to go; interpret the lie of the land when you're there; and provide a lasting souvenir of your journeys.

The Maps

There are fifty-two numbered maps whose layout is shown by the Route Planner inside the front cover. Maps 1 to 25 cover the "Warwickshire Ring" circuit commencing at Napton and following the ring in a clockwise direction via Kingswood, Bordesley, Salford, Fazeley, Hawkesbury and Braunston junctions. Maps 26 to 29 cover the Grand Union Canal between Braunston and Stoke Bruerne; Maps 30 to 34 cover the Ashby Canal; Maps 35 to 37 cover the Worcester & Birmingham Canal between Tardebigge and Birmingham; Maps 38 to 43 cover the Stratford Canal; and Maps 44 to 50 cover the Trent & Mersey Canal between Derwent Mouth and Fradley. The maps - measured imperially like the waterways they depict, and not being slavishly north-facing - are easily read in either direction. Users will thus find most itineraries progressing smoothly and logically from left to right or vice versa. Figures quoted at the top of each map refer to distance per map, locks per map and average cruising time. An alternative indication of timings from centre to centre can be found on the Route Planner. Obviously, cruising times vary with the nature of your boat and the number of crew at your disposal, so quoted times should be taken only as an estimate. Neither do times quoted take into account any delays which might occur at lock flights in high season. Walking and cycling times will depend very much on the state of individual sections of towpath and the stamina of those concerned.

The Text

Each map is accompanied by a route commentary placing the waterway in its historic, social and topographical context. As close to each map as is feasible, gazetteer-like entries are given for places passed through, listing, where appropriate, facilities of significance to users of this guide. Every effort is made to ensure these details are as up to date as possible, but - especially where pubs/restaurants are concerned - we suggest you telephone ahead if relying upon an entry to provide you with a meal at any given time.

Walking

The simplest way to go canal exploring is on foot along the towpaths originally provided so that horses could 'tow' boats. Walking costs little more than the price of shoe leather and you are free to concentrate on the passing scene; something that boaters, with the responsibilities of navigation thrust upon them, are not always at liberty to do. The maps set out to give some idea of the quality of the towpath on any given section of canal. More of an art than a science to be sure, but at least it reflects our personal experiences, and whilst it does vary from area to area, none of it should prove problematical for anyone inured to the vicissitudes of country walking. We recommend the use of public transport to facilitate 'one-way' itineraries but stress the advisability of checking up to date details on the telephone numbers quoted, or on the websites of National Rail Enquiries or Traveline.

Cycling

Bicycling along towpaths is an increasingly popular pastime, though one not always equally popular with other waterway users such as boaters, anglers and pedestrians. It is important to remember that you are sharing the towpath with other people out for their own form of enjoyment, and to treat them with the respect and politeness they deserve. A bell is a useful form of diplomacy; failing that, a stentorian cough or the ability to whistle tunefully; light operatic extracts go down very well in our experience.

Boating

Boating on inland waterways is an established, though relatively small, facet of the UK tourist industry. It is also, increasingly, a chosen lifestyle. There are approximately 38,000 privately owned boats registered on the canals, but in addition to these, numerous firms offer boats for hire. These range from small operators with half a dozen boats to sizeable fleets run by companies with several bases.

Most hire craft have all the creature comforts you are likely to expect. In the excitement of planning a boating holiday you may give scant thought to the contents of your hire boat, but at the end of a hard day's boating such matters take on more significance, and a well equipped, comfortable boat, large enough to accommodate your crew with something to spare, can make the difference between a good holiday and one which will be shudderingly remembered for the wrong reasons.

Traditionally, hire boats are booked out by the week or fortnight, though many firms now offer more flexible short breaks or extended weeks. All reputable hire firms give newcomers tuition in boat handling and lock working, and first-timers soon find themselves adapting to the pace of things 'on the cut'.

Navigational Advice

Newcomers, hiring a boat on the inland waterways for the first time, have every right to expect sympathetic and thorough tuition from the company providing their boat. Boat-owners are, by definition, likely to be already adept at navigating. The following, however, may prove useful points of reference.

Locks are part of the charm of canal cruising, but they are potentially dangerous environments for children, pets and careless adults. Use of them should be methodical and unhurried, whilst special care should be exercised in rain, frost and snow when slippery hazards abound.

The locks included in this guide fall into two distinct types: narrow and wide. The wide locks are to be found on the Grand Union between Napton and Knowle (Maps 1 to 6), and on the Trent & Mersey Canal between Derwent Mouth and Stenson Maps 44 to 46. These locks can accept narrowbeam craft side by side and it helps save water (not to mention workload) if they are shared with other boats travelling in the same direction.

Finally, it behoves us all to be on our best behaviour at locks. Remember to exercise a little 'give and take'. The use of foul mouths or fists to decide precedence at locks is one canal tradition not worthy of preservation.

Mooring on the canals featured in this guide is per usual practice - ie on the towpath side, away from sharp bends, bridge-holes and narrows. A 'yellow' bollard symbol represents visitor mooring sites; either as designated officially or, in some cases as recommended by our personal experience. Of course, one of the great joys of canal boating has always been the ability to moor wherever (sensibly) you like. In recent years, however, it has become obvious, particularly in urban areas, that there are an increasing number of undesirable locations where mooring is not to be recommended for fear of vandalism, theft or abuse. It would be nice if local authorities would see their way to providing pleasant, secure, overnight facilities for passing boaters who, after all, bring the commerce of tourism in their wake. Few boaters would object to making a small payment in such circumstances, as is the custom on a number of river navigations.

Turning points on the canals are known as 'winding holes'; pronounced as the thing which blows because in the old days the wind was expected to do much of the work rather than the boatman. Winding holes capable of taking a full length boat of around seventy foot length are marked where appropriate on the maps. Winding holes capable of turning shorter craft are marked with the approximate length. It is of course also possible to turn boats at junctions and at most boatyards, though in the case of the latter it is polite to request permission before doing so. It would be helpful if CRT signed official winding holes (as they do on the southern Oxford) quoting maximum lengths.

Boating facilities are provided at regular intervals along the inland waterways, and range from a simple water tap or refuse disposal skip, to the provision of sewage disposal, showers and laundry. Such vital features are also obtainable at boatyards and marinas along with repairs and servicing. An alphabetical list of boatyards appears on pages 111-112.

Closures (or 'stoppages' in canal parlance) traditionally occur on the inland waterways between November and April, during which time most of the heavy maintenance work is undertaken. Occasionally, however, an emergency stoppage, or perhaps water restriction, may be imposed at short notice, closing part of the route you intend to cruise. Up to date details are available on *www.canalrivertrust.org.uk*

Canal & River Trust

The Trust controls the bulk of the inland waterways network, and all day-to-day enquiries regarding the upkeep of the canals should be addressed to them. Their Head Office is located in Milton Keynes. Tel: 0303 040 4040 *www.canalrivertrust.org.uk*

Societies

The Inland Waterways Association was founded in 1946 to campaign for the retention of the canal system. Many routes now open to pleasure boaters may not have been so but for this organisation. Membership details, together with details of the IWA's regional branches, may be obtained from: Inland Waterways Association, Island House, Moor Road, Chesham HP5 1WA. Tel: 01494 783453. *www.waterways.org.uk*

A number of the canals featured in this guide are also supported by individual societies such as the Ashby Canal Association, the Coventry Canal Society, the Stratford-on-Avon Canal Society, Trent & Mersey Canal Society, and Worcester & Birmingham Canal Society. Further details can be found on the internet.

Amendments

Updates to current editions can be found on our website: *www.jmpearson.co.uk*. Feel free to email us if you spot anything worth notifying others about.

Acknowledgements

Much appreciation to: Karen Tanguy for all her work 'behind the scenes'; Meg Gregory for her *third* South Midlands cover; Tamar Lumsden for her charming Cicely Pickering image; Andrew Denny for alerting us to Tatenhill's place in the history of screw making; Jackie Pearson for home and hearth; regular correspondents David Hymers, Chris & Terry Rigden and Jenny Tyte; and all involved in the printing of this book at the estimable Short Run Press in Exeter.

Boat Hire

ABC BOAT HIRE Kings Orchard, Coventry Canal, Map 13 WS13 8SP; Springwood Haven, Coventry Canal, Map 18 CV10 0RZ; Gayton, Grand Union Canal, Map 28 NN7 3ER; Alvechurch, Worcester & Birmingham Canal Map 35, B48 7SQ. HQ, Worcester, WR1 2SD. Tel: 0330 333 0590. Day boats at Alvechurch and Kings Orchard (Map 13). *www.abcboathire.com*

ANGLO WELSH WATERWAY HOLIDAYS Stockton, Grand Union Canal, Map 2, CV47 8HN; Tardebigge, Worcs & B'ham Canal, Map 35, B60 1LR; Wootton Wawen, Stratford Canal, Map 42, B95 6BZ. HQ, Bristol, BS2 0BH. Tel: 0117 304 1122. *www.anglowelsh.co.uk*

AQUA NARROWBOATS Barton Marina, Barton, Trent & Mersey Canal, Map 49, DE13 8DZ. Tel: 01283 585718. *www.aquanarrowboats.co.uk*

ARMADA BOAT HIRE Harborough Magna, Oxford Canal, Map 22, CV23 0HA. Tel: 0788 066 0660. *www.armadaboathire.co.uk*

ASHBY BOAT CO Stoke Golding, Ashby Canal, Map 31, CV13 6EY. Tel: 01455 212671. *www.ashbyboats.com*

BLACK PRINCE HOLIDAYS Napton Junction, Oxford Canal, Map 1, CV47 8NL. HQ Stoke Prior, Bromsgrove, B60 4LA. Tel: 01527 575115. *www.black-prince.com*

BOOT WHARF BOAT HIRE Nuneaton, Coventry Canal, Map 18, CV10 7BE. Tel: 0247 634 4766. *www.star-line-boats.co.uk* (Day Hire Only)

BOSWORTH MARINA Market Bosworth, Ashby Canal, Map 32, CV13 6PG. Tel: 01455 291111. *www.bosworthmarina.co.uk* (Day Hire Only)

CALCUTT BOATS Stockton, Grand Union Canal, Map 1. CV47 8HX. Tel: 01926 813757. *www.calcuttboats.com*

BOATING DIRECTORY

CLIFTON CRUISERS Rugby, Oxford Canal, Map 23, CV23 0EY. Tel: 01788 543570. *www.cliftoncruisers.com*

COPT HEATH WHARF Copt Heath, Grand Union Canal, Map 7, B91 2SX. Tel: 0785 034 4412. *www.coptheathwharf.co.uk* (Day Hire Only)

DEBBIE'S DAY BOATS Birmingham & Fazeley Canal Map 12, B78 3RY. Tel: 0752 216 9241. (Day Hire Only)

GRAND UNION NARROWBOATS - Weedon, Grand Union Canal, Map 27, NN7 4QD. Tel: 01327 342418. *www.grandunionnarrowboats.co.uk*

KATE BOATS Stockton, Grand Union Canal, Map 2, CV47 8HN; Warwick, Grand Union Canal, Map 4, CV34 5JB. Tel: 01926 492968. *www.kateboats.co.uk*

LIME FARM MARINA Cathiron, Oxford Canal, Map 22, CV23 0JH. Tel: 01788 570131. *www.limefarmmarina.co.uk* (Day Hire Only)

LYONS BOATS Warstock, Stratford Canal, Map 38, B14 4SP. Tel: 0121 474 4977. *www.lyonsboats.co.uk* (Day Hire Only)

NAPTON NARROWBOATS Napton, Oxford Canal, Map 1, CV47 8HX. Tel: 01926 813644. *www.napton-marina.co.uk*

ROSE NARROWBOATS Brinklow, Oxford Canal, Map 22, CV23 0PU. Tel: 01788 832449 *www.rose-narrowboats.co.uk*

SALTISFORD CANAL TRUST Warwick, Grand Union Canal, Map 4, CV34 5RJ. Tel: 01926 490006. *www.saltisfordcanal.co.uk* (Day Hire Only)

STREETHAY WHARF Lichfield, Coventry Canal, Map 13, WS13 8RJ. Tel: 01543 414808 *www.streethaywharf.co.uk* (Day Hire Only)

UNION CANAL CARRIERS Braunston, Grand Union, Map 25, NN11 7HJ. Tel: 01788 890784. *www.unioncanalcarriers.co.uk*

WILLOW WREN Rugby, Oxford Canal, Map 23, CV21 1PB. Tel: 01788 562183. *www.willowwren.co.uk*

WILLOW WREN TRAINING Stockton, Grand Union Canal, Map 1, CV47 8AA. Tel: 0797 077 0565. *www.willowwrentraining.co.uk* (Day Hire Only)

Boatyards

ALVECHURCH MARINA (ABC) Alvechurch, Worcs & B'ham, Map 35. Tel: 0121 445 1133. B48 7SQ

ALVECOTE MARINA Alvecote, Coventry Canal, Map 16. Tel: 01827 898585. B78 1AS

ANGLO WELSH Tardebigge, Worcs & B'ham Canal, Map 35. Tel: 01527 873898. B60 1LR

ANGLO WELSH Wootton Wawen, Stratford Canal, Map 42. Tel: 01564 793427. B95 6BZ

ASHBY BOAT CO Stoke Golding, Ashby Canal, Map 31. Tel: 01455 212671 CV13 6EY

ASHBY CANAL CENTRE Stoke Golding, Ashby Canal, Map 31. Tel: 01455 212636. CV13 6EU

BARBY MOORINGS Barby, Oxford Canal, Map 24. Tel: 01788 890486. CV23 8UJ

BARTON MARINA Barton-under-Needwood, T & M Canal, Map 49. Tel: 01283 711666. DE13 8DZ

BLISWORTH MARINA - Blisworth, Grand Union Canal, Map 28. Tel: 01604 879827. NN7 3FG

BLISWORTH TUNNEL - Blisworth, Grand Union Canal, Map 29. Tel: 01604 858868. NN7 3BN

BOSWORTH MARINA Market Bosworth, Ashby Canal, Map 32. Tel: 01455 291111. CV13 6PG

BRAUNSTON BOATS - Grand Union Canal, Map 25. Tel: 01788 891079. NN11 7HJ

BRAUNSTON MARINA Grand Union Canal, Map 25. Tel: 01788 891373. NN11 7JH

BRIDGE 32 SUPPLIES - Nether Heyford, Grand Union Canal, Map 27. Tel: 01327 341202. NN7 3JY

BRINKLOW BOAT SERVICES Stretton-u-F, Oxford Canal, Map 22. Tel: 01788 833331. CV23 0PR

BRINKLOW MARINA (CASTLE) Brinklow, Oxford Canal, Map 22. Tel: 07711 803430. CV23 0JH

CALCUTT BOATS Grand Union Canal, Map 1. Tel: 01926 814091. CV47 8HX

CLIFTON CRUISERS Rugby, Oxford Canal, Map 23. Tel: 01788 543570. CV23 0DG

COPT HEATH WHARF Copt Heath, Grand Union Canal, Map 7. Tel: 0121 704 4464. B91 2SX

DELTA MARINE Warwick, Grand Union Canal, Map 4. Tel: 01926 499337. CV34 5JB

DUNCHURCH POOLS MARINA - Oxford Canal, Map 24. Tel: 0749 165 0909. CV23 8AN

FAZELEY MILL (ABC) Fazeley, B'ham & Fazeley, Maps 12/15. Tel: 01827 261138. B78 3SE

FRADLEY MARINA - Fradley, Trent & Mersey Canal, Map 50. Tel: 0794 116 7087. DE13 7EW

FRADLEY MARINE SERVICES Fradley Junction, Trent & Mersey Canal, Map 50. Tel: 0797 168 6516. DE13 7DN

GAYTON MARINA (ABC) - Gayton, Grand Union Canal, Map 28. Tel: 01604 858685. NN7 3ER

GLASCOTE BASIN BOATYARD - Glascote, Coventry Canal, Map 15. Tel: 01827 311317. B77 2AH

GRAND JUNCTION BOAT CO - Gayton, Grand Union Canal, Map 28. Tel: 01604 858043. NN7 3EF

GRAND UNION NARROWBOATS - Weedon, Grand Union Canal, Map 27. Tel: 01327 342418. NN7 4QD

GRANTHAM'S BRIDGE Hillmorton, Oxford Canal, Map 23. Tel: 01788 578661. CV21 4PP

HEYFORD FIELDS MARINA - Bugbrooke, Grand Union, Map 28. Tel: 01604 833599. NN7 3NP

HILL FARM MARINA Wootton Wawen, Stratford Canal, Map 42, B95 6DE. Tel: 01564 627280.

HILLMORTON WHARF Hillmorton, Oxford Canal, Map 24. Tel: 01788 540149. CV21 4PW

KATE BOATS - Warwick, Grand Union Canal, Map 4. Tel: 01926 492968. CV34 5JB

KINGS ORCHARD MARINA (ABC) - Huddlesford, Coventry Canal, Map 13. Tel: 01543 433608. WS13 8SP

KNOWLE HALL WHARF Knowle, Grand Union Canal, Map 6. Tel: 01564 778210. B93 0JJ

LADY LANE WHARF - Earlswood, Stratford Canal, Map 39. Tel: 01564 702552. B94 6AH

LIME FARM MARINA Cathiron, Oxford Canal, Map 22. Tel: 01788 570131. CV23 0JH

LYONS Warstock, Stratford Canal, Map 38. Tel: 0121 474 4977. B14 4SP

MANCETTER MARINA - Mancetter, Coventry Canal, Map 17. Tel: 01827 215716. CV9 2RD

MERCIA MARINA Willington, Trent & Mersey Canal, Map 47. Tel: 01283 703332. DE65 6DW

NAPTON NARROWBOATS Napton, Oxford Canal, Map 1. Tel: 01926 813644. CV47 8HX

ROSE NARROWBOATS Brinklow, Oxford Canal, Map 22. Tel: 01788 832449. CV23 0PU

RUGBY BOAT SALES - Weedon, Grand Union Canal, Map 27. Tel: 01327 342211. NN7 4SF

SALTISFORD CANAL CENTRE Warwick, Grand Union Canal, Map 4. Tel: 01926 490006. CV34 5RJ

SAWLEY MARINA (AQUAVISTA) - Sawley, River Trent, Map 44. Tel: 0115 907 7400. NG10 3AE

SHARDLOW MARINA - Shardlow, Trent & Mersey Canal, Map 44. Tel: 01332 792832. DE72 2GL

SHERBORNE WHARF - Birmingham, Birmingham Canal, Maps 9B/37. Tel: 0121 455 6163. B16 8DE

SHOBNALL MARINA Burton-on-Trent, Trent & Mersey Canal, Map 48. Tel: 01283 542718. DE14 2AU

SPRINGWOOD HAVEN (ABC) - Nuneaton, Coventry Canal, Map 18. Tel: 0247 639 3676. CV10 0RZ

STAR LINE BOATS Nuneaton, Coventry Canal, Map 18. Tel: 0247 634 4766. CV10 7BE

STENSON MARINA Stenson, T & M Canal, Map 46. Tel: 0739 140 8069. DE73 7HL

STOCKTON TOP MARINA Stockton, Grand Union Canal, Map 2. Tel: 01926 492968. CV47 8HN

STREETHAY WHARF Lichfield, Coventry Canal, Map 13. Tel: 01543 414808. WS13 8RJ

SWALLOW CRUISERS Hockley Heath, Stratford Canal, Map 40. Tel: 01564 783442. B94 5NR

TRINITY MARINA (CASTLE) Hinckley, Ashby Canal, Map 31. Tel: 01455 896820. LE10 0NF

UNION CANAL CARRIERS Braunston, Grand Union, Map 25. Tel: 01788 890784. NN11 7HJ

VENTNOR FARM MARINA Calcutt, Grand Union Canal, Map 1. Tel: 01926 815023. CV23 8HY

WARINGS GREEN WHARF Illshaw Heath, Stratford Canal, Map 39. Tel: 0787 981 8456. B94 6BU

WARWICKSHIRE FLYBOAT Long Itchington, Grand Union, Map 2. Tel: 01926 812093. CV47 8LD

WELTONFIELD NARROWBOATS - Welton, GUC Leicester Section, Map 26. Tel: 01327 842282. NN11 2LG

WIGRAMS TURN (CASTLE) Napton Junction, Oxford Canal, Map 1. Tel: 01926 817175. CV47 8NL

WILLOW WREN Rugby, Oxford Canal, Map 23. Tel: 01788 562183. CV21 1PB

WITHYBED MOORINGS - Alvechurch, Worcs & B'ham Canal, Map 35. Tel: 0121 447 7313. B48 7BX

WHILTON MARINA - Whilton, Grand Union Canal, Map 26. Tel: 01327 842577. NN11 2NH

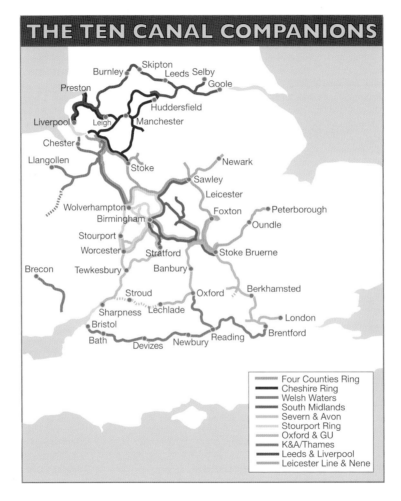

THE TEN CANAL COMPANIONS

Skipton
Burnley
Leeds Selby
Preston
Goole
Huddersfield
Liverpool Leigh Manchester
Chester
Llangollen
Stoke
Newark
Sawley
Leicester
Wolverhampton Foxton Peterborough
Birmingham Oundle
Stourport
Worcester Stratford Stoke Bruerne
Brecon Tewkesbury Banbury
Stroud Oxford Berkhamsted
Sharpness Lechlade
Bristol London
Bath Reading Brentford
Devizes Newbury

- Four Counties Ring
- Cheshire Ring
- Welsh Waters
- South Midlands
- Severn & Avon
- Stourport Ring
- Oxford & GU
- K&A/Thames
- Leeds & Liverpool
- Leicester Line & Nene